Catechism of the Summa Theologica of Saint Thomas Aquinas, for the Use of the Faithful

By

R. P. Thomas Pegues

Published by Forgotten Books 2012

Originally Published 1922

PIBN 1000636249

Catechism of the "Summa Theologica"

of

Saint Thomas Aquinas

For the Use of the Faithful

BY

R. P. THOMAS PEGUES, O.P.

MASTER IN THEOLOGY
MEMBER OF THE ROMAN ACADEMY OF ST. THOMAS AQUINAS
FORMERLY PROFESSOR OF ST. THOMAS AT THE COLLEGIO ANGELICO, ROME
NOW REGENT OF STUDIES AT ST. MAXIMIN, FRANCE

ADAPTED FROM THE FRENCH AND

DONE INTO ENGLISH BY ÆLRED WHITACRE, O.P.

*" Deriventur fontes tui foras ; et in plateis aquas tuas divide."—*PROV. V. 16.

New York, Cincinnati, Chicago

Benziger Brothers

Printers to the | Publishers of
Holy Apostolic See | Benziger's Magazine

1922

BRIEF OF
HIS HOLINESS POPE BENEDICT XV.

*To our well-beloved son Thomas Pegues of the Order
of Friars Preachers.*

BELOVED SON,

Greeting and Apostolic Benediction.

The manifold honours paid by the Holy See to St. Thomas Aquinas exclude for ever any doubt from the mind of Catholics with regard to his being raised up by God as the Master of Doctrine to be followed by the Church through all ages. It was therefore fitting that the singular wisdom of the Holy Doctor should be made accessible not only to the clergy but to the faithful in general, and to whomsoever desired to make a deeper study of the things of religion; for in very truth, the nearer one approaches to the light, so much the more is one enlightened.

Much praise is therefore due to you first of all because you have undertaken to write a commentary in your mother tongue* upon the greatest work of the Angelic Doctor, viz., the *Summa Theologica* (the volumes already published of this work show what success has attended your labours); and, secondly, because you have recently published the *Summa Theologica* in the form of a catechism. Therein you have aptly accommodated the riches of the great genius to the understanding of the less instructed

* French.

as well as of the learned; briefly and succinctly you have expounded the doctrine, and in the same luminous order as that of the Angelic Doctor whose treatise is more lengthy and more detailed.

We congratulate you sincerely on this fruit of your labours which shows your masterly knowledge of St. Thomas' doctrine. We hope, therefore, through your love of Holy Church that this work will bring many souls to a sound knowledge of Christian doctrine.

As a mark of the divine largess and in testimony of our own special good will we impart in all affection to you and to your pupils the Apostolic Benediction.

Given at Rome at St. Peter's the fifth day of February, 1919, in the fifth year of our Pontificate,

POPE BENEDICT XV.

FOREWORD

THE author of the original work asked me personally to translate his book into English. I have done so; but the genius of the English language did not permit a literal translation. The present book is therefore in some sense rather an adaptation than a literal translation, although the latter has been strictly adhered to wherever possible.

In the original work the answer always repeats the whole question word for word; in the cause of brevity and sometimes for clearness' sake, I have adopted the simple answer of " yes " or " no " lest the reader tire with the insistency of the ceaseless repetition.

Those readers who wish to study the doctrine more deeply will find much help in the references quoted at the end of most of the answers to the questions; they refer to the *Summa Theologica* itself, which has been translated literally into English* by the Dominican Fathers of the English Province. To take an example: On p. 9 of this book there is the question: *Does the Providence of God extend also to inanimate things?* And the answer: *Yes, for they are a part of God's handiwork* (XXII. 2, *Obj.* 5). The reference here quoted means that the doctrine in its every detail is to be found in the reply to the 5th Objec tion of the 2nd Article of the 22nd Question of the First

* To be had of Burns, Oates and Washbourne.

vii

Part of the *Summa*. It should be noted that the citation
of " First Part " is not added to the quotation for the
simple reason that the particular " part " of the *Summa*
to which the quotation refers may easily be found by
consulting the table of Contents. Moreover, whenever
necessary and in order to give additional strength to the
doctrines of St. Thomas, reference has been made to the
new Code of Canon Law; *e.g.*, on p. 289 (*Code*, Canon
1036). Thus this work is brought up to date.

Æ. W.

Rome,
Feast of St. Nicholas
(*December* 6, 1921).

CONTENTS

THE FIRST PART

OF GOD

(SOVEREIGN BEING; CAUSE AND LORD OF ALL THINGS)

THE SECOND PART

OF MAN

(Who came from God and Who must return to Him)

FIRST SECTION

General View of Man's Return to God

SECOND SECTION

Detailed View of Man's Return to God

THE THIRD PART

JESUS CHRIST

(GOD MADE MAN IN ORDER TO LEAD MAN TO GOD)

CONTENTS

CHAPTER   PAGE

   XV. OF THE TAKING PLACE OF THE INCARNATION IN THE
        WORLD - - - - - - 236

  XVI. OF CHRIST'S ENTRANCE INTO THE WORLD; OF HIS
        BIRTH: OF OUR BLESSED LADY - - - 236

 XVII. OF THE NAME "JESUS CHRIST" - - - 238

XVIII. OF CHRIST'S BAPTISM - - - - 238

  XIX. OF CHRIST'S TEMPTATION; OF HIS PREACHING; OF HIS
        MIRACLES; AND OF HIS TRANSFIGURATION - 239

   XX. OF CHRIST'S DEPARTURE FROM THIS WORLD; OF HIS
        PASSION AND DEATH; OF HIS BURIAL - 241

  XXI. OF CHRIST'S DESCENT INTO HELL - - 243

 XXII. OF CHRIST'S RESURRECTION - - - 244

XXIII. OF CHRIST'S ASCENSION; OF HIS POWER AT THE
        RIGHT HAND OF THE FATHER - - - 245

 XXIV. OF THE SACRAMENTS INSTITUTED BY JESUS CHRIST;
        OF THEIR NATURE, NECESSITY, AND EFFICACY - 246

  XXV. OF "BAPTISM"; OF THE MINISTER OF THIS SACRA-
        MENT - - - - - - 249

 XXVI. OF THOSE WHO MAY RECEIVE BAPTISM; AND OF ITS
        NECESSITY FOR ALL - - - - 251

XXVII. OF THE EFFECTS OF THIS SACRAMENT - - 253

XXVIII. OF THE DIGNITY AND DUTIES OF THOSE WHO HAVE
        RECEIVED IT - - - - - 254

 XXIX. OF "CONFIRMATION"; OF THE DUTIES IMPOSED
        THEREBY; OF THE RELIGIOUS INSTRUCTION NECES-
        SARY FOR ITS RECEPTION - - - - 255

  XXX. WHETHER MORE INSTRUCTION IS NECESSARY FOR THE
        RECEPTION OF CONFIRMATION THAN FOR THE
        RECEPTION OF THE HOLY EUCHARIST - - 257

 XXXI. OF THE "HOLY EUCHARIST" - - - 257

 XXXII. OF THE MATTER AND FORM OF THIS SACRAMENT; OF
        TRANSUBSTANTIATION; OF THE REAL PRESENCE; OF
        THE EUCHARISTIC ACCIDENTS - - - 259

XXXIII. OF THE EFFECTS OF THIS SACRAMENT - - 261

XXXIV. OF THE RECEPTION OF THE HOLY EUCHARIST - 264

 XXXV. OF THE MINISTER OF THIS SACRAMENT - - 266

XXXVI. OF THE HOLY SACRIFICE OF THE MASS - - 268

XXXVII. OF "PENANCE" - - - - - 270

XXXVIII. OF THE EFFECTS OF THIS SACRAMENT - - 272

XXXIX. OF THE PART OF THE PENITENT; OF CONTRITION,
        CONFESSION, AND SATISFACTION - - - 274

THE FIRST PART

OF GOD

(THE SOVEREIGN BEING; THE SOURCE AND MASTER OF ALL THINGS)

The Divine Nature and Attributes.
The Blessed Trinity.
The Creation: Angels, the World, Man.
The Divine Government.

CATECHISM OF THE "SUMMA THEOLOGICA"

I.—OF GOD'S EXISTENCE

Does God exist?

Yes, God exists (II.).

Why do you say that God exists? (II. 3).

Because if God did not exist, nothing would exist.

How do you prove that if God did not exist nothing would exist?

It is proved by this argument: That which exists through God only, would not exist if God did not exist. But whatever exists that is not God, exists through God only. Therefore, if God did not exist nothing would exist.

But how do you prove that whatever exists that is not God, exists through God only?

By this argument: Final analysis shows that that which does not exist of itself, can only exist through some other which exists of itself; and this latter we call God. But whatever exists that is not God, does not exist of itself. Therefore final analysis shows that whatever exists that is not God, exists through God only.

But how do you prove that whatever exists that is not God, does not exist of itself?

By this argument: That does not exist of itself, which has need of some other. But whatever exists that is not God, has need of some other. Therefore whatever exists that is not God, does not exist of itself.

But why is it that whatsoever has need of another, does not exist of itself?

Because that which exists of itself, neither depends nor could it depend upon anything or anybody; on the other hand, whatever has need of something or somebody, depends upon this something or this somebody.

3

But why do you assert that what exists of itself neither depends nor could depend on something or on somebody?

Because, existing of itself, it has everything in itself and through itself, and can receive nothing either from anything or from anybody.

Therefore every existing thing that has need of some other, manifestly proves by its very existence that God exists?

Yes.   Every existing thing that has need of some other manifestly proves by its very existence that God exists.

What then do those say who deny the existence of God?

They say that what has need of all has need of nothing, and conversely.

But surely that is a contradiction?

Precisely; one cannot deny God without falling into contradiction.

Is it then foolish to deny the existence of God?

Yes, it is indeed foolish to deny the existence of God.

II.—OF GOD'S NATURE AND ATTRIBUTES

(A)

Who is God?

God is a spirit, in three persons, the creator and sovereign Lord of all things.

What is meant by saying that God is a spirit?

By this is meant that He has no body, as we have, and that He is free from all matter, and that in Him there is nothing distinct from His being (III. 1-4).

What does this imply in God?

It implies that God is not a being like any other being which is this or that determined being; for He is in the true sense of the word most transcendental and most absolute; He is Very Being (III. 4).

Is God perfect?

Yes, God is perfect, for He lacks nothing (IV. 1).

Is God good?

Yes, God is Very Goodness; for He is the beginning and the end of all love (VI.).

Is God infinite?

Yes, God is infinite, for He has no limits (VII. 1).

Is God everywhere?

Yes, God is everywhere, for all that is, is in Him and through Him (VIII.).

Is God unchangeable?

Yes, God is unchangeable because possessing all things He can acquire nothing (IX.).

Is God eternal?

Yes, God is eternal because in Him there is no succession (X.).

Are there several Gods?

No, there is only one God (XI.).

(B)

Why are these divers attributes affirmed of God?

Because if He had them not, He would not be God.

How do you prove that if God did not have these attributes He would no longer be God?

Because God would no longer be God if He were not He who exists of Himself. But He who exists of Himself must be perfect, since He contains all in Himself; and if He is perfect He is good of necessity. He must be infinite, for if not something or other could act on Him, and thereby limit Him; and, if He is infinite, He must be everywhere. He must be unchangeable, for if not there would be something whereof He had need, and if He is unchangeable He is Eternal, since time implies succession which involves change. On the other hand, since He is infinitely perfect He can be only one; for two things infinitely perfect are absolutely impossible, since there would be nought in one whereby it was distinguished from the other (III.–XI.).

(C)

Can we see God in this life?

No, we cannot see God in this life, the obstacle being our mortal body (XII. 11).

Can we see God in heaven?

We can see God in heaven with the eyes of the glorified soul (XII. 1-10).

How can we know God in this life?

We can know God in this life by reason and by faith (XII. 12, 13).

What is meant by knowing God in this life by our reason?

It is to know God through the creatures He has made (XII. 12).

What is it to know Him in this life by faith?

It is to know God by what He has told us Himself about Himself (XII. 13).

Of these two kinds of knowledge that we can have of God, which is the more perfect?

Without doubt, the more perfect is the knowledge we have of Him by faith. For by it we see God in a light wherein the eye of reason fails; moreover, even though there are shadows and sometimes an impenetrable dark ness for us here below, nevertheless the light of faith is none other than the dawn of heaven's vision which is to be our happiness through all eternity (XII. 13).

(D)

When we speak of God, or endeavour to express our thoughts concerning Him, have the words we use a correct meaning?

Most certainly: for these words, although used prim arily to designate the perfections in a creature, can be transferred to designate what in God corresponds to these very perfections (XIII. 1-4).

When applied to God and to creatures, have these words the same meaning or one wholly different?

When applied to God they have the same meaning but in a superlative degree, that is, when used to designate perfections in creatures in the fulness of their meaning, they truly signify these perfections: whereas when used to designate the divine perfections, or whatever is attrib uted to God, if all that they tell is verily in God they do not tell fully the perfections they express in God (XIII. 5).

*Then whatever we may tell of God, and however exalted
be our expressions concerning Him, for us God ever remains
unutterable?*

Yes; but in this life we cannot do anything more salu
tary, more perfect, and more noble than speak of Him and
of all that concerns Him even though our thoughts fall
short of Him and our speech fail (XIII. 6-12).

III.—OF THE DIVINE OPERATIONS

What is the life of God?
He lives in His knowledge and in His love (XIV.-XXVI.).
Does God know all things?
Yes (XIV. 5).
Does God know all that happens on earth?
Yes (XIV. 11).
Does God know our secret thoughts?
Yes (XIV. 10).
Does God know the future?
Yes (XIV. 13).
How is this knowledge in God?
The reason is because God who is utterly immaterial
has a mind that is infinite. Hence no thing that is, that
will be, or can be in no matter what being is hidden from
Him, since everything is related to His knowledge as
effects are related to their causes (XIV. 1-5).

(A)

Has God a will?
Yes; for wheresoever there is mind, there also must be
will (XIX. 1).
Do all things depend on the will of God?
Yes; because God's will is the first and supreme
cause of all things (XIX. 4-6).

(B)

Does God love all His creatures?
Yes, for He made them out of love only (XX. 2).

Does God's love for His creatures produce any effect in them?

Yes, the effect of God's love in His creatures is the good found in them (XX. 3, 4).

(c)

Is God just?

Yes, God is Very Justice (XXI. 1).

Why is God Very Justice?

God is Very Justice because He gives to each creature what is due to its nature (XXI. 1-2).

Is there any special kind of God's justice towards men?

Yes; and it consists in this, that He rewards the good and punishes the wicked (XXI. 1, *Obj.* 3).

Does God reward the good and punish the wicked in this life?

Only in part does God reward the good and punish the wicked in this life.

Where does God fully reward the good and punish the wicked?

In heaven God fully rewards the good, and in hell fully punishes the wicked.

(D)

Is God merciful?

Yes (XXI. 3).

In what does the mercy of God consist?

It consists in this, that He gives to each thing even more than is due to its nature; likewise He rewards the good more fully than they deserve and punishes the wicked even less than they deserve (XXI. 4).

(E)

Has God any care of the world?

Yes; and it is called providence (XXI. 1).

Does the providence of God extend to all things?

Yes, for there is nothing in the world that God has not foreseen and pre-ordained from all eternity (XXII. 2).

Does it extend also to inanimate things?

Yes, for they are a part of God's handiwork (XXII. 2, *Obj.* 5).

Does it extend to the free acts of man?

Yes; and by this is meant that every free act of man is subject to the ordering of Divine Providence, and in these acts there is nothing but what God ordains or permits; for in no sense does man's liberty imply man's independence of God (XXII. 2, *Obj.* 4).

(F)

Has God's providence in regard to the elect any special name?

Yes, it is called predestination (XXIII. 1).

What does predestination imply with regard to those whom it concerns?

It implies that these one day shall possess the happiness of heaven (XXIII. 2).

What are those called who never attain to this happiness?

They are called the reproved or the non-elect (XXIII. 3).

Why is it that the predestined attain this happiness while the reproved or the non-elect do not?

It is because God chooses the predestined by a love of predilection, in virtue of which He so arranges all things in this life that ultimately they reach the happiness of heaven (XXIII. 4).

And why is it that the reproved or the non-elect do not ultimately reach the same happiness?

It is because God does not love them with the same love as He loves the predestined (XXIII. 3, *Obj.* 1).

But surely this is unjust on God's part?

No, it is not unjust, because no one has a right to the happiness of heaven; and those who reach heaven do so by the grace of God only (XXIII. 3, *Obj.* 2).

But those who do not reach heaven, will they be punished for not getting there?

They will not be punished for not getting there except

in so far as their sins prevented them from getting there
(XXIII. 3, *Obj.* 3).

*Is it true that man is prevented from reaching heaven by
his own fault?*

Yes, it is through man's own fault if he does not reach
the happiness of heaven which God offers to all; man who
is free either does not respond to the offer made him by
God or he spurns it by seeking his own ends (*ibid.*).

*Does this despisal or the choosing of one's own ends
outrage God?*

Yes, such is an outrage against God; moreover when
this is due to one's own personal sin, it merits the most
severe chastisement (*ibid.*).

*Do those who respond to God's offer and who reach the
happiness of heaven owe it to God that they responded to His
offer, and is it due to Him that they merit their happiness?*

Yes, they owe it all to the predestination of God
(XXIII. 3, *Obj.* 2).

Does God make this choice from all eternity?

Yes (XXIII. 3, *Obj.* 2).

*What does this choice imply with regard to those whom
it concerns?*

It implies that God has fixed for them a place in heaven
and that by His grace He guides them towards heaven,
which eventually they reach (XXIII. 5-7).

*What should men do at the thought of this eternal choice
of predestination?*

They should rely completely on the grace of God in
the endeavour to know for certain, in so far as this is
possible on earth, that they are among the elect (XXIII. 8).

(G)

Is God almighty?
Yes (XXV. 1-6).
Why is God almighty?
Because since God is Very Being, whatever is not
opposed to the idea of being is dependent upon Him
(XXV. 3).

(H)

Is God happy?

Yes, God is Very Happiness; for He enjoys in an infinite manner the infinite good which is none other than Himself (XXVI. 1-4).

IV.—OF THE DIVINE PERSONS

(A)

What is meant by saying that God is a spirit in three persons?

By this is meant that each of these three persons is the self-same spirit, who is God, with all the attributes of divinity (XXX. 2).

What are the names of the three persons?

They are called the Father, the Son, and the Holy Ghost.

Who is God the Father?

God the Father is He who, without principle Himself, begets the Son, and from whom proceeds the Holy Ghost.

Who is God the Son?

God the Son is He who is begotten of the Father, and from whom (with the Father as co-principle) proceeds the Holy Ghost.

Who is God the Holy Ghost?

The Holy Ghost is He who proceeds from the Father and the Son.

Are these three divine persons distinct from God Himself?

No.

Are they distinct from each other?

Yes.

What is understood by saying that the divine persons are distinct from each other?

By this is understood that the Father is not the Son nor the Holy Ghost; that the Son is not the Father nor the Holy Ghost; and that the Holy Ghost is not the Father nor the Son.

Can these three persons be separated from each other?
No.

Were they together from all eternity?
Yes.

Has the Father, in relation to the Son, all that we have affirmed of God?
Yes.

And have the Son in relation to the Father, and the Father and Son in relation to the Holy Ghost, all that we have affirmed of God?
Yes.

And in relation to the Father and the Son, has the Holy Ghost likewise all we have affirmed of God?
Yes.

Are these three, thus related to each other from all eternity, three Gods?
No.   They are not three Gods, but three persons, each of whom is identified with the self-same God, and yet withal remain distinct from each other.

Do these three persons form a veritable society?
Yes, they form a veritable society, and such as is the most perfect of all societies (XXXI., *Obj.* 1).

Why is this society the most perfect of all societies?
The reason is because each of these three is alike infinite in perfection, in duration, in knowledge, in love, in power, and in happiness; and hence their joy in each other is infinitely rapturous.

(B)

How do we know there are three persons in God?
We know this by faith.

Could reason, without the help of faith, know that there are three persons in God?
No (XXXII. 1).

When faith tells us there are three persons in God, can reason understand this?
No.   Even though faith tell us this, reason fails to understand (XXXII. 1, *Obj.* 2).

What are these truths called that are beyond reason's grasp and are known by faith only?

They are called mysteries.

Is the doctrine of the three Divine Persons a mystery?

Yes; and it is the most inscrutable of all mysteries.

What is this mystery of the three Divine Persons called?

It is called the mystery of the Holy Trinity (XXXI. 1).

Shall we ever come to know the Holy Trinity in itself?

Yes, some day we shall know the Holy Trinity in itself, for this knowledge will constitute our eternal happiness in heaven.

Is it possible on earth to get a glimpse of the beauties of this mystery of the Holy Trinity by a consideration of those actions which are proper to intellectual beings?

Yes, for these actions imply in an intellectual being the twofold relation of principle and term whether the action be one of thought or of love; for faith teaches us that in God in the act which is thought, the Father has the nature of the principle that expresses and the Word the nature of the term expressed; and in the act which is loving, the Father and the Son are co-principles of love in relation to the Holy Ghost who has the nature of the one loved.

What then is the ultimate reason of the mystery of the Holy Trinity in God?

It is the infinite richness or fecundity of the divine nature which demands the existence of these mysterious processions, which are called processions of origin (XXVII. 1).

(c)

What are these processions of origin called in God?

They are called generation and procession.

What is the consequence of this generation and this procession in God?

The consequence is that between the two terms of generation and the two terms of procession there are real relations which are constituted by these different terms.

What are these relations in God?

They are four in number, and are called Paternity, Filiation, Active Spiration, and Procession (or Passive Spiration) (XXVIII. 4).

Are these divine relations the same as the Divine Persons?

Yes (XL. 1).

Why is it then that there are four divine relations and yet only three Divine Persons?

The reason is because one of these relations, viz., Active Spiration, not being relatively opposed either to Paternity or Filiation, but on the contrary belonging to both Father and Son as one principle, it follows that the two persons, Father and Son, the one constituted by Paternity the other by Filiation, can be the subject of Active Spiration, which thereby does not constitute a separate person but which belongs equally to the person of the Father and the person of the Son (XXX. 2).

(D)

Is there any kind of order among the Divine Persons?

Yes, there is the order of origin, owing to which the Son can be *sent* by the Father, and the Holy Ghost can be *sent* by the Father and the Son (XLII., XLIII.).

When the Divine Persons produce acts other than those known as notional acts (which are the acts of generation and spiration), are these acts produced by the three persons in common?

Yes; and this is the reason why the act of thinking and the act of loving belong to all the three persons; and likewise all those actions which produce an effect *outside* God (XXXIX., XLI.).

(E)

But are there not certain actions or certain sources of action which are attributed more particularly to this or that person?

Yes.   There are what are called certain *attributions* of this kind to which these acts or sources of act give rise according to the distinctive character of this or of that person: for this reason by way of *appropriation* we attribute power to the Father, for instance, wisdom to the Son, and goodness to the Holy Ghost, although these belong equally to all three (XXXIX. 7, 8; XLV. 6).

When therefore we speak of God in His relation to the world, do we always imply that it is God as one in nature and as three in person that acts?

Yes, except when we speak of the person of God the Son in the mystery of the Incarnation (XLV. 6).

V.—OF THE CREATION

What is meant by saying that God is the Creator of all things?

It is meant that God made all things out of nothing (XLIV., XLV.).

There was then nothing at all beside God before He made all things?

Of a truth there was nothing beside God before He made all things, He Himself being by Himself, and all things else through Him (XLIV. 1).

When did God thus make all things out of nothing?

God made all things out of nothing when it pleased His will (XLIV.).

Had He so wished then, He need not have created the things He has made?

It is even so.

Why therefore did God wish to create at some given moment the things He has made?

God created the things He has made to make manifest His glory (XLIV. 4).

What is meant by this?

It is meant that God wished to make manifest the abundance of His goodness by communicating to others in part something of the infinite goodness which is none other than Himself.

It was not then through need, nor in order to acquire some perfection, that God created the things that He has made?

No, on the contrary, it was merely to give unto others something of what He Himself possesses in an infinite degree and out of sheer goodness that He created the things He has made.

VI.—OF THE WORLD

What name is given to the sum of God's creation?

It is called the world or the universe (XLVII. 4).

Is then the world or the universe the work of God's hand?

Yes (XLVII. 1, 2, 3).

Of what is the world or universe composed?

It is composed of three categories of being: pure spirits, bodies, and spirits joined to body.

Is God Himself the Creator of these pure spirits, these bodies, and these spirits joined to body?

Yes, God Himself is the Creator of all these.

Did God alone, by Himself, create these things?

Yes, for God alone can create (XLV. 5).

How did God, alone and by Himself, make the world of spirits and bodies?

He did it by His Word together with His Love (XLV. 6).

VII.—OF THE ANGELS: THEIR NATURE

(A)

Why did God wish there should be pure spirits in His work of creation?

He willed there should be pure spirits because they were destined to be the crowning of His work (L. 1).

Why are these pure spirits the crowning of God's work?

Because they are the highest, the most perfect, and the most beautiful part of His creation (*ibid.*).

What is the nature of these pure spirits?

Pure spirits are substances free from all body and from all matter (L. 1, 2).

Are these pure spirits very numerous?

Yes (L. 3).

Is their number greater than that of all other created things?

Yes (*ibid.*).

But why are they so numerous?

Because the most beautiful part of God's creation ought to dominate by its grandeur all the rest of His creation (*ibid.*).

What are these pure spirits called?

They are called angels.

Why are they called angels?

Because they are the messengers whom God employs for the administering of the rest of His creation.

(B)

Can the angels take to themselves a body like ours?

No, the angels cannot take to themselves a body like ours; if at any time they reveal themselves to men in a bodily form, this form has only the external appearance of a body (LI. 1, 2, 3).

(C)

Do the angels exist somewhere?

Yes (LII. 1).

Ordinarily speaking, where are the angels?

Their ordinary place is in heaven (LXI. 4.)

Can angels pass from one place to another?

Yes (LIII. 1).

. *Is time necessary for their passing from one place to another?*

In an instant the angels can pass from one place to another no matter the distance (LIII. 2).

Are they also able to leave one place gradually and to be present gradually in another place according to will?

Yes, they can do this, for their movement is nought else

but a successive application of their power or their activity upon different things or on different parts of the same thing (LIII. 3).

VIII.—THE INNER LIFE OF THE ANGELS

(A)

What is the life of the angels in so far as they are pure spirits?

Their life as pure spirits consists in knowledge and love.

What kind of knowledge have the angels?

Their knowledge is intellectual (LIV.).

Have the angels a knowledge through sense as we have?

No, there is no such knowledge in the angels (LIV. 5).

Why is there no knowledge through sense in the angels as in us?

Because knowledge through sense is acquired through a body; and the angels have no body (*ibid.*).

Is the intellectual knowledge of the angels more perfect than ours?

Yes.

Why is this?

Because their intellectual knowledge is not acquired like ours from the exterior world; moreover they attain to the truth of a thing at a single glance without need of reasoning (LV. 2; LVIII. 3, 4).

(B)

Do the angels know all things?

No, for their nature is finite; God alone knows all things because He is infinite (LIV. 1, 2, 3).

Do they know the totality of creatures?

Yes; for their nature of pure spirit demands that this be so (LV. 2).

Do the angels know all that passes in the external world?

Yes. For the ideas in their minds manifest to them these things according as the latter come into being (*ibid.*).

Do they know our secret thoughts?

No. For these thoughts depend on our free will, and thereby are not necessarily linked up with external events (LVII. 4).

Is there no means at all whereby the angels can know our secret thoughts?

Yes. Our secret thoughts can become known to them by the revelation of God, or by the person himself revealing them (*ibid.*).

Do the angels know the future?

No, unless God reveal it to them (LVII. 3).

What kind of love is connatural to the angels?

Connaturally there is in the angels a perfect love of God, love of themselves and of all creatures unless sin, in the supernatural order, does not denaturalize what is free in their love in the natural order (LX.).

IX.—OF THE CREATION OF THE ANGELS

Were all the angels created by God Himself?

Yes, for each of them is a pure spirit which can come into being only by way of creation (LXI. 1).

When were all the angels created by God?

The angels were created by God instantaneously at the same time when He created all the contents of the corporal world (LXI. 3).

Were the angels created by God in a locality?

Yes, the harmony of the divine work demanding this (LXI. 4, *Obj.* 1).

What is the locality where the angels were created called?

We call it heaven simply, and sometimes the empyrean heaven (LXI. 4).

What does the empyrean heaven mean?

It means a place full of glory and splendour which is the most beautiful part of the corporal world (*ibid.*).

Is the empyrean heaven the same as the heaven of the blessed?

Yes (*ibid. Obj.* 3).

X.—OF THE PROBATION OF THE ANGELS

In what state were the angels created?

They were created by God in a state of grace (LXII. 3).

What is meant by saying the angels were created in a state of grace?

By this is meant that at the instant of their creation they received from God a nature adorned with sancti fying grace which made them God's children, and which gave them the wherewith to attain to the glory of life eternal (LXII. 1, 2, 3).

Was it by an act of their free will that the angels could attain the glory of life eternal?

Yes (LXII. 4).

In what consisted this act of their free will?

This act consisted in responding to the impulse of grace which inclined them to submit to God and to receive from Him with love and acknowledgment the gift of His glory which He offered to them (*ibid.*).

Under this impulse of grace, was time at all necessary for the angels to make the choice proposed to them by God?

No, this choice was made by them instantaneously (*ibid.*).

Did the angels attain to glory as soon as ever they had made this choice?

Yes, they attained to glory on the instant (LXII. 5).

XI.—OF THE FALL OF THE BAD ANGELS

Did all the angels make the choice deserving of heaven offered to them by God?

No, for some of them turned away from God (LXIII. 3).

Why did certain angels refuse to turn to God?

Because they were prompted through pride and through the desire of self-sufficiency making themselves like unto God (LXIII. 2, 3).

Was this pride a great sin?

Yes, it was a heinous sin which provoked God's anger on the instant.

What was the result of God's just anger in regard to this sin of the angels?

On the instant God cast the bad angels into hell; and this place will be for ever the scene of their punishment (LXIV. 4).

What are these bad angels who revolted against God and were cast into hell called?

They are called the devils (LXIII. 4).

XII.—OF THE CREATION OF MATERIAL SUBSTANCES, AND THE WORK OF THE SIX DAYS

(A)

After the creation of pure spirits, what is the second category of beings created by God in the universe?

The second category of beings created by God was bodily substance.

Were all the bodily substances in the world created by God?

Yes (LXV. 5).

Was it then God Himself who created the earth and all that we see in the heavens   the sun, the moon, the stars—and did He create the sea and all contained therein?

Yes, of a truth God created all these things Himself.

When did God create this material world?

God created this material world and all contained therein at the same time that He created the world of spirits (LXI. 3; LXVI. 4).

Did God create both the world of matter and the world of spirit in an instant?

Yes, God created both in an instant and at the same time (*ibid.*).

Was the material world in the first instant the same as we see it to-day?

No (LXVI. 1).

In what state then was the material world created by God?
It was created in a state of chaos.

What is meant by saying it was created in a state of chaos?

By this is meant that God first of all created the elements only, from which the world evolved such as we see it to-day (LXVI. 1, 2).

Who was the cause of this evolution of the world from the primary elements, such as we see it to-day?
God was the cause thereof.

Did God so create the material world that straightway it evolved from the primary elements?

No, for this evolution lasted through several succeeding stages, each of which was due to His divine intervention.

How many such interventions were there whereby the material world was brought to that state in which we see it to-day?

There were six divine interventions.

What are these six interventions called?

They are called the six days of creation (LXXIV. 1, 2).

(B)

What did God create on the first day?
On the first day God created the light (LXVII. 4).

On the second day?
The firmament (LXVIII. 1).

On the third day?
On the third day God separated the waters from the land; He also created the vegetable kingdom (LXIX.).

On the fourth day?
On this day God created the sun, the moon, and the stars (LXX. 1).

On the fifth day?
The fishes and the birds (LXXI.).

On the sixth day?
On this day God created the beasts of the earth; and lastly He created man (LXXII.).

How do we know that God thus created the world such as we see it?

We know that God thus created the world such as we see it because He Himself has said so.

Where does God say that He created the world in this wise and such as we see it?

In the first chapter of Genesis, at the very beginning of the Holy Scriptures, God tells us that He made the world in this wise and such as we see it.

Are the sciences in accord with this first chapter of Genesis?

There is no doubt that sciences worthy of the name are and will always be in accord with the first chapter of Genesis.

Why do you say sciences worthy of the name?

Because sciences worthy of the name give true explana tions of things as they are; but no science knows better than God Himself the things that He Himself made; and it is God who tells us how He made them in the first chapter of Genesis.

Can there be then any contradiction between the sciences and Holy Scripture on the subject of the creation of the material world?

No, it is not possible for any contradiction to exist between the sciences worthy of the name and Holy Scripture on the subject of the creation of the material world (LXVII.–LXXIV.).

XIII.—OF MAN: HIS NATURE; HIS SPIRI-TUAL AND IMMORTAL SOUL

(A)

Is there anything in this world which forms as it were a world apart, a being that is wholly distinct from the rest of the world created by God?

Yes; and this being is man.

What is man?

Man is a composite of spirit and body, in whom the world of spirits and the world of bodies in some sort coalesce (LXXV.).

What is the spirit called that is in man?

It is called the soul (LXXV. 1-4).

Is man the only being in the world of bodies that has a soul?

No. Besides man plants and animals have souls.

What is the difference between the soul of man and the souls of plants and animals?

There is this difference, the soul of a plant has only vegetative life, the soul of an animal has both vegetative and sensitive life, whereas the soul of man has in addition an intellective life.

Is it then by intellective life that man is distinct from all other living beings in this world?

Yes

Is this intellective life of the soul of man, in itself, independent of his body?

Yes (LXXV. 2).

Can any reason be given to establish this truth?

Yes; and the reason is because the object of thought is something wholly immaterial.

But how does it follow from this that the human soul in its intellective life is, in itself, independent of body?

This follows because if the soul itself were not wholly immaterial it could not attain by thought to an object wholly immaterial (*ibid.*).

What follows from this truth?

It follows that the soul of man is immortal (LXXV. 6).

(B)

Can it be shown that the immortality of man's soul follows from this truth?

Yes. Because if in the soul there is an act wholly independent of bodily matter, it must itself be independent of bodily matter.

What follows from this truth that the soul is, in itself, independent of bodily matter?

It follows that if the body perishes by separation from the soul, the soul itself does not perish (*ibid.*).

Will the human soul live for ever?

Yes.

Why then is the human soul united to a body?

The human soul is united to a body in order to make a substantial whole called man (LXXVI. 1).

Is it not then accidental that the soul is united to a body?

No, for the soul was made to be joined to a body (LXXVI. 1).

What are the effects of the soul upon the body to which it is united?

The soul gives to the body every perfection that the body has, that is it gives to it being, life, and sense; but thought it cannot give, for this is proper to the soul itself (LXXVI. 3, 4).

XIV.—OF THE VEGETATIVE AND SENSITIVE POWERS

(A)

Are there in the soul divers powers corresponding to the divers acts it produces?

Yes, with the only exception of the first perfection which the soul gives to the body, namely, existence; but it gives this not through some power or faculty, but immediately, of itself (LXXVII.).

What powers of the soul give life to the body?

The vegetative powers.

What are these powers?

They are three in number, viz., the power of nutrition, of growth, and of reproduction (LXXVIII. 2).

(B)

What faculties of the soul give sense to the body?

The sensitive powers.

What are these powers?

They are twofold: the powers of knowing and the powers of loving.

What are the sensitive powers through which the body knows?

The five external senses (LXXVIII. 3).

What are these powers called?

They are called the powers of seeing, hearing, smelling, tasting, and touching.

And the five external senses, what are they called?

They are called sight, hearing, smell, taste, and touch (*ibid.*).

Are there also any internal sensitive powers of knowing that do not appear externally?

Yes, they are the common (or central) sense, the imagination, instinct (or estimative sense), and memory (LXXVIII. 4).

XV.—OF THE MIND AND ITS ACT OF UNDERSTANDING

(A)

Are there any other powers of knowing in man?

Yes, there is another faculty of knowing and it is man's chief power.

What is this chief power of knowing in man called?

It is called his reason or intellect (LXXIX. 1).

Is reason and intellect one and the same power of knowing in man?

Yes (LXXIX. 8).

Why are these two names given to the same power?

It is because in the act of knowing man sometimes understands at a glance as it were without reasoning, whereas at other times he must reason (*ibid.*).

Is reasoning an act proper to man?

Yes, because of all beings that are, man alone is able to reason, or has need of reasoning.

Is it a perfection in man to be able to reason?

Yes, but it is an imperfection to have need of reasoning.

Why is it a perfection in man to be able to reason?

Because in this wise man can attain to truth; whereas no creature inferior to man, such as animals which are without reason, can do this.

Why is it, on the other hand, an imperfection in man to have need of reasoning?

Because in this wise he attains to truth by slow degrees only, and he is thereby liable to err; whereas God and the angels who have no need of reasoning attain to truth straightway without fear of making a mistake.

(B)

What is it to know truth?

To know truth is to know things as they are.

What then is it not to know things as they are?

It is to be in ignorance or in error.

Is there any difference between being in ignorance and being in error?

Yes, there is a great difference; to be in ignorance is merely not to know things as they are; whereas to be in error is to affirm that a thing is, when it is not, or conversely.

Is it an evil for man to be in error?

Yes, it is a great evil, because man's proper good consists in knowledge of the truth which is the good of his intellect.

Has man a knowledge of the truth at birth?

No, at birth man has no knowledge of the truth; for though he then has an intellect it is in an entirely undeveloped state; its unfolding, necessary for the attainment of truth, awaits the development of the powers of sense which are its handmaids (LXXXIV. 5).

When then does man begin to know truth?

Man begins to know truth when he has attained the use of reason, that is at about the age of seven years.

(C)

Can man know all things by his reason?

No, man cannot know all by his reason adequately, that is if one considers his reason within the limits of its natural powers (XII. 4; LXXXVI. 2, 4).

What things can man know by the natural force of his reason?

By the natural power of his reason man can know all things attainable by his senses and all that these things manifest.

Can man know himself by the natural power of his reason?

Yes, because he himself is a thing attainable by the power of sense, and by the help of other things that fall within the scope of his senses, he is able, by reasoning, to come to a knowledge of himself (LXXXVII.).

(D)

Can man know the angels or pure spirits?

Yes, but he can know them only imperfectly.

Why can he know them only imperfectly?

It is because he cannot know them in themselves by reason of their nature; for they do not belong to the category of things attainable by sense, which things are the proper object of man's reason (LXXXVIII. 1, 2).

(E)

Can man know God in Himself?

No, man cannot know God in Himself by the natural force of his reason, for God is infinite above all things of sense, which alone are the objects proportionate to the natural power of man's reason (LXXXVIII. 3).

Left then to his natural powers man can know God only imperfectly by his reason?

Yes.

Is it nevertheless a good thing for man to be able to know God only imperfectly by his reason?

Yes. Indeed it is a great perfection for man to know

God by his reason however imperfect the knowledge be; because thereby man is lifted up in an eminent degree above the rest of creatures that are devoid of reason; it is moreover owing to the possibility of this knowledge that God has raised man to the sovereign dignity of being a child of His grace; in this happy state man's reason knows God as He is in Himself, at first imperfectly by the light of faith, but at length perfectly by the light of glory (XII. 4, *Obj.* 3, 5, 8, 10, 13).

By the fact that man can be raised to the dignity of becoming a child of God by grace, is he placed on a level with the angels?

Yes. Raised to the dignity of a child of God by grace, man is in some sort on an equal footing with the angels; indeed he can even ascend higher than they in this order of grace, although in the order of nature he always remains inferior to them (CVIII. 8).

XVI.—OF MAN'S POWERS OF LOVING: FREE WILL

(A)

Are there any other powers in man beside those of knowing?

Yes, there are also the powers of loving.

What is understood by these powers?

By the powers of loving we understand that there is in man a power by which he is drawn through the medium of his powers of knowing to seek whatsoever presents itself as a good, and to turn away from whatsoever presents itself as an evil.

Are there several powers of loving in man?

They are twofold by reason of the two kinds of knowledge in man.

What are these powers of loving called?

The first is called the heart or the affections in the material sense of the word (LXXXI.); the second is called the will (LXXXII.).

May not man's will also be called the heart?

Yes, but in a higher and wholly immaterial sense of the word.

Which is the more perfect of these two powers of loving?

The will.

(B)

Is it because man has a will that he is said to be free?

Yes, for his will is not drawn of itself or of necessity to a good except under the general aspect of good; hence provided the good presented to the will is only some particular good the will is master of its own act in so far as it is able to choose or not to choose that particular good (LXXXIII.).

Is man's free will dependent upon his will only?

No, man's free will results from a combination of his will with his reason or intellect.

Is man by his intellect and will, and his power of freedom, the king of all creatures in this world?

Yes, this is so; for all things else by their very natures are inferior to man and were made to serve him.

XVII.—OF MAN'S ORIGIN OR HIS CREATION BY GOD

(A)

Do all men on earth, and all those who preceded them, come from one father and one mother?

Yes.

This first man and this first woman from whom all men come, what were they called?

They were called Adam and Eve.

Who was the author of Adam and Eve?

Almighty God.

How did God make Adam and Eve?

By giving them a body and a soul.

How did God give a soul to Adam and Eve?

By creation (XC. 1, 2).

How did God give a body to Adam and Eve?

God tells us that He made the body of Adam from the slime of the earth and that He built up Eve's body from a rib of Adam (XCI., XCII.).

(B)

Must we say that man was made to God's own image and likeness?

Yes (XCIII.).

What is understood by this?

By this is understood that God has given to man a nature and corresponding actions of such a kind that in their highest reach man is enabled to enter in some measure into the spiritual life of God and appreciate the inner life of the three august persons; and owing to this he is enabled to imitate the perfection proper to the Divine Persons (XCIII. 5-9).

Is it possible to show how the nature of man and his actions, viewed in their highest endeavour, enable him to know God in His spiritual nature and to catch a glimpse even of the intimate life of the three Divine Persons?

The reason is because man's soul as regards its highest faculties is also spiritual in nature; moreover its supreme acts are those of thinking and loving, which are capable of reaching to the First Truth and the First Good which is God Himself (XCIII. 5-7).

In these acts of thought and of love how can we catch a glimpse of the inner life of the three Divine Persons?

By these acts we can attain even unto this because when our mind thinks of God it forms within itself an interior word wherein it reads an object; and under the very impulse of the thought which conceives the word there is begotten an act of love for this same object con ceived by the mind (XCIII. 6).

How can we imitate the perfection proper to the Divine Persons?

We can do this, as God Himself does, by making God conceived in our mind and loved by our will the first object of our life of thought and of our life of love (XCIII. 7).

In the corporeal world is man only made to the image and likeness of God?

Yes; and this by reason of his spiritual nature (XCIII. 2).

Do not other creatures in this world resemble their Creator in some way?

Yes, all creatures in the world bear a mark or a trace of God who made them, by reason of their perfections which are of a lower order (XCIII. 6).

XVIII.—OF THE STATE OF HAPPINESS IN WHICH MAN WAS CREATED

(A)

Was man created by God in a state of great perfection?
Yes.

What did the state of perfection in which man was created comprise?

It comprised the mind's complete knowledge void of error; original justice with all the virtues of mind and will; entire command of the soul over the body and over every creature inferior to man (XCIV., XCV., XCVI.).

Was this state of perfection proper to the first man only, or ought it to have been common to all who are descended from Adam by generation?

It was proper to Adam as regards the gift of knowledge only; but since original justice and the gifts of integrity and complete moral rectitude are inseparable from human nature as such these would have been transmitted to all by way of origin or generation had not sin stood in the way (XCIV., CI. 1).

In this state in which man was created, would he have been subject to death?

No, in this state man would not have died (CXVII. 1).

Would man have suffered in this state?

No, for by a special privilege man's body was guarded

from all evil by the soul which itself was incapable of
suffering so long as it remained subjected to God by its
will (XCVII. 2).

(B)

Was man created by God in a state of happiness?
Yes.

Was this state that of his final and perfect happiness?
No, it was only temporary, and would have been fol
lowed by another state which was final (XCIV. 1, *Obj.* 1).

*What then may one call this state of happiness in which
man was created by God?*
It may be called a state of initial happiness which was
to prepare man by way of merit to enter into the state
of his final and perfect happiness in token of reward
XCIV. 1, *Obj.* 2; XCV. 4).

*Where would man have acquired this state of final and
perfect happiness had he remained faithful?*
He would have acquired this happiness in the glory
of heaven in the company of the angels, whither God
would have transferred him after a certain period of
probation (XCIV. 1, *Obj.* 1).

*Where was man placed while awaiting to be transferred
to the glory of heaven?*
He was placed in a garden of delights prepared by God
for him (CII.).

What was this garden of delights called?
It was called the Garden of Eden (*ibid.*).

XIX.—OF THE CONSERVATION OF THINGS
AND THEIR GOVERNMENT

*What is meant by saying that God is the sovereign lord
of all things?*
By this is understood that in the world created by God
all things are subjected to the exclusive, supreme, and
absolute dominion of God Himself (CIII. 1, 3).

What is meant by this?
By this is meant that there is nothing in the spirit

world, or in the material world, or in man, which can evade the action of God maintaining and leading all things to the end for which He created them (CIII. 4-8).

What is this end towards which God by His dominion maintains and guides all created things?

This end towards which God by His sway leads and maintains all created things is Himself or His glory (CIII. 2).

What is meant by saying that God and His glory are the end of the entire universe thus maintained and ruled by Him?

By this is meant that God and His glory are the end of the whole universe because God directs all things therein that He might make known in the very order of the uni verse the designs of His holy will (*ibid.*).

It is then in the very order of the universe that the glory of God shines forth and is manifested outwardly?

Yes.

Could there be anything greater and more perfect outside God than this order of the universe which is created, main tained, and ruled by Him?

No, in the present dispensation of things there could be nothing greater or more perfect (XXV. 5, 6).

Why in the present dispensation of things?

Because, since God is infinite and almighty, no created order however perfect could ever exhaust His infinite power (*ibid.*).

XX.—OF GOD'S ACTION IN THE GOVERN MENT OF THE UNIVERSE; AND OF MIRACLES

(A)

How does God govern this universe which was created by Him?

By maintaining it and directing it to its end (CIII. 4).

Does God maintain all created things Himself?

Yes, God Himself maintains all created things; although He uses certain of His creatures to maintain others in

existence according to the order of dependence which
He established among things when He created them
(CIV. 1, 2).

*What is meant by saying that He Himself maintains all
created things?*

By this is meant that that which is at the basis of all
beings in the universe and which makes existence the
common connecting link of all is communicated to them
by the direct action of God Himself (CIV. 1).

*Is the act of maintaining all things in existence also proper
to God as is the creation of things?*

Yes, because the direct and immediate result of both
phenomena is the inflow of being which is an effect
proper to God (CIV. 1, *Obj.* 4; VIII. 1).

(B)

*Could God effect that all things that are should cease
to be?*

Yes.

*What action on God's part would be necessary to effect
that all things that are should cease to be?*

It would be sufficient for Him to cease willing to give
them the being they have, and which they continue to
receive from Him every instant (*ibid.*).

*Without ceasing, therefore, the being of all things that
are in the world depends absolutely upon God?*

Yes, without ceasing things depend absolutely on God;
much in the same way as the light of the day depends
absolutely upon the presence of the action of the sun;
except that the action of the sun is a necessary action,
whereas the action of God is wholly free (*ibid.*).

Has God ever annihilated anything He has made?

No (CIV. 4).

Will God ever annihilate anything?

No (*ibid.*).

*Why has God never annihilated and will never annihilate
anything He has created?*

Because God acts for His glory only; and His glory

demands not that He annihilate, but rather that He preserve things in existence (*ibid.*).

(c)

Can there be any change in things made by God?

Yes, and changes more or less radical according to the difference of natures, and according to the difference of states of the same nature.

Do these changes which sometimes come about in the things made by God, enter into the plan of His divine government?

Yes, since all such can and should advance the end of His government which is the glory of God and the well-being of His work.

Are there any changes in creatures that are due to the special action of God?

Yes (CV. 1-8); and they are those changes which affect directly the ultimate basis of material things, or the affective part of spiritual beings, and also that which is fundamental in every action of the creature (CV. 1, 4, 5).

Is this action which is proper to God and to which we must attribute the changes that come about in material things " outside" the action of secondary causes which in the ordinary course of nature is proportionate to these changes?

Yes, and such changes are called miracles (CV. 6, 7).

(D)

Are there any such miracles performed by God?

Yes, it is most certain that there are miracles performed by God in the material world. They can be graded in three categories according as the events are beyond the power of nature to effect—in themselves, or in the subject in which they are effected, or in the manner of their production (CV. 8).

Why has God performed such miracles, and does He still perform them?

God has performed, and may perform again as it pleases Him, such miracles in order to arouse the minds of men, and to make them acknowledge His divine power which is brought into play for their well-being and for His own glory.

XXI.—OF THE ACTION OF CREATURES IN THIS GOVERNMENT; AND OF THE ORDER OF THE UNIVERSE

(A)

As regards the changes that come about, or can come about in created things, can creatures act and do they act one upon the other?

Yes; and it is indeed the action of one creature upon another which constitutes, properly speaking, the order of the universe (XLVII. 3).

Is this action of creatures, one upon the other, subjected also to the action of the divine government?

Yes; and in the most intimate way (CIII. 6).

What is meant by this?

By this is meant that by the action of creatures one upon the other, God directs the whole assemblage of His creatures to the end He has fixed for them (*ibid.*).

Could God alone, and by His own activity, lead each one of His creatures to its end?

Without doubt He could do this; but it was better for Him to have willed to employ thus the actions of creatures one upon the other in order to lead them to their end; for thereby creatures are more perfect and God's power is made more manifest.

Why are creatures thereby more perfect?

Because, thus, creatures participate in the sovereign activity of God, whereby He directs them to their end (CIII. 6, *Obj.* 2).

And why is God's power made more manifest?

Because it is a mark of power and greatness for a sovereign to have in his service a throng of ministers to put his orders into execution (CIII. 6, *Obj.* 3).

*When creatures then act one upon the other they are
simply executing the orders of God?*

Yes, for their actions can never evade the perfect and
sovereign sway of the divine government (CIII. 8,
Obj. 1, and *Obj.* 2).

(B)

*Is it altogether impossible for there to be any disorder
in the activity of creatures, one upon the other, when
they act as instruments of God in the government of the
world?*

Yes, it is impossible, for no matter what their action be
it is also always directed in co-operating under the transcend
ing action of God towards the good of the universe
(CIII. 8, *Obj.* 1, and *Obj.* 3).

*Can creatures, in their action one upon the other, be the
cause of any particular evil?*

Yes; and this both in the physical order and the moral,
for they can disturb this or that particular subalternate
order among creatures, or even among the divers mani
festations thereof which come under the designs and
wishes of God (CIII. 8, *Obj.* 1).

*Can any such particular evil happen contrary to the
order of divine government?*

No, if understood in its entirety.

What is meant by this?

By this is meant that God who is ineffably mighty
effects that such a particular evil is subordinate to a
higher order in virtue of which even this particular evil
helps towards the universal good (*ibid.;* XIX. 6; XXIII.
5, *Obj.* 3).

*Everything then that happens by the action of creatures
one upon the other falls in a marvellous manner under the
supreme control of the divine government?*

Yes, for even if one thing seems to be disarranged in
its own subalternate order, there is always to be found
a wise and searching reason for the disarrangement in
some higher sphere.

Can we, in this life, come to understand this wonderful ordering of divine government in the world?

No, we can never come to understand this, since for such knowledge it would be necessary to be acquainted not only with the whole of creation but also with the divine plans.

Where shall we come to see in all its splendour the beauty and the harmony of God's government of the world?

Only in heaven shall we see it in all its splendour.

XXII.—OF THE ANGELS: THE HIERARCHIES AND THE ORDERS

(A)

Do the pure spirits or the angels also act one upon the other?

Yes.

What is this action of one angel upon another called?

It is called illumination (CVI. 1).

Why is it called illumination?

Because angels act one upon the other only for the reason of transmitting the light (knowledge) they receive from God concerning the course of His government (*ibid.*).

Is this light, imparted by God to angels, communicated to them in some graduated and ordered scale?

Yes.

What is meant by this?

By this is meant that God imparts this light first of all to those who are nearer to Him, and these in their turn impart the light to other angels; thus, from the highest to the lowest the light is communicated in such wise that the first imparts it to the last by the action of those who are midway (CVI. 3).

There is then in this action of the angels whereby they communicate one to the other the light imparted by God to them the subordination of first, midway, and last?

Yes (CVIII. 2).

*Is it possible to give some illustration of this subordina
tion of this action of pure spirits one upon the other
whereby they communicate the light imparted to them
by God?*

One might compare it to a stream of light which falls
translucently from rock to rock, and is fed everlastingly
by the waters of some beautiful lake situate in the heights
of the mountain.

(B)

*Does this subordination among the angels comprise divers
groups?*

Yes (CVIII. 1).

How many kinds are there of these groups?

These groups are of two kinds.

What are these two kinds of groups called?

They are called the hierarchies and orders or the
angelic choirs.

What is meant by the word "hierarchy? "

The word " hierarchy " is derived from the Greek and
means " sacred principality."

What does the word " principality " entail?

The word " principality " entails two things: a prince
and a multitude organized under him (CVIII. 1).

*When one speaks of a " sacred principality " what is
meant by that?*

" Sacred principality " understood in its strict and
full sense means the whole assemblage of rational
creatures called to participate in things holy under the
sole government of God, who is the Supreme Prince and
Sovereign King of them all (*ibid.*).

*There ought then to be only one sacred principality and
only one hierarchy in the world governed by God?*

Yes, if one considers the sacred principality on the
part of God, who is the Supreme Prince and Sovereign
King of all rational creatures governed by Him, there is
only one sacred principality or only one hierarchy which
embraces both angels and men (CVIII. 1).

Why then and in what sense does one speak of hierarchies in the plural, and even in a certain way of hierarchies in the world of pure spirits or angels only?

Because on the part of the multitude organized under a prince the principality differs according as that multitude in different ways is subject to the governing of the prince (CVIII. 1).

Is it possible to give an illustration of this diversity in things human?

Yes, for under the same king are to be found cities or provinces differing from each other in that they are ruled by different laws and by different ministers of state (*ibid.*).

Is there one hierarchy for human beings and another for the angels?

Yes, as long as there are human beings on earth, there is one hierarchy for them and another for the angels (*ibid.*).

Why as long as there are human beings on earth?

Because in heaven men are included in the hierarchy of the angels (CVIII. 8).

(c)

Are there several hierarchies among the angels?
Yes (CVIII. 1).

How many hierarchies are there?

There are three hierarchies among the angels (*ibid.*).

Is it possible to say how these hierarchies among the angels are differentiated?

These three hierarchies among the angels are differentiated according to the threefold way of knowing the reasons of things which relate to the divine government (*ibid.*).

In what way does the first hierarchy know the reasons of things which relate to the divine government?

It knows them according as these reasons proceed from the First Universal Principle, which is God (*ibid.*).

What does this import on the part of the angels of this first hierarchy?

On the part of the angels of this first hierarchy, this imports that their place is near to God in such wise that all the orders of this hierarchy are named from some office which has for its object God Himself (CVIII. 1, 6).

In what way does the second hierarchy know the reasons of things which relate to the divine government?

It knows them according as this kind of reasons depend upon created universal causes (CVIII. 1).

What does this import on the part of the angels of this second hierarchy?

For the angels of the second hierarchy, this imports that they receive their illumination (knowledge) from the first hierarchy, and that their orders are named from some office having reference to the universality of creatures governed by God (CVIII. 1, 6).

In what way does the third hierarchy know the reasons of things which relate to the divine government?

It knows them according as they are applied to par ticular things in so far as these things depend from their proper causes (CVIII. 1).

What does this imply on the part of the angels of this third hierarchy?

For the angels of this third hierarchy, this imports that they receive the divine light, according to certain par ticular forms which enable them to have communion with our minds in this life—and it further implies that their orders are named from acts relating to some one human being as, for instance, the guardian angels, or to some one province as, for instance, the Principalities (CVIII. 1, 6).

Is it possible to find some illustration of this threefold kind of hierarchy in the things of this world?

Yes, there are illustrations of this threefold kind of hierarchy in the things of this world; for instance, among the ministers of a king there are chamberlains, coun cillors, and attendants who are always near the person of the prince; further, there are officers of the royal court whose duty it is to look after the affairs of the whole kingdom in a general way; lastly, there are officers whose duty it is to look after this or that particular section of the kingdom (CVIII. 6).

Are the orders distinct from the hierarchies among the angels?

Yes (CVIII. 2).

In what consists this distinction?

It consists in this, that the hierarchies constitute divers multitudes of angels forming divers principalities under the same divine government, whereas the orders constitute divers classes in each multitude which forms a hierarchy (CVIII. 2).

(D)

How many orders are there in each hierarchy?

There are three orders in each hierarchy (*ibid.*).

Why are there three orders in each hierarchy?

Because even with us the different classes which dis tinguish men in one city are reduced to three principal classes, namely, the nobles, the commoners, and the peasantry (CVIII. 2).

There are then in each hierarchy the higher angels, the lower angels, and the angels that come between?

Yes, and these form what are called the three orders of each hierarchy (CVIII. 2).

One must distinguish then, in all, nine angelic orders?

Yes, there are nine principal angelic orders (CVIII. 5, 6).

Why nine " principal " angelic orders?

Because in each order there are yet other subordina tions almost without number, each angel having his proper place and his particular duty; but it is not for us to know all this in this life (CVIII. 3).

Are the nine orders the same as the nine choirs of angels?

Yes.

Why is the name " choirs " given to the angelic orders?

Because each order in fulfilling its duties in the divine government constitutes a class replete with harmony which makes manifest in a wonderful way the glory of God in this work.

What are the names of the nine choirs of angels?

They are, descending from the higher to the lower, the Seraphim, the Cherubim, the Thrones, the Domina tions, the Virtues, the Powers, the Principalities, the Archangels, and the Angels (CVIII. 5).

Do these orders still exist among the devils?

Yes, for the orders are consequent upon the very nature of the angels; and nature in the devils remains the same.

Is there then a subordination among the devils just as there was before their fall?

Yes (CIX. 1, 2).

Is this order among them ever used for good?

No, it is never used except for evil (CIX. 3).

There is then no illumination among the devils?

Among the devils there is only the darkness of evil; and for this reason their empire is called the kingdom of darkness (*ibid.*).

XXIII.—OF THE ACTION OF THE GOOD ANGELS ON THE CORPOREAL WORLD

Does God employ His angels in the administration of the corporeal world?

Yes, for this corporeal world is inferior to the angels, and in every ordered government the lower is ruled by the higher (CX. 1).

To what order belong the angels who govern the corporeal world?

They belong to the Order of the Virtues (CX. 1, *Obj.* 3).

What is the duty of the angels who exercise control over the corporeal world?

The angels who exercise control over the corporeal world see to the perfect accomplishment of the intent of divine providence and to the fulfilment of the divine will in all that passes among the divers beings which make up the corporeal world (CX. 1, 2, 3).

Is it through the medium of these angels of the order of the virtues that God performs all changes which come about in the corporeal world, even the performance of miracles?

Yes, it is through the medium of these angels of the Order of the Virtues that God performs all changes which come about in the corporeal world, even the performance of miracles (CX. 4).

When God employs His angels for the performance of some miracle, is it by the personal power of the angel that the miracle is performed?

No, a miracle is performed by the power of God only; but an angel may help therein either by way of inter cession or in the capacity of instrument (CX. 4, *Obj.* 1).

XXIV.—OF THE ACTION OF THE GOOD ANGELS UPON MAN; THE GUARDIAN ANGELS

(A)

Can an angel have any action upon man?

Yes, an angel can act upon man by reason of man's spiritual nature, which is of a high order (CXI.).

Can an angel illumine the thought and the mind of man?

Yes, an angel can illumine the thought and the mind of man by strengthening his power of vision and by bringing within his reach some truth which the angel himself contemplates (CXI. 1).

Can an angel move the will of man by influencing it directly?

No, an angel cannot move the will of man by acting upon it directly, since the movement of the will is an interior inclination which depends only upon the will itself directly or upon God who is its author (CXI. 2).

Only God then can move the will of man by acting upon it directly?

Yes, only God can change the will of man by acting upon it directly (CXI. 2).

Can an angel act upon the imagination of man and upon his other sensitive faculties?

Yes, an angel can act upon the imagination of man and upon his other sensitive faculties; for these faculties function by means of organs, and consequently they depend for their activity upon the corporeal world which is under the control of the angels (CXI. 3).

Can an angel act upon man's senses?

Yes, for the same reason an angel can act upon man's external senses; moreover he can affect them as he wills unless it is a question of the bad angels whose activity can be checked by the action of the good angels (CXI. 4).

Can then the good angels check and counteract the action of the bad angels?

Yes, the good angels can check and counteract the action of the bad angels, for the order of Divine Justice determined that on account of their sin the bad angels should be subject to the control of the good angels (CIX. 4).

Can the good angels be sent by God to minister to men?

Yes, the good angels can be sent by God to minister to men, since God makes use of their activity in order to promote man's good, or in order to put His plans into execution with regard to men (CXII. 1).

Can all the good angels be sent by God in this way to minister to men?

No, not all of them can be sent thus (CXII. 2).

Which of them are never sent to minister to men?

All those of the first hierarchy (CXII. 2, 3).

Why are not any of these angels sent to minister to men?

Because it is the privilege of this hierarchy to stand always before God (CXII. 3).

By reason of this privilege, what are these angels of the first hierarchy called?

They are called the assisting angels (CXII. 3).

Can all the angels of the other two hierarchies be sent to minister to men?

Yes, in this wise however, that the Dominations superintend the execution of the divine plans, whereas the Virtues, Powers, Principalities, Archangels, and Angels put them directly into execution (CXII. 4).

(B)

Are there any angels sent by God to protect men?

Yes, there are certain angels sent by God to protect men, for it is a part of the ruling of Divine Providence that man, whose thoughts and wishes are so changeable and so inconstant, should be assisted in his journey towards heaven by one of the blessed spirits whose wills are for ever rooted in good (CXIII. 1).

Has God deputed one and the same angel to be the guardian of several men, or has he deputed a guardian angel for each separate man?

God has deputed a guardian angel to assist each separ ate man; for every single human soul is more dear to God than the divers species of material creatures over which, however, presides an angel who is mindful of them, and promotes their welfare (CXIII. 3).

To what order belong the angels which are thus deputed by God, separately, to be the guardian angels to men?

The angels which are thus deputed by God, separately, to be the guardian angels to men belong all to the last of the nine choirs of angels (CXIII. 3).

Are all men without exception thus committed by God to the care of one of His angels?

Yes, all men without exception are thus committed by God to the care of one of His angels, as long as they live on this earth, and the reason is because of the perilous way through which all must pass before they come to the end of their lives (CXIII. 4).

Did Christ our Lord, as man, also have a guardian angel?

No, it was not fitting that Christ our Lord should have a guardian angel, seeing that in person He was God; but certain angels were appointed to the great honour of ministering to Him (CXIII. 4, *Obj.* 1).

When is an angel personally appointed by God to be the guardian of some man?

It is at the instant of man's coming into the world that God deputes an angel to be his guardian (CXIII. 5).

Does it happen that sometimes an angel quits a man to whose guardianship he has been appointed?

No, a guardian angel never leaves a man over whom he has charge, and he continues to watch over him, without ceasing, until the last moment of his life on earth (CXIII. 6).

Do the angels ever sorrow because of the sins of those over whom they have charge?

No, for after doing what lies in their power to prevent sin, should sin nevertheless prevail, they adore, in this as in all things else, the inscrutability of the divine plans (CXIII. 7).

Is it a commendable thing to counsel the practice of committing oneself often and in all things to the protection of one's guardian angel?

Yes, to counsel the practice of commending oneself often and in all things to the protection of one's guardian angel is an excellent thing, and should be recommended in every way.

May one be infallibly certain of this protection, should one invoke it?

Yes, provided that our demand is consistent with the eternal counsels of God, and according as our concerns are ordained to the glory of God (CXIII. 8).

XXV.—OF THE ACTION OF THE BAD ANGELS OR OF THE DEMONS

Can the devils attack and tempt men?

Yes.

Why is it possible for the devils to attack and tempt man?

The devils are able to attack and to tempt man by reason of their wickedness, and because God can make use of the very temptation for the good of his chosen ones (CXIV. 1).

Is it proper to the devils alone to tempt man?

Yes.

In what sense is it said that it is proper to the devils alone to tempt man?

It is proper to the devils to tempt man in this sense, that they alone tempt man always with the object of doing him harm and in the hope that man might be lost (CXIV. 2).

Can the devils perform miracles in order to tempt and to seduce man?

No, the devils are unable to perform true miracles in order to tempt and to seduce man, but they can perform things that have the appearance of miracles.

What is meant by the words : appearance of miracles?

By these words are understood prodigies which exceed the manner of acting of the things around us as far as our knowledge of them goes, but which, however, do not exceed the natural power of the whole of creatures (CXIV. 4).

By what sign above all may one detect these spurious miracles performed by the devils?

Above all one may detect them by this, that they are always related to something that is bad, and consequently God cannot be their author as He is of true miracles (CXIV. 4, *Obj*. 3).

XXVI.—OF THE ACTION OF THE MATERIAL WORLD OR OF THE WHOLE OF THE COSMOS

Is it only the good or evil spirits that God employs in the government of the world?

No, it is not only the good or evil spirits that God employs in the government of the world.

What other beings are there which concur in this government?

All the cosmic agents whose activities are brought into play by God help also towards the accomplishment of His rule (CXV. 1).

Is then the whole course of nature thus in the hands of God for the ruling of the world?

Yes, the whole course of nature with all its laws is in the hands of God for the ruling of the world (CXV. 2).

It is then for the realization of the plans of God and for the help thereof, that every day the sun rises, that day follows night, that the seasons come and go, and this in such order that nothing ever disturbs the coming and the going of the days, the months, the years, and the centuries?

Yes, it is for the fulfilment of the designs of God and for help thereof that the sun rises each day, that night follows day, that the seasons follow each other in order, and this in such a way that nothing ever disarranges the coming and the going of the days, the months, the years, and the centuries.

May one say that it is for man and for his welfare that God has thus ordained and maintains in a regular order the course of the world of nature?

Yes, one may and indeed must say that it is for man and for his welfare that God has thus ordained and maintains in a regular order the course of the world of nature.

Man then is the creature for whom God in some wise has arranged that all other creatures should be subservient to his needs?

Yes, man is the creature for whom God in some wise has arranged that all other creatures should be subservient to his needs.

Why has God thus acted towards man?

God has acted thus towards man because man is the weakest of His creatures who has need of all other things for the good of his soul and body.

XXVII.—OF THE ACTION OF MAN HIMSELF

Can man, weak though he be, also help in the action of God towards the government of the world?

Yes, in spite of his weakness, man also can help in a very great degree in the activity of God in the govern ment of the world

How can man thus concur with the action of God in the government of the world?

Man can concur with the action of God in the govern ment of the world in co-operating himself for the good of man.

In what way can man co-operate himself for the good of man?

Man co-operates towards the good of man in being used by God as an instrument for the welfare of the soul and body of man.

How can man serve as an instrument in God's hands for the benefit of the soul and body of man?

Man serves as an instrument in God's hands for the benefit of the soul of man, because it is due to the opera tion of man that God creates the soul of each child born into the world; and because this soul develops and grows in perfection under the action of the master who is its teacher (CXVII., CXVIII.).

And how does man serve as an instrument in God's hands as regards the body of man?

Because, according to the laws of nature fixed by Him, God has arranged that the body of the child is formed and is brought forth into the world by the tender care of a father and a mother (CXIX.).

XXVIII.—OF THE POINT UPON WHICH THE WHOLE COURSE OF DIVINE GOVERN MENT IS CENTRED

It is then at the cradle of the child, among men, that we see shine forth, as from a central point, all the graciousness of God's government in the world?

Yes, it is at the child's cradle, among men, that we see shine forth, as from a central point, all the sweetness of God's government in the world; for all in the world is ordained for the welfare of the child: the loving care of the parents, the whole of nature which helps its life, the angels who have care of it, and the goodness of God who destines it for the glory of heaven.

Was there a cradle or the birth of a child among men around which all the splendours of God's government in the world shone forth in a way beyond compare?

Yes; and this happened at the birth of a Child, who, as we shall see shortly, is the means or the way of man's return to God (CXIX. 2, *Obj.* 4).

What happened, in effect, at the birth of this Child?

At the birth of this Child there was a conception wholly due to the supernatural action of the Holy Spirit, a Mother who remained virgin, kings and wise men led to the cradle by a star, and a multitude of celestial spirits praising God and singing: " Glory to God in the highest; and on earth peace to men of good will."

How is this Child of benediction called?

He is none other than Emmanuel, or God-with-us, and He is called Jesus.

THE SECOND PART

OF MAN

(WHO CAME FROM GOD AND WHO MUST RETURN TO GOD)

FIRST SECTION: General outline of Man's return to God.

End of man—Human acts—Passions—Virtues and Vices—Law and Grace.

SECOND SECTION: Detailed view of Man's return to God.

Theological virtues: Faith—Hope—Charity.

Moral virtues: Prudence—Justice (Religion)—Fortitude—Temperance.

Gratuitous Graces—Active and Contemplative life—States of life.

FIRST SECTION

GENERAL OUTLINE OF MAN'S RETURN TO GOD

I.—OF MAN'S RESEMBLANCE TO GOD IN THE FREE ADMINISTRATION OF ALL THAT CONCERNS HIM

Has man any special likeness to God in his actions?
Yes, man in his actions has a special likeness to God.
In what consists this special likeness of man to God?
It consists in this, that just as God disposes of all the universe which depends upon Him, at His will and in all liberty, so in the same way man disposes at his will and in all liberty of all things that depend upon him (*Pro logue*).

II.—OF THE LAST END OR HAPPINESS OF MAN VIEWED IN ALL HIS ACTIONS

(A)

Has man always an end in view when he acts?
Yes, man has always an end in view when he acts, that is when he acts as man and not as a machine, or by impulse, or by any reaction which is purely physical or instinctive (I. 1).
In the material world, is it only man that can act for an end?
Yes, only man in the material world can act for an end (I. 2).
Does it then follow that all other beings in the material world act without an end?
No, it does not follow that all other beings in the material world act without an end; on the contrary, all

55

beings act for an end that is very definite; but they are incapable of fixing an end for themselves; it is God who knows the end and who fixes it for them (I. 2).

All other beings then act in view of attaining some end which has been fixed for them by God?

Yes, all other beings act in view of attaining some end which has been fixed for them by God (I. 2).

Has not God also fixed for man the end for which he acts?
Yes.

What then is the difference between man when he acts and other creatures in the material world?

The difference is this, that man under the higher action of God and dependently upon this action, can fix for himself the end for which he acts; whereas other creatures of the material world put into execution blindly, naturally, or instinctively the end fixed to their action by God (I. 2).

What is the reason of this difference between man and other beings in the matter of actions?

The reason is because man is endowed with mind, whereas other creatures are not (I. 2).

(B)

Is there some supreme object or some last end which man has in view whenever he acts?

Yes, there is always some supreme object or some last end man has in view whenever he acts; since without some such supreme object or last end he would be unable to will anything at all (I. 4, 5).

Does man in his actions ordain all to this supreme object or last end which he has in view whenever he acts?

Yes, man ordains all to this supreme object or last end whenever he acts; if he does not do this consciously and explicitly, he does it at least implicitly and by a sort of natural instinct in the order of reason (I. 6).

What is the last end or what is the supreme object which man always has in view and to which he ordains all when ever he acts?

This last end or supreme object which man always has

in view when he acts and to which he ordains all is happiness (I. 7).

Man then necessarily desires to be happy?

Yes, of necessity man desires to be happy.

Is it absolutely impossible to find a man who desires to be unhappy?

Yes, it is quite impossible to find a man who desires to be unhappy (V. 8).

Can man deceive himself as to the object of his happiness?

Yes, man can thus deceive himself, because since he can seek his welfare among so many and divers good things, he can deceive himself as to the object of his true happiness (I. 7).

What happens if man deceives himself as to the object of his true happiness?

If man deceives himself as to the object of his true happiness, it follows that instead of finding happiness at the end of his life, he finds nought but the worst evil.

It is then supremely important for man not to deceive himself as to the object of his happiness?

There is nothing of greater import for man than that he deceive not himself as to the object of his happiness.

III.—OF THE OBJECT OF THIS HAPPINESS

What is the object of the happiness of man?

The object of the happiness of man is a good higher than himself and in which he can find his perfection (II. 1-8).

Are riches the object of this happiness of man?

No, it is not riches, for these are beneath man; nor are they sufficient to guarantee his entire welfare and his perfection (II. 1).

Are honours?

No, not honours; because honours do not bring perfec tion, but rather presuppose it, that is when they are not false honours; and if they be false they avail nothing (II. 2).

Is it glory or renown?

No, for these are of no worth unless they be merited; moreover among men these things are often foolish and ill-judged (II. 3).

Is it power?

No, because power is for the good of others, and is subject to their whims and disobedience (II. 4).

Is it health or bodily beauty?

No, because these good things are too unstable ; furthermore they belong only to the external perfection of man and not to his internal perfection or that of his soul (II. 5).

Does it consist in pleasures of the body?

No, it does not consist in pleasures of the body, since these are of small account in comparison with the higher pleasures of the mind which are proper to the soul (II. 6).

Does the happiness of man consist in something which is a good of the soul?

Yes, the happiness of man consists in some good of the soul (II. 7).

What is this good of the soul in which the happiness of man consists?

The good of the soul in which the happiness of man consists is God, the Supreme Good, Sovereign and Infinite (II. 8).

IV.—OF THE POSSESSION OF THIS HAPPINESS

How can man come to possess God, his Supreme Good, and to enjoy Him?

Man can come to possess God, his Supreme Good, and to enjoy Him, by an act of his intellect which is moved to this by his will.

What must man do in order to attain his perfect happiness by this act of his intellect?

In order for man to attain to his perfect happiness by this act of his intellect, it is necessary that God should be reached by him, as He is in Himself, and not merely in the way He can be reached by the aid of creatures what soever these creatures may be (III. 5-8).

What is this act called whereby God is reached by the intellect as He is in Himself?

This act is called the " vision of God " (III. 8).

Does then the perfect happiness of man consist in the vision of God?

Yes, it is in the vision of God that the perfect happiness of man consists (III. 8).

When man has attained to this vision of God in all its perfection, does it bring with it whatsoever is of perfection to man, in his soul, body, and in everything that concerns him?

Yes, when man has attained to this vision of God in all its perfection of necessity it brings with it all that can be of perfection to man in his soul, body, and in all that concerns him; for since it is the good of man in its highest source, from it come all things felicitous for his supreme perfection (IV. 1-8).

This vision then means for man the possession of all good to the exclusion of all evil?

Yes, this means for man the possession of all good to the exclusion of all evil (*ibid.*).

V.—OF THE MEANS OF REALIZING THIS POSSESSION, OR OF THE GOOD ACTS WHICH ARE DESERVING OF IT, AND OF EVIL ACTS WHICH BRING ABOUT ITS LOSS

Can man on earth and in this life come to possess this perfect happiness which is the vision of God?

No, on earth and in this life it is impossible for man to come to possess the vision of God which is his perfect happiness, for the conditions of this life and the miseries thereof are incompatible with such fullness of happi ness (V. 3).

How can man attain to the vision of God which con-stitutes his perfect happiness?

Man can only attain to the vision of God which con stitutes his perfect happiness by the help of God from whom he receives it (V. 5).

Does God confer this boon upon man if man do not by merit prepare himself thereto?

No, God will not confer this boon upon man unless by merit he make himself worthy to receive it (V. 7).

What then has man to do on earth and in this life?

On earth and in this life man has only to prepare him self by way of merit to receive from God some day the beatific vision and all that it entails; and this shall come about when God gives to man his reward.

VI.—OF WHAT IS IMPLIED IN A HUMAN ACT FOR IT TO BE A GOOD MERITORIOUS ACT, OR A BAD DEMERITORIOUS ACT; AND OF MERIT AND DEMERIT IN GENERAL

(A)

Is it possible to say by what means man on earth and in this life can prepare himself, by way of merit, to receive from God some day in token of reward the beatific vision in which consists man's eternal happiness?

Yes, this he can merit solely by his *acts* (VI., *Prologue*).

Of what kind of acts is there question?

Of virtuous acts.

What is meant by " acts of virtue "?

They are those " acts which man performs by his own free will in conformity with God's will under the action of grace " (VI.-CXIV.).

What is necessary that man's acts should proceed from his will?

It is necessary that he perform them spontaneously and with the knowledge that he is their cause (VI. 1-8).

What is meant by saying that he must perform them spontaneously?

It is meant that he must perform them without con-straint or force (VI. 4, 5, 6).

How can man be coerced or forced to do something against his will?

Man can be coerced or forced to do something against his will in two ways: by violence and by fear (VI. 4, 5, 6).

What is understood by violence?

By violence is understood a force exterior to man which fetters his members and impedes him from acting as he wills, or makes him do exteriorly what his will rejects (VI. 4, 5).

What is understood by fear?

By fear is understood an interior movement which makes man will a thing he would not otherwise will, but to which he consents in the present circumstances in order to avoid some evil that threatens (VI. 6).

Is that which one does under violence wholly involuntary?

Yes, that which one does under exterior violence is wholly involuntary (VI. 5).

Why under " exterior " violence?

Because sometimes the word " violence " is taken to signify the internal movement of anger.

In this case and in the case of other interior movements which excite or incline the will may one also speak of in-voluntariness?

No, in these divers cases one may not speak of in-voluntariness unless perchance these interior movements be so vehement as to deprive man of the use of his reason (VI. 7).

And when one acts through fear, is the act also in-voluntary?

When one acts through fear the act is voluntary, but with it there is an admixture of involuntary in this sense, that that which is done is indeed willed, but it is willed with reluctancy and by reason of some evil from which man shrinks (VI. 6).

(B)

It has also been said that for man's acts to be voluntary they must be done with knowledge of what is being done?

Yes; and this means that if one performs an act, without the knowledge of what one is really doing, the act done is not voluntary (VI. 8).

Is such an act then involuntary?

Yes, provided that if one knew the true facts, one would not have performed the act (VI. 8).

Can that which one does or which one does not owing to ignorance or to some error, be nevertheless sometimes voluntary?

Yes; it is always so if one is responsible for one's ignorance or one's error (VI. 8).

And when is one responsible for one's ignorance or one's error?

When one wills these directly, or when they are the outcome of culpable negligence (VI. 8).

(C)

Must not one take into account the circumstances which accompany a human act, since upon them depends so much the character of the act?

Yes; and nothing is more important than the weighing of the circumstances of a human act in order to appreciate its true value (VII. 1, 2).

Is it possible to enumerate these circumstances?

Yes, these circumstances are those of person, of object, or of effect produced, of place, of motive, of the means employed, and of time (VII. 3).

What is meant by these different circumstances?

These different circumstances bear on the character or condition of the person who acts, on what he does, or on what results from his act, on the place where he does the act, on the end for which he acts, on those things which he uses as means, and on the time when he acts (VII. 3).

Which is the most important of these circumstances?

It is the motive for which a person acts or the end which he has in view when he acts (VII. 4).

Is it always the will which produces human acts?

Yes, it is always the will; sometimes the will only; at other times it is some other faculty or even the ex terior members of the body, but always under the impulse and by order of the will (VIII.-XVII.).

(D)

The will of man then is the central point of all those acts that constitute his life as a rational being, and have direct bearing upon the reward of his life which is the winning or the losing of the happiness of heaven?

Yes, the will of man is the central point of all those acts that constitute his life as a rational being, and have direct bearing upon the reward of his life which is the gain or the loss of the happiness of heaven; and this implies that the act of a human being is of no account except in so far as it proceeds from the will; whether it be the will itself that produces the act, or whether the will move some other faculty of the soul or even member of the body to produce the act (VIII.-XXI.).

Of all the interior acts of the will which is the most im portant and the one which is the root of responsibility in man?

It is the act of choosing or " choice " (XIII. 1-6).

Why has the act of choosing or " choice " this importance?

It is because this act effects that the will fixes with full knowledge and after deliberation upon some determined good, which it accepts and makes its own in preference to any other (XIII. 1).

Is choice properly speaking the act of the free will?

Yes (XIII. 6).

It is then by the choice that he makes with regard to all things that man derives his true moral character and his real value in view of the gain or the loss of his eternal happiness?

Yes, it is by the choice that he makes in regard to all

things that man derives his true moral character and his real value in view of the gain or the loss of his eternal happiness.

How is choice divided as regards man's true character and moral worth in view of the gain or loss of his eternal happiness?

It is divided into " good choice " and " bad choice " (XVIII.–XXI.).

What is a " good choice "?

It is one that bears upon a good object, in view of some good end, and as regards which all the accompanying circumstances are good (XVIII.–XIX.).

(E)

Whence is derived the goodness of an object, of an end, and of the circumstances?

This goodness is derived from the relation that all these things have with right reason (XIX. 3-6).

What is meant by right reason?

By this is understood the reason enlightened by all the lights that come from God, or which at least is not knowingly at variance with them.

When man then wills or chooses something in conformity with right reason for an object or an end of which right reason approves, and of which all the accompanying circum stances accord with right reason, the act willed or chosen by man is a good act?

Yes; then, and then only, is man's act a good act. If on any one of these counts whatsoever man's act is not conformed with right reason it ceases to be a good act, and it becomes in a less or great degree, as the case may be, a bad act (XVIII.–XXI.).

What is a bad act called?

A bad act is called a " fault " or a " sin " (XXI. 1).

VII.—OF THE AFFECTIVE MOVEMENTS IN MAN WHICH ARE CALLED THE PASSIONS

(A)

Are there not in man certain other affective acts which can contribute towards the reward of his life, other than the acts of his will?

Yes, there are other affective acts in man.

What are they called?

They are called the " passions " (XXII.–XLVIII.).

What is understood by the passions?

By passions are understood affective movements of the sensitive part of man's soul.

Is it only man that has these affective movements in the sensitive part of his soul?

No, these affective movements of the sensitive part are to be found in all animals (XXII. 1, 2, 3).

Have these affective movements of the sensitive part in animals any moral worth?

No, these affective movements of the sensitive part in animals have no moral value; only in man have they a moral value.

Why is it that only in man these affective movements of the sensitive part are of moral value?

Because it is in man only that they are related with the higher acts of the free will in that they are subject to their rule (XXV. or XXIV. 1-4).

What precisely are these affective movements of the sensitive part in man and to which is given the name of passions?

These affective movements of the sensitive part in man and to which is given the name of passions, are movements of the heart which bear towards a good or withdraw from an evil tendered by the senses (XXIII., XXIV., or XXV.).

(B)

How many kinds are there of these movements of the heart?

There are *eleven* (XXII. 4).

What are they called?

Their names are: " love," " desire," " delight " or " joy "; " hate," " abhorrence," " sadness," " hope," " courage," " fear," " despair," and " anger " (XXII. 4).

Do these movements of the heart occupy an important part in man's life?

Yes, these movements of the heart occupy a very important part in man's life.

Why is it that they occupy a very important part in man's life?

Because in man there is a twofold nature: rational and sensitive; the sensitive nature is the one that is moved first by the action of the external world in the midst of which we live and from which we derive even all the data of our rational life.

Are not then the movements of the heart or the passions always, of themselves, bad?

No, the movements of the heart or the passions are not of themselves always bad.

When are these movements of the heart or the passions bad?

When they are not in accord with the rulings of right reason.

And when are they not in accord with the rulings of right reason?

When they bear towards a sensible good or withdraw from a sensible evil by forestalling the judgment of the reason or by coming into play contrary to this judgment (XXV. or XXIV. 3).

(c)

Is it only in the sensitive part of man that there are movements of love, desire, delight, hate, aversion, sadness, hope, daring, fear, despair, and anger?

These same movements are to be found also in the will.

What difference is there between these movements in so far as they are in the sensitive part, and in so far as they are in the will?

There is this difference, that in the sensitive part they

always imply the co-operation of the organism or of the body, whereas in the will they are purely spiritual (XXXI. 4).

When one speaks of movements of the heart, of which affective movements is there question, of those of the sensitive part or of those of the will?

Properly speaking, there is question of the movements of the sensitive part; but in a metaphorical sense there is a question also of those of the will.

When then one speaks of the heart of man, can there be question of this twofold sort of movement?

Yes, when one speaks of the heart of man, there can be question of this twofold kind of movement.

And when it is said of a man that he has heart, what is meant by that?

When it is said of a man that he has heart, one means to imply that at times he is affectionate and tender hearted, of whatever kind of affection there may be question, whether of the purely sensitive or of the spiritual order, and at other times one means to imply that he is courageous and virile.

Why is it sometimes said and what is meant by saying that one must watch over one's heart?

When it is said that one must watch over one's heart, one means that it is necessary to take care lest one follow indiscreetly the first affective movements, especially of the sensitive order, which tend to make us seek what is pleasing and to shrink from what is displeasing.

One speaks sometimes of the training of the heart ; what does this mean?

This means that one must endeavour to have only good affective movements.

This education of the heart, thus understood, is it of any importance?

Yes, for this education of the heart, thus understood, embraces the whole of man's activity in the acquisition of virtue and the shunning of vice.

VIII.—OF THE VIRTUES WHICH CAN AND OUGHT TO BE THE PRINCIPLE OF MAN'S GOOD ACTS

(A)

What is meant by the acquiring of virtue?

By this is meant the acquiring or the bringing to perfec tion of all the " good habits which make man act well " (XLIX.–LXVIII.).

What are the good habits which make man act well?

They are dispositions or inclinations which are seated in divers faculties, and which render good the acts of these faculties (LV. 1-4).

Whence in man's divers faculties come these dispositions or inclinations which are conducive to their acting well?

At times they come, in part, from nature herself; sometimes they come from the person who acts for virtue's sake; and sometimes they come directly from God, who produces them in the soul supernaturally (LXIII. 1-4).

(B)

Are there any such dispositions or good habits or virtues in man's intellect?

Yes, there are suchlike dispositions or good habits or virtues in man's intellect (LVI. 3).

What is the effect of these virtues in man's intellect?

They make man's intellect to seek the truth only (LVI. 3).

What are these virtues in man's intellect called?

They are called " intuition " or " insight," " science," " wisdom," " art," and " prudence " (LVII. 1-6).

What is the object of each of these virtues in man's intellect or reason?

Intuition or insight gives a knowledge of principles (self-evident truths); science a knowledge of conclusions; wisdom a knowledge of the highest causes; art gives directions for the execution of external works; and pru dence directions for the whole of the moral life (LVII. 1-6).

Prudence then is most important in the exercise of a virtuous life?

Yes, prudence is most important in the exercise of a virtuous life (LVII. 5).

(c)

Are these the only virtues in man's intellect?

There is another virtue in man's intellect but it is of an altogether higher order (LXII. 1-4).

What is this virtue in man's intellect of an altogether higher order?

It is the virtue of " faith " (*ibid.*).

(D)

Are there also virtues of the same order in the will?
Yes (*ibid.*).

What are these virtues of the same order in the will called?
They are called " Hope " and " Charity " (*ibid.*).

Have these virtues of Faith, Hope, and Charity any special name?

Yes, they are called the " theological virtues " (*ibid.*).

What is understood by the words : theological virtues?

By these words is meant that the virtues of Faith, Hope, and Charity have reference to God alone, and that they have also their sole source in God (LXII. 1).

Is there any other virtue in the will?

Yes, there is also the virtue of " justice " in the will; and the other virtues which spring from justice (LVI. 6; LIX. 4; LX. 2, 3).

Are there to be found virtues in the other faculties of man?

Yes, there are virtues which reside in the affective sensitive faculties of man.

(E)

What are the virtues to be found in the affective sensitive faculties?

They are the virtues of " fortitude " and " temperance," and the other virtues which arise from them.

What are the virtues of justice, fortitude, temperance, and prudence called?

They are called the moral virtues (LVIII. 1).

Are they not also called by the name of the " cardinal " virtues?

Yes, they are also called the cardinal virtues (LXI. 1-4).

What is meant by the words : cardinal virtues?

By these words is implied that they are virtues of particular importance, which are as it were the hinges (in Latin *cardo, cardinis*) upon which, setting aside the theological virtues, turn all the other virtues (*ibid.*).

In man must the virtues of the natural order, or the acquired virtues, intellectual or moral, have corresponding virtues of the supernatural order, infused by God in order that man may be perfected in every act of his moral life?

Yes; for only these infused virtues are proportionate to those acts in the supernatural moral life of man which the supernatural end demands; an end held out for man's attainment by the theological virtues (LXIII. 3, 4).

(F)

Are all these virtues, theological and cardinal, necessary in order that man may live well?

Yes, all these virtues are necessary that man may live well (LXV. 1-5).

And suppose man is lacking in any one of these virtues, could he not be called virtuous?

No; for if man is found wanting in any one of these virtues, whatsoever other virtues he may have they would never, in him, possess the true character or nature of perfect virtue (LXV. 4).

IX.—OF THE GIFTS WHICH CROWN AND PERFECT THE VIRTUES

Does it suffice for man to possess all the virtues spoken of above in order for his life to be what it ought to be in view of gaining heaven?

No; he must also have the gifts of the Holy Ghost (LXVIII. 2).

What is understood by the gifts of the Holy Ghost?

By these are understood habitual dispositions which are given to man by the Holy Ghost, and which make man yielding and docile to all the inspirations of the Holy Spirit that help man towards the possession of God in heaven (LXVIII. 1, 2, 3).

Why are these gifts of the Holy Ghost necessary in addition to all the virtues above mentioned?

Because man called to live as a child of God, is unable to attain to the perfection of this life unless God Himself, by His own action, makes perfect what man's action could achieve only incompletely through the virtues (LXVIII. 2).

How many gifts of the Holy Ghost are there?

There are seven gifts of the Holy Ghost (LXVIII. 4).

What are the seven gifts of the Holy Ghost?

They are the gifts of " wisdom," " understanding," " knowledge," " counsel," " piety," " fortitude," and " fear of the Lord " (LXVIII. 4).

X.—OF THE BEATITUDES AND OF THE FRUIT OF THE HOLY SPIRIT, WHICH ARE EFFECTS OF THE VIRTUES AND THE GIFTS

(A)

When man is thus endowed with the virtues and the gifts, has he, on his part, all that is required to live a perfect life in view of winning heaven?

Yes, when man is thus endowed with the virtues and the gifts he has, on his part, all that is required to live a perfect life in view of winning heaven.

May not one even say that he has already, in some sort, begun to live the life of heaven here on earth?

Yes, one may even say that he has already, in some sort, begun to live the life of heaven here on earth; and with this in mind one speaks of the beatitudes on earth, and of the fruit of the Holy Spirit (LXIX., LXX.).

(B)

What is understood by the beatitudes?

By the beatitudes is meant the acts of the virtues and the gifts enumerated by our Lord Jesus Christ in the gospel, which by their presence in the soul or by the merits which result there, give to us as it were a guarantee of the future beatitude promised to each of them (LXIX. 1).

And what is meant by the fruit of the Holy Spirit?

By the fruit of the Holy Spirit is understood those good acts whose nature it is to give joy to the virtuous man in that he acts in the supernatural order under the impulse of the Holy Spirit (LXX. 1).

Is this fruit distinct from the beatitudes?

If the fruit is all that is most perfect in the absolute sense of the word, for man it is identified with the fruit *par excellence* which is the beatitude of heaven. It is also identified with the beatitudes in this life; but it is distinct from them in this sense, that without needing the essential perfection or excellence of the beatitudes, its nature of goodness is sufficient (LXX. 2).

What are the beatitudes and what are their rewards?

They are: " Blessed are the poor in spirit, because theirs is the kingdom of heaven "; " Blessed are the meek, because they shall possess the land "; " Blessed are they who weep, because they shall be comforted "; " Blessed are they who thirst and hunger for justice sake, because they shall be filled "; " Blessed are the merciful, because they shall obtain mercy "; " Blessed are the pure of heart, for they shall see God "; " Blessed are the peaceful, because they shall be called the children of God " (LXIX. 2-4).

(c)

What is the fruit of the Holy Ghost?

The fruit of the Holy Ghost is: " charity," " joy," " peace," " patience," " benignity," " meekness,"

" faithfulness," " modesty," " continency," and " chastity " (LXX. 3).

Where is the fruit of the Holy Ghost spoken of?

It is to be found in the Epistle of St. Paul to the
Galatians (v. 22, 23).

And where are the beatitudes enumerated?

They are enumerated in the Gospel of St. Matthew
(v. 3-10), and in a manner less complete, in St. Luke
(vi. 20-22).

*Is there not also an eighth beatitude in St. Matthew, to be
found also in St. Luke?*

Yes, it is the beatitude of those who suffer persecution
for justice sake; but it is included in the other seven
beatitudes of which it is, as it were, the resume or the
consequence (LXIX. 3, *Obj.* 5).

*There can then be nothing better for man on earth than to
live thus the life of the virtues and of the gifts, from which
spring the beatitudes and the fruit of the Holy Ghost?*

No, there can be nothing better for man on earth than
to live thus the life of the virtues and of the gifts, from
which spring the beatitudes and the fruit of the Holy
Ghost.

XI.—OF VICES WHICH ARE THE PRINCIPLE OF MAN'S BAD ACTIONS

*Is there another life man can lead on earth other than a
virtuous life?*

Yes, it is the life of sin or vice (LXXI.–LXXXIX.).

What is understood by vice?

By vice is understood the state of man who lives in sin
(LXXI. 1-6).

What is sin?

Sin is an act or a voluntary omission which is bad
(LXXI. 5-6).

When is an act or a voluntary omission bad?

When this act is contrary to the good of God, or of our
neighbour, or of man himself (LXXII. 4).

How comes it that man can thus wish a thing which is opposed to the good of God, to the good of his neighbour. or to his own good?

It is because man can will some good which is opposed to the good of God, or to the good of his neighbour, or to his own good (LXXI. 2; LXXVII. 4).

What is this other good which man can will?

It is the good that gratifies his senses, or his ambition, or his pride (LXXII. 2, 3; LXXVII. 5).

Whence comes it that man can thus will a good that gratifies his senses, or his ambition, or his pride?

The reason is because the senses can be borne towards what is agreeable to them by forestalling or by enticing the reason and the will which do not oppose this move ment of the senses when they might and when they should (LXXI. 2, *ad* 3).

It is then the unlawful seeking after sensible and temporal goods which is, for man, the beginning and, in some sort, the reason of all his sins?

Yes, it is the unlawful seeking after sensible and temporal goods that is, for man, the beginning and, in some sort, the reason of all his sins.

What is this inclination in man to seek unlawfully sensible and temporal goods called?

It is called concupiscence (LXXVII. 1-5).

XII.—OF ORIGINAL SIN, AND OF ITS CONSE QUENCES, OR OF THE WOUNDING OF HUMAN NATURE

(A)

Did this concupiscence exist in man in the first state in which he was created by God?

No.

Why then does it exist now in man?

It exists in man now because of his fall (LXXXI.- LXXXIII.).

What do you mean by the fall of man?

By this is meant that state which followed upon the first sin of the first man, and which is the effect of this first sin (LXXXI. 1; LXXXII. 1).

Why are we now all in this state which followed upon the sin of Adam?

We are all in this state now because we received our nature from Adam (LXXXI. 1).

If Adam had not sinned would we have received our nature from him in another state?

Yes, if Adam had not sinned we would have received our nature from him in the state of integrity, or original justice (LXXXI. 2).

Is the state in which we now receive our nature from Adam a state of sin?

Yes, the state in which we now receive our nature from the first man is a state of sin (LXXXI. 1; LXXXII. 1).

Why is this nature which we now receive from Adam in a state of sin?

Because we receive it from him such as it really is, that is as affected by his sin (LXXXI. 1).

And what is this state called?

It is called the state of original sin (*ibid.*).

By the very fact then that we receive our nature in this state from Adam, original sin is transmitted to each one of us?

Yes, it is by the very fact that we receive our nature in this state from Adam that original sin is transmitted to each one of us (*ibid.*).

What does this state of sin in which each one of us is born, and which is called original sin, entail?

It entails the privation of all the supernatural or gratuitous gifts which God had implanted in our nature in the person of Adam, our common father (LXXXII. 1).

What were these supernatural or gratuitous gifts, the privation of which constitutes in us the state of original sin?

These supernatural or gratuitous gifts were: first of

all, sanctifying grace with the supernaturally infused
virtues and the gifts of the Holy Spirit; and also the
privilege of integrity which was associated with these
supernatural gifts.

*What did this privilege of integrity granted to the soul
imply?*

It implied the entire subordination of the senses to the
reason and of the body to the soul.

*What was the effect of this perfect subordination of the
senses to reason and of the body to the soul?*

The effect was that in man's sensitive appetite there
could be no inordinate movement; and his body was
rendered impassable and immortal.

Are death and all other bodily ailments the result of sin?

Yes, death and all other bodily ailments are the result
of sin (LXXXIV. 5).

(B)

What are the consequences of this sin in the soul called?

They are called the wounds of the soul.

What are these wounds in the soul?

They are ignorance, malice, weakness, and concupiscence (LXXXV. 3).

What is meant by ignorance?

By this is meant that state in which the reason is de
prived of that inherent relation it had towards the truth
in the state of integrity (LXXXV. 3).

What is meant by malice?

By this is meant that state of the will in which it is
deprived of the inherent relation it had to good in the
state of integrity (LXXXV. 3).

What is meant by weakness?

By this is meant that state of the sensitive appetite
in which it is deprived of the inherent relation to all that
is arduous and difficult which it had in the state of
integrity (LXXXV. 3).

What is meant by concupiscence?

By this is meant that state of the sensitive appetite

in which it is deprived of the inherent relation towards
sensitive pleasures tempered by reason which it had in
the state of integrity (LXXXV. 3).

*Are the four wounds in our nature the effects, properly
speaking, of the sin of Adam?*

Yes, these four wounds in our nature are the effects,
properly speaking, of the sin of Adam (LXXXV. 3).

*Are they rendered worse by the personal sins of parents
and of individuals?*

Yes (LXXXV. 1, 2).

*Are there certain personal sins which in particular
have an evil influence upon man by leading him to commit
other sins?*

Yes, they are the capital sins.

What are the capital sins?

They are pride, avarice, gluttony, lust, idleness, envy,
and anger.

(c)

*In spite of all these causes of sin in man which come either
from the sin of Adam, or from the personal sins of man,
may we yet say that man is free in his moral acts, and that
he is never necessitated to commit sin?*

Yes, in spite of all these causes of sin in man which
come either from the first sin of the first man, or from
the personal sins of man, we are bound to say that he
is still free in his moral acts, and that he is never necessi
tated to commit sin.

*What would be necessary for man to cease to be free in
his acts considering all these consequences of sin?*

It would be necessary for them to affect man in such
a way as to make him lose his reason (LXXVII. 7).

*Unless man then loses his reason he always remains free
in his acts in such wise that it depends upon him whether
he sin?*

Yes, unless man loses his reason his acts always remain
free in such wise that it depends upon him whether
he sin.

Can this liberty, however, become less perfect and less virile on account of the consequences of sin, even to the extent that when man relapses into sin he is less culpable?

Yes, man's liberty becomes less perfect and less virile owing to the effects of sin, so much so that when he relapses into sin he is less culpable, unless his personal sins are themselves in part cause of this abatement of his perfect liberty (LXXVII. 6).

XIII.—OF THE DIVERSE GRAVITY OF SINS, AND OF THE PUNISHMENT DUE TO THEM

(A)

All the sins that man commits are not then equally grave?
No.

Whence arises the degree of gravity in the sins that man commits?

A sin is more or less grave according as it is opposed to the degree of good which should be sought by man, and according as the sin is in a greater or a lesser degree voluntary (LXXIII. 1-8).

(B)

Does every sin, as such, deserve to be punished?

Yes, every sin, as such, deserves to be punished (LXXXVII. 1).

Why does every sin, as such, deserve to be punished?

Because every sin, as such, is a trespassing of the free will upon ground to which it has no right of entry; and punishment is as it were a restitution, made by the will, of this violation of right (LXXXVII. 1).

The punishment therefore of sin is a question of strict justice?

Yes.

(C)

Who inflicts the punishment due to sin?

It is always one of three principles which rule the order against which sin revolts.

*What are these three principles which rule the order
against which sin revolts?*

The divine law always; human authority in those
things dependent upon it; and the reason of the sinner
according to the degree of his responsibility in sinning
(LXXXVII. 1).

*As regards the punishment inflicted on sin, in what way
does the reason of the sinner punish sin?*

The reason of the sinner can punish sin in two
ways: by remorse and by self-inflicted punishment
(LXXXVII. 1).

How does human authority punish sin?

Human authority punishes sin by chastisement
(LXXXVII. 1).

And how does the divine law punish sin?

The divine law punishes sin in two ways: mediately
and immediately (LXXXVII. 1).

*What is meant by saying that the divine law punishes
sin mediately?*

By this is meant that it inflicts punishment on sin
through the medium of the reason of the sinner and of
human authority (LXXXVII. 1).

*Why does the divine law punish sin through the medium
of the sinner's reason and of human authority?*

Because the reason of the sinner and human authority
act dependently on the divine law, and are in some
sort its instruments (LXXXVII. 1).

(D)

*Is there not also another way in which the divine law
can punish sin as it were mediately?*

Yes, through the medium of creatures or the order
of things which the sinner disturbs by his sin
(LXXXVII. 1).

*Is it in this sense that one may speak of a certain immanent
justice?*

Yes; in this sense there is a kind of immanent justice,
which effects that things used as instruments of divine

justice avenge the sin committed in that they thwart the sinner at every turn (LXXXVII. 1).

What is meant by saying that the divine law punishes sin immediately?

By this is meant a special supernatural intervention by which God Himself avenges man's violation of the supernatural order (LXXXVII. 3-5).

What does this supernatural intervention imply in par-ticular?

As regards certain sins, it implies eternal punishment (LXXXVII. 3, 5).

XIV.—OF MORTAL SINS AND VENIAL SINS

(A)

For what sins does God inflict eternal punishment?
For mortal sins (LXXXVII. 3).

What are mortal sins?

Mortal sins are those which kill the soul, in that, by them, charity is lost, which is the principle of the super natural life (LXXXVIII. 3).

Why does God inflict eternal punishment on these sins?

Because these sins, making the soul lose that life which God alone can give, render the sinner incapable of making reparation for his sin; and thus, since the sin remains always, the punishment must likewise remain always (*ibid.*).

(B)

Are all the sins man commits mortal sins?
No (LXXXVIII. 1, 2).

What are the sins called that are not mortal?
They are called venial (*ibid.*).

What does the word " venial " mean?

It means a sin less grave which does not take away the principle of the supernatural life, which is charity or grace, and for which, consequently, reparation can be made under the ordinary action of grace by a contrary movement of the sinner himself, and on this head its punishment is only temporal: hence it is called " venial," or easily " pardonable " (from the Latin word *venia*, which means *pardon*) (LXXXVIII. 1).

Supposing venial sins are committed by a man who is in the state of mortal sin, and this man were to die in this state, would his venial sins be punished by eternal punishment?

Yes, by reason of his state of soul, and because not having charity, he would be incapable of making repara tion for these sins, which, after his death, are eternally irreparable.

Whence does it arise that some sins are mortal, whereas others are only venial?

This arises from the nature of the disorder brought about by different sins, and from the greater or lesser voluntariness of sin (LXXXVIII. 2).

What is meant by saying that this difference of mortal from venial sin arises from the nature of the disorder brought about by sin?

This means that there are sins which, of themselves, are directly opposed to the supernatural love of God, which is the principle of the life of the soul, or that they are incompatible with this love; whilst other sins bring about a lesser disorder of an accidental nature which is compatible with the supernatural love of God existing habitually in the soul (*ibid.*).

What are those sins which, of themselves, are directly opposed to the supernatural love of God, the principle of the soul's life, or which are incompatible with this love?

They are those sins which reject the supernatural love of God, or which imply an evil and a disorder that disturb the very essence of man's relation to God, or the mutual relation of men, or the relation of man to himself.

What are these sins?

These sins are the spurning of the supernatural love of God, or the sins that violate the honour of God, or

6

the sins of theft, homicide, and adultery, or the sins against nature.

(c)

What is the best means of knowing exactly these divers sins and their gravity?

The best means is to consider them in their relation with the different virtues taken in specific detail.

Shall we have occasion to study this relation of sins with each of the virtues taken in specific detail?

Yes, we shall consider this after having seen, in general, what is required for man to live a virtuous life by avoiding a life of sin.

What further remains to be seen, after having considered, in general, what is required for man to live a virtuous life by avoiding a life of sin?

There remains to be considered the exterior helps necessary for man to attain this end.

What are these exterior helps necessary for man to attain this end?

They are laws which direct him, and grace which helps him on his journey (XC.–CXIV.).

XV.—OF THE EXTERIOR PRINCIPLE WHICH DIRECTS MAN'S ACTIONS; OR OF LAW

What is meant by law?

By law is meant an order of reason, for the com mon good, made and promulgated by one in authority (XC. 1-4).

An order then contrary to reason could not be a law?

No, an order or a commandment contrary to reason can never be a law; it is an act of despotism or of tyranny (XC. 1, *ad* 3).

What is meant by saying that law is an order of reason ordained to the common good?

This means that a law provides first of all for the good of the whole community, and does not concern itself with a part thereof or of the individual, except in so far as a part or an individual concurs in the general good (XC. 2).

From what authority does law emanate?

It emanates from him upon whom it is incumbent to be mindful of the common good as if it were his own private good (XC. 3).

For a law to bind, is it necessary that it be promulgated and known?

Yes, for a law to bind it is necessary that it be promulgated in such a way that it come to the knowledge of those whom it concerns (XC. 4).

And if, through one's own fault, one is ignorant of the law, is one excused for not obeying the law?

No; if, through one's own fault, one is ignorant of the law, one is not excused from obeying the law.

It is then very important to learn fully the laws that concern us?

Yes, it is very important to study the laws that concern us.

XVI.—OF DIVERS LAWS; AND FIRST, OF THE ETERNAL LAW

Are there several kinds of law that concern us?
Yes.

What are these different kinds of law?
They are the eternal law, the natural law, human law, and the divine law (XCI. 1-5).

What is the eternal law?
The eternal law is the supreme law which rules all things, and on which all other laws depend, for these latter are only derivations or particular manifestations thereof (XCIII. 1, 3).

Where is the eternal law?
The eternal law is in God (XCIII. 1).

How is this law manifested in things?
It is manifested by the very order of things such as is found in the world (XCIII. 4-6).

XVII.—OF THE NATURAL LAW

(A)

Is the eternal law to be found in man by participation?
Yes (XCIII. 6).

What is this participation or manifestation of the eternal law in man called?

It is called the natural law (XCIV. 1).

What is meant by the natural law?

By the natural law is meant that inborn light of man's practical reason by which he is able to direct himself and to act with knowledge consciously in such wise that his acts execute the eternal law, just as the natural actions of things produced by virtue of their natural inclination execute this same law unconsciously (XCIV. 1).

Is there a first principle of this practical reason, or a first precept of the natural law in man?

Yes, it is that which is founded upon the very nature of *good* in the metaphysical sense of the word, just as the first principle of the speculative reason is founded upon the nature of *being* (XCIV. 2).

In what does the first principle of the practical reason or the first precept of the natural law in man consist?

It consists in this, that man must seek what is good and avoid what is evil (XCIV. 2).

Does this first principle or first precept embrace all others?

Yes; for the rest are only applications thereof more or less immediate (XCIV. 2).

What are the first applications thereof in man?

The first applications thereof in man are the proclamation by man's reason of the threefold good touching his nature (XCIV. 2).

What is this proclamation of man's reason concerning the threefold good touching his nature?

It is this: whatever is beneficial for or perfects his physical life is good; also, whatever helps towards the conservation of the human species; and also whatever conduces to the welfare of his life as a rational being (XCIV. 2).

What follows from this threefold proclamation of man's practical reason?

There follows from this that whatever is essential for the conservation of this threefold life, or that can help towards its perfection, is proclaimed a good thing by the practical reason of every man, in such a way, however, that among the three goods there is a certain subordination, so that by way of dignity the good of the reason comes first, then the good of the species, and then the good of the individual (XCIV. 2).

(B)

As regards the good of the individual, what does the first principle of the natural law proclaim as essential?

This principle proclaims that man must eat for the sustenance of his body, and that he may never attempt his life (XCIV. 2).

As regards the good of the species, what does the first principle of the natural law proclaim as essential?

This principle proclaims that there must be human beings who concern themselves with the conservation of the species by taking upon themselves the burden as well as the joys of fatherhood and motherhood; and that it is never lawful to do anything which tends to frustrate the object of fatherhood and motherhood (XCIV. 2).

As regards the good of reason, what does the first principle of the natural law proclaim as essential?

This principle proclaims that man, who is the work of God from whom he has received his all, and who was made to live in the society of other men, should honour God as his Sovereign Lord and Master, and should act towards his fellow-beings according as the nature of his relations with them demands (XCIV. 2).

(c)

Are all other precepts of man's practical reason consequent upon these three first principles and their subordination?

Yes, all other precepts or determinations of the practical

reason which affirm that this or that thing is or is not good for this or for that man, and binding him to do or to refrain from doing, are consequent more or less remotely upon these three first principles and their subordination (XCIV. 2).

Are these other precepts or determinations of the practical reason, which are consequent, more or less remotely, upon the three first principles of the natural law, identical for all men?

No, these other precepts or determinations are not the same for all; for according to the degree one recedes from first principles, or from those things, which for all are essential as regards the good of the individual, the good of the species, and the good of reason, one enters the sphere of positive precepts, which can vary almost with out end according to the diversity of individual conditions of different human beings (XCIV. 4).

Who makes these other precepts which can vary almost without end according to the diversity of the individual conditions of different men?

They are made by the individual reason of each human being or by a competent authority in each of the different groups of human beings that form some society in particular.

XVIII.—OF HUMAN LAW

(A)

Can these other precepts become the subject-matter of law?

Yes.

Of what laws are they the subject-matter?

They are the subject-matter, properly speaking, of human laws (XCV.–XCVII.).

What is meant by human laws?

By human laws are meant those ordinations of reason made for the common good of this or that society of human beings, which are enacted and promulgated by the supreme authority of every society (XCVI. 1).

Must these ordinations be obeyed by all who belong to this society?

Yes (XCVI. 5).

Is there here entailed a duty of conscience that binds before God?

Yes (XCVI. 4).

Are there certain cases in which one is not obliged to obey?

Yes, there can be certain cases in which one is not obliged to obey (XCVI. 4).

What are these cases in which one is not obliged to obey?

In the case of impossibility, or in the case of dispensation (XCVI. 4).

(B)

Who can dispense from obeying a law?

He only can dispense from obeying a law who is the maker of the law, or he who has the same authority as the maker of the law, or he who has received from this authority the power to dispense (XCVII. 4).

(C)

Is one bound to obey an unjust law?

No, one is not bound to obey an unjust law, unless the refusal to obey cause scandal or grave trouble (XCVI. 4).

What is meant by an unjust law?

It is one made without authority, or contrary to the common good, or one that injures the lawful rights of members of the society (XCVI. 4).

If a law is unjust in that it offends the rights of God or of His Church, is one bound thereto?

No, if a law is unjust in that it offends the rights of God or the essential rights of the Church, one is never bound thereby (XCVI. 4).

What is meant by the rights of God and the essential rights of the Church?

By the rights of God is meant whatever touches the honour and the worship of God, the Creator and Sovereign Master of all things; by the essential rights of the

Church is meant whatever touches the mission of the Catholic Church as regards the sanctification of souls by the preaching of the truth and the administration of the sacraments.

If then a human law attacks religion one is not bound to obey this law?

If a human law attacks religion one is not bound to obey at any cost (XCVI. 4).

Would such a law be a true law?

No, such a law is a hateful tyranny (XC. 1, *ad* 3).

XIX.—OF THE DIVINE LAW—THE DECALOGUE

(A)

What is meant by the divine law?

By the divine law is meant the law given to men by God who manifests Himself supernaturally (XCI. 4, 5).

When did God give this law to men?

God gave this law to men in the first place in a very simple way before their fall in the Garden of Eden; but He also gave it in a much more elaborate way, later on, through the medium of Moses and the Prophets, and in a way much more perfect by Jesus Christ and the Apostles (XCI. 5).

What is the divine law given by God to men through Moses called?

It is called the Old Law (XCVIII. 6).

And what is the divine law called that was given by God to men through Jesus Christ and the Apostles?

It is called the New Law (CVI. 3, 4).

Was the Old Law made for all men?

No, the Old Law was made for the Jewish people only (XCVIII. 4, 5).

Why did God give a special law to the Jewish people?

Because this people was destined to prepare in the old

world the coming of the Saviour of men who was to be born of the Jewish nation (XCVIII. 4).

What were the precepts called that were given to the Jewish people and that regarded them only?

They were called the " judiciary " precepts, and the " ceremonial precepts " (XCIX. 3, 4).

Are there not also in the Old Law certain precepts which have remained in the New Law?

Yes, and they are called the " moral " precepts (XCIX. 1, 2).

Why have these precepts of the Old Law been kept in the New Law?

Because they constitute what is essential and absolutely obligatory concerning the conduct of every man, from the very fact that he is man (C. 1).

These moral precepts then have always been and always will be the same for all men?

Yes, these moral precepts have always been and always will be the same for all men (C. 8).

Are they identified with the natural law?

Yes, these moral precepts are identified with the natural law.

How then are they part of the divine law?

They are part of the divine law because in order to give them more force and to hinder the human reason from forgetting or corrupting them, God Himself promulgated them solemnly when He manifested Himself to His chosen people at the time of Moses; and also because God promulgated them in view of the super natural end to which every man is called by Him (C. 3).

(B)

What are these moral precepts thus solemnly promulgated by God at the time of Moses called?

They are called the " Decalogue " (C. 3, 4).

What does the word Decalogue mean?

It is a Greek word which means the ten words, for the number of precepts given by God is ten.

What are the ten commandments of the Decalogue?

The ten commandments of the Decalogue are the following:

1. Thou shalt have no other God beside Me.
2. Thou shalt not take the name of the Lord thy God in vain.
3. Thou shalt keep holy the Sabbath day.
4. Honour thy father and thy mother.
5. Thou shalt not kill.
6. Thou shalt not commit adultery.
7. Thou shalt not steal.
8. Thou shalt not bear false witness against thy neighbour.
9. Thou shalt not covet thy neighbour's wife.
10. Thou shalt not covet thy neighbour's goods (C. 4, 5, 6).

(c)

Do these ten commandments suffice to guide the whole moral life of man in the way of virtue?

Yes, they suffice as regards the principal virtues which have reference to the essential duties of man towards God and his neighbour; but for the perfection of all the virtues it was necessary for them to be further explained and completed by the teaching of the prophets in the Old Law, and still further by the teaching of Jesus Christ and the Apostles in the New Law (C. 3, 11).

What is the best way to understand these precepts fully and to understand that which explains or completes them for the perfection of the moral life?

It is to study them by help of each of the virtues considered in detail.

Will the study of them thus be made easy?

Yes, for the very nature of the virtue will explain the nature and the obligation of the precept.

Will this be at the same time a good way to understand the whole perfection of the New Law?

Yes; because the perfection of this law consists precisely in its relation with the excellence of all the virtues (C. 2; CVIII.).

(D)

Has this excellence of all the virtues any special character in the New Law?

Yes, it has a special character inasmuch as the counsels are added to the precepts (CVIII. 4).

What is meant by the counsels being added to the precepts?

By this is meant certain invitations offered by Jesus Christ to all souls of good will, to detach themselves from earthly things for love of Him and in order to obtain a more perfect enjoyment of Him in heaven, things that they might indeed desire and possess without detriment to virtue, but which might prove an obstacle to the perfection of virtue (CVIII. 4).

How many counsels are there?

There are three: poverty, chastity, and obedience (CVIII. 4).

Is there any special state wherein one may practise these counsels in a very perfect way?

Yes, the religious state (CVIII. 4).

XX.—OF THE EXTERNAL PRINCIPLE WHICH HELPS MAN TO PRACTISE GOOD ACTS; OR OF GRACE

(A)

Is law a sufficient guide for man to live a virtuous life and to avoid the contrary life of sin?

No, the help of grace is also necessary (CIX., CXIV.).

What is meant by grace?

By grace is meant a special help from God that assists him to do good and to avoid evil.

Is this special help from God always necessary for man?

Yes.

Is not man of himself ever able to do any good thing or to avoid any bad thing?

Yes, of himself, that is relying on the principle of his nature given to him by God, and upon the other natural helps around him, man can accomplish certain good acts and avoid certain evil acts even in the moral order or in the domain of virtue; but if God by His grace does not heal human nature which was wounded by sin, man would never be able to accomplish even in the order of natural virtue all the good required of him or to avoid all evil; moreover, in the order of supernatural virtue or as regards the good life that is to win heaven, man by his sole nature, without grace, can do absolutely nothing (CIX. 1-10).

(B)

What does this grace of the supernatural order imply?

This grace of the supernatural order implies two things: a supernatural state of soul, and supernatural motions of the Holy Spirit (CIX. 6).

What is meant by this supernatural state of soul?

By this is meant certain qualities introduced and preserved therein by God which in a sense make the very being and faculties of man divine (CX. 1-4).

What is the fundamental quality which makes man's very being divine?

It is called habitual or sanctifying grace (CX. 1, 2, 4).

What are the supernatural qualities which divinize man's faculties?

They are the virtues and the gifts (CX. 3).

Are the virtues and the gifts associated with habitual or sanctifying grace?

Yes, the virtues and the gifts are associated with habitual or sanctifying grace in such wise that they issue from this grace which can never exist in the soul unless they also exist in the faculties.

Are this grace, and these virtues and gifts, which sanctify the soul and its faculties something very estimable?

Yes, for they make man a child of God, and give him the power to act as such.

Is man, endowed with grace and the accompanying virtues and gifts, more perfect than the whole created world in the order of nature?

Yes, he is more perfect even than the angels if we consider them in their nature only (CXIII. 9, *ad* 2).

There is then nothing on earth more to be desired by man than to possess and keep, and by making daily progress in this grace of God together with the virtues and the gifts.

(c)

How can man thus possess and keep the virtues and the gifts and make daily progress in this grace of God?

By responding faithfully to the supernatural motion of the Holy Spirit, who solicits man to prepare himself to receive grace if he has it not, or to make daily progress therein if he already possesses it (CXII. 3; CXIII. 3, 5).

What is this action of the Holy Spirit called?

This action of the Holy Spirit is called actual grace (CIX. 6; CXII. 3).

It is then with this help or through the motion of actual grace that we dispose ourselves to receive habitual or sanctifying grace if we have it not already, or if we have it, to make progress therein?

Yes, it is with this help or through the motion of actual grace that we dispose ourselves to receive habitual or sanctifying grace if we have it not already, or if we have it, to make progress therein.

(d)

Can actual grace produce its full effect in us, in spite of us, and without our response?

No, actual grace cannot produce its full effect in us, in spite of us, and without our response (CXIII. 3).

It is necessary then for our free will to co-operate with the motion of actual grace?

Yes, our free will must co-operate with the motion of actual grace.

What is the co-operation of the free will with the motion of actual grace called?

It is called correspondence with grace.

(E)

When our free will corresponds thus with actual grace, and we have habitual grace in our soul, has the act any special character?

Yes, it is always a meritorious act (CXIV. 1, 2).

Are there several kinds of merit?

Yes, there is merit *de condigno* and merit *de congruo* (CXIV. 2).

What is understood by merit " de condigno "?

It is the merit that demands recompense by right and in strict justice (CXIV. 2).

What is required for man's act to be meritorious "de condigno"?

The act must be done under the impulse of actual grace; it must proceed from sanctifying grace by the virtue of charity; and it must tend towards the acquisition of eternal life for itself alone, or further, towards the increase of grace and of the virtues (CXIV. 2, 4).

Is it possible to merit for others life eternal, or sanctifying grace, or the increase of this grace by merit which is " de condigno "?

No, it is impossible to merit this kind of boons for others except by merit *de congruo;* for to merit *de condigno* for others is proper to Jesus Christ, the Head of the Church (CXIV. 5, 8).

What is understood by merit " de congruo "?

By this it is understood that merit which effects that God by reason of the friendship that unites Him to the just, deems it fitting and in accord with His wishes, to respond to the joy that they seek to give Him by their good works, in Himself giving joy to them by granting what they ask or what they desire of Him (CXIV. 6).

Then the whole " raison d'etre " of merit is reduced to this, that God moves intimately in the life of the just through grace and the virtues under the action of the Holy Ghost?

Yes, it is always in the intimacy between God and the just, or in their life of grace and the virtues under the action of the Holy Spirit, that consists the whole *raison d'etre* of merit; moreover, whatever man does outside this life, even though in itself it is not evil, is altogether vain and will avail him nothing at the last day (CXIV. 6).

Can this life of grace and the virtues to be lived by man on earth be explained in detail?

Yes, all this will be explained in its proper place when we study man's return to God by his good acts.

SECOND SECTION

A DETAILED SURVEY OF MAN'S RETURN TO GOD

I —OF THE SPECIES OF GOOD AND BAD ACTS CONSIDERED IN DETAIL AND ACCORDING TO THE CONDITIONS HABI TUALLY FOUND AMONG MEN; AND OF THE THEOLOGICAL VIRTUES

What virtues are of the greatest import?
The theological virtues.
Why are these of the greatest import?
Because they are those whereby man attains his final end as far as he can and ought to attain it in this life so as to merit the possession of his final end in heaven.
It is then impossible for man to perform any super-naturally good act without the theological virtues?
Yes, it is quite impossible.
What are the theological virtues?
The theological virtues are faith, hope, and charity.

II —OF FAITH AND ITS NATURE: OF THE CONDITIONS NECESSARY FOR AN ACT OF FAITH; OF THE " I BELIEVE " AND THE FORMULA OF AN ACT OF FAITH; OF THE SINS OPPOSED TO FAITH: VIZ., INFIDELITY, HERESY. APOSTASY, AND BLASPHEMY

(A)

What is faith?
Faith is a supernatural virtue which makes our mind, even though it understand not, adhere most firmly and

96

without fear of deception to what God has revealed principally about Himself, and of His will to give Himself to us some day as the object of our perfect happiness (I., II., IV.).

How can our mind not understanding what God has revealed adhere firmly thereto and without fear of deception?

By relying on the authority of God who can neither deceive nor be deceived (I. 1).

Why is it that God cannot deceive nor be deceived?

Because He is Truth itself (I. 1 ; IV. 8).

(B)

But how do we know that God has revealed truths?

We know this through them to whom He has revealed these truths, and through them to whose care He has confided the deposit of His revelation (I. 6-10).

Who are they to whom God has revealed these truths?

First of all God revealed them to Adam to whom He manifested Himself directly; subsequently to the Prophets of the Old Testament; and lastly, to the Apostles at the time of Jesus Christ (I. 7).

How do we know that God thus revealed Himself to Adam, to the Prophets, and to the Apostles?

We know this through history which narrates this fact, and which speaks also of prodigies or miracles done by God to convince men of His supernatural intervention.

(C)

Does the miracle prove absolutely the intervention of God?

Yes, for it is proper to God only, no creature being able to perform a miracle by its own power.

(D)

Where is the history of these supernatural interventions of God and of His revelation to be found?

In particular this history is to be found in the Holy Scriptures or the Bible.

7

What is meant by the Holy Scriptures or the Bible?

It is a collection of books divided into two groups, which are called the Old and the New Testaments.

Do these books resemble other books?

No, for other books are written by men, whereas these were written by God.

What is meant by saying that these books were written by God?

By this is meant that God is the principal author of these books, and that He chose certain men, as so many instruments, to write them.

Of whatever then is contained in these books God is the author?

Yes, God is the author of all that is contained in these books, that is if we speak of the original autograph written by the holy writers; whereas all copies of this autograph are only divine in their authorship in so far as they con form with the original.

Whenever then we read these books, it is as though we heard God Himself speaking to us?

Yes.

But is it not possible for us to misunderstand the sense of this word of God?

Yes, for there are passages that are obscure.

Why is it that there is obscurity in the Holy Scriptures?

This obscurity is due first of all to the mysteries con tained therein, since the Bible treats essentially of truths that God Himself alone knows, such as are beyond the reach of every created mind; this obscurity also arises from the antiquity of these books, which were written primarily for people whose tongue was other than ours and whose lives and customs differed from ours; and, lastly, this obscurity arises from mistakes that have crept either into the copies of the original language, or into the translations made thereof and into the copies of these translations.

(E)

Is there anyone who unerringly interprets the right sense of the word of God whether contained in the Scriptures or elsewhere?

Yes, the Sovereign Pontiff, and through him the Catholic Church in its universal teaching (I. 10).

Why cannot the Sovereign Pontiff and through him the Catholic Church in its universal teaching be deceived as to the sense of the word of God in the Holy Scriptures or wherever it is to be found?

Because God Himself has wished that they should be infallible.

And why did God wish that they should be infallible?

Because, otherwise, men would not have the necessary means of reaching, without fail, the supernatural end to which He has called them (I. 10).

Is this what is meant by saying that the Pope and the Church are infallible in matters of faith and morals?

Yes, this is the precise sense of these expressions; the Pope and the Church can never be deceived, nor can they deceive us, when they give or interpret the word of God, in matters that treat of the essential truths which regard faith or conduct.

(F)

Is there a resume of these essential truths which treat of faith and conduct?

Yes, it is the Apostles' Creed or the " I believe " (I 6).

What is the Apostles' Creed?

It is the following, such as the Catholic Church recites every day:

I believe in God,

the Father Almighty,

Creator of Heaven and earth;

And in Jesus Christ, His only-begotten Son, our Lord,

Who was conceived by the Holy Ghost;

was born of the Virgin Mary;

suffered under Pontius Pilate, was crucified, dead, and
buried;
He descended into Hell;
the third day He arose again from the dead;
He ascended into Heaven, and sitteth at the right hand of
God the Father Almighty;
He shall come to judge the living and the dead.
I believe in the Holy Ghost;
The Holy Catholic Church, the communion of Saints,
the forgiveness of sins;
the resurrection of the body, and life everlasting.

Amen.

*Is the recitation of the Apostles' Creed an act of faith
" par excellence "?*

Yes, indeed it cannot be sufficiently recommended to
the faithful for their daily practice.

Is it possible to make a short and concise act of faith?

Yes; the following in the form of an act of homage to
God is excellent: " O my God, I believe, on Thy word,
all that Thou hast revealed to us, because of Thyself who
hast promised to be some day our perfect happiness."

(G)

Who are able to make this act of faith?

Those only who have the supernatural virtue of faith
(IV., V.).

Then unbelievers cannot make this act of faith?

No, for they do not believe what God has revealed with
a view to their supernatural happiness; and this either
because they are ignorant thereof, or do not trust in the
will of God, who is able to give to them the good that He
thinks fit; or because having known His revelation they
refuse to give their assent to it (X.).

Can the impious make this act of faith?

No, because even though they may hold to be true
what God has revealed by reason of the authority of
God, who can neither deceive nor be deceived, their

assent is not the effect of a supernatural love for the word
of God; on the contrary, the word of God is hateful to
them, although in spite of themselves they are forced to
admit its truth (V. 2, *ad* 2).

*Are there men who believe the word of God, and yet do
not make an act of the supernatural virtue?*

Yes, and in this they imitate the devils (V. 2).

Can heretics make an act of faith?

No, for even though in their minds they assent to such
and such a point of revealed doctrine, they do not give this
assent on the word of God, but on their own private
judgment (V. 3).

*As regards the act of faith, are heretics more to be blamed
than the impious or the devils?*

Yes, because the word of God or His authority is not
the motive of their assent.

Can apostates make an act of faith?

No, because their mind rejects entirely what formerly
they believed on the word of God (XII.).

Can sinners make an act of faith?

Yes, provided they actually have this virtue; and they
can have it, although imperfectly, when they have not
charity, that is when they are in the state of mortal sin
(IV. 1, 4).

Every mortal sin then is not a sin against faith?

No (X. 1, 4).

(H)

In what consists precisely a sin against faith?

A sin against faith consists in not wishing to submit
one's mind to the word of God through homage or
through love for God's word (X. 1-3).

*Is it always man's own fault if he does not thus submit his
mind to the word of God through homage or through love for
God's word?*

Yes, it is always man's own fault, because he resists the
actual grace God offers inviting him to make this act of
submission (VI. 1, 2).

Is this actual grace offered to all men on earth?

Yes, all men always have this grace, although in different degrees and as it pleases God to distribute it according to the designs of His Providence.

Is it a great grace of God to have the virtue of supernatural faith?

Yes, to have the supernatural virtue of faith is in some sense the greatest grace of God.

Why is the gift of faith the greatest grace of God?

Because, without supernatural faith one can do abso lutely nothing towards salvation; moreover, heaven is lost unless one receive the gift of faith from God before death (II. 5-8; IV. 7).

(1)

Would it then be a great sin to expose oneself to the danger of losing the happiness of its possession by reading books or by listening to conversations opposed thereto?

Yes, it would be a great sin to place oneself knowingly in this danger; and even when it is not one's own fault, it is a deplorable thing to have to run such danger.

It is then an extremely important thing to choose our acquaintances and our reading with prudence so as not to expose ourselves to this danger, but, on the contrary, so as to preserve and to increase the great gift of faith?

Yes, this is extremely important, especially seeing that in the world, what with the liberty of the press and so forth, one meets so many things that are dangerous to faith.

(J)

Is there any other sin against faith?

Yes, the sin of blasphemy (XIII.).

Why is blasphemy a sin against faith?

Because it militates directly against the exterior act of faith which is the confession of faith by words; all blas phemy, in fact, consists in the uttering of some word that dishonours God or His saints (XIII. 1).

Is blasphemy a great sin?

Blasphemy is always of its nature a great sin (XIII. 2-3).

Does the habit of blaspheming excuse or lessen the gravity of the sin?

On the contrary, this habit aggravates the sin somewhat, for instead of endeavouring to correct oneself of the habit, the grave evil is allowed to become rooted firmly (XIII. 2, *ad* 3).

III.—OF THE GIFTS OF THE HOLY GHOST THAT CORRESPOND TO FAITH: OF UNDERSTANDING, AND KNOWLEDGE: OF THE SINS OPPOSED TO THEM, NAMELY, OF IGNORANCE, OF BLINDNESS OF MIND, AND OF HEBETUDE OF THE SENSES

Does this virtue of faith suffice to attain to the knowledge of God such as is necessary in this life?

Yes, it suffices provided there are present also certain gifts of the Holy Ghost which aid faith (VIII. 2).

What gifts of the Holy Ghost aid the virtue of faith?

They are the gifts of understanding and knowledge (VIII., IX.).

(A)

How does the gift of understanding succour the virtue of faith in knowing God?

The gift of understanding succours the virtue of faith in knowing God, by making our mind, under the direct action of the Holy Ghost, discern the sense of the words which express the divine messages, and of all propositions pertaining thereto, so as, provided they are not beyond the reach of our minds, to understand them in their full meaning; or if it is a question of mysteries this gift helps us to hold them securely in spite of all difficulties.

This gift of understanding then is " par excellence " a gift of enlightenment?

Yes; and all the intellectual lucidity that we have concerning supernatural truth and the joy resulting therefrom, are due primarily to this gift of under standing (VIII. 2).

Does the gift of understanding also help us in the matter of behaviour?

Yes, the gift of understanding helps us in the greatest degree in the matter of behaviour, because it throws light on the reasons of supernatural good that are contained in the revealed truth that we hold by faith; thus does the gift of understanding enlighten the mind, in order that man's will made divine by charity may be drawn to act well as it behoves (VIII. 3. 4, 5).

Can it be shown how the gift of understanding is distin guished from faith and from the other gifts, such as the gifts of wisdom, knowledge, and counsel?

Yes, in a few words thus: Faith proposes to man's mind under the form of propositions uttered by God certain truths of which the principal surpass his under standing. Some of these truths have reference to God alone, others to creatures, and others to man's conduct. If man by faith assents to these truths as it behoves, he can never live these truths by good behaviour unless he fully understand them; and it is the proper office of the gift of understanding to make man's mind understand these truths fully, whereas the gift of wisdom enlightens the mind with regard to truths that have reference to the things of God, the gift of knowledge to truths relating to creatures, and the gift of counsel to truths relating to man's behaviour (VIII. 6).

(B)

What is the importance and the role of the gift of know-ledge in relation to the virtue of faith?

By the gift of knowledge, the faithful soul, under the direct action of the Holy Ghost, judges with absolute certainty and infallibly, not by the natural process of reasoning, but by instinct as it were and intuitively, the true character of created things in their relation to faith according as they are to be believed, or according as they are directive of our conduct. Thus immediately man sees in creatures what is and what is not, in harmony with the First Truth which is the object of faith and the last end of our acts (IX. 1-3).

(c)

Is this gift of special importance to the faithful in these days?

Yes, for it carries with it the remedy *par excellence* for one of the greatest evils that has afflicted humanity since the Renaissance.

Of what evil is there question?

It is the prevalence of false science which fails to under stand the true relation between creatures and God, who is the First Truth and the last end of man: in the specula tive order it has made the study of creatures an insur mountable obstacle to the truths of faith; and in the practical order it has renewed the old pagan depravity which is all the more pernicious seeing that it succeeded the peerless lives of virtue practised by the saints.

Is this one of the principal causes of the evil that is rife in the world and is the bane of modern society?

Yes, without doubt.

The virtue of faith then with the accompanying gifts of understanding and knowledge is one of the most powerful remedies against the impiousness and the aloofness from God of modern society?

Yes, the virtue of faith with these gifts is one of the most powerful remedies against this evil.

(D)

What are the vices opposed to the gifts of understanding and knowledge?

They are ignorance, which is opposed to knowledge,

and blindness of mind, and the hebetude of the senses, which are opposed to understanding (XV. 1, 2).

What are the causes of these vices, and of the last two in particular?

The causes of these vices are, in particular, sins of the flesh which stifle the life of the mind (XV. 3).

IV.—OF THE PRECEPTS RELATING TO FAITH —OF THE CATECHISM, AND OF THE SUMMA OF ST. THOMAS AQUINAS

(A)

Are there in God's law any precepts relating to faith?

Yes, in God's law there are certain precepts relating to faith, especially in the New Law (XVI. 1, 2).

Why especially in the New Law?

Because in the Old Law there were no precepts treating in detail the things to be believed; God thought it not yet necessary to impose these truths in their details on the faith of all people (XVI. 1).

These truths that are now expanded in detail, at least those that regard the mysteries of the Trinity and the Incarnation. and are imposed on the faith of all, why were they not imposed on all in the Old Testament?

Because in the Old Testament the mysteries relating to Jesus Christ existed only in the state of promise as it were or of figure, and it was reserved to Jesus Christ Himself to reveal to men in their plenitude the two essential mysteries of our faith, namely, those of the Trinity and the Incarnation.

What then were the people under the Old Law bound to believe?

As regards these two mysteries they were not bound to believe anything explicitly; but they believed them in an implicit way by believing in the perfection of God and in His repeated promises of salvation (XVI. 1).

Was this sufficient for them to be able to make an act of supernatural faith?

Yes.

Is our state to be preferred to that of the people under the Old Law?

There is no comparison between our state and that under the Old Law.

In what does this superiority consist?

It consists in this, that these mysteries are now mani fested to us directly as they are in themselves, although in a way that is veiled and obscure; whereas under the Old Law they were unknown except implicitly, and in a vague and figurative sense.

(B)

Have we not then, under the New Law, a special duty to live in the thought of these great mysteries, and to endeavour to understand them more and more by the use of the gifts of knowledge and understanding?

Yes, this is a duty incumbent on all the faithful under the New Law; it is to help them to this end that the Church endeavours with so much care to instruct the faithful in the things of faith.

What form of teaching that is within the reach of all does the Church use in particular?

It uses that form of teaching known as the Catechism.

It is then a duty of all the faithful to learn the teaching of the Catechism as far as lies in their power?

Yes, this is a strict duty for all the faithful.

Has the Catechism any special value and authority?

Yes, the Catechism brings within the reach of all, all that is sublime and enlightening in the greatest truths which are the food of our minds.

Who is the author of this teaching?

The Church in the person of its learned Doctors.

May one say that this Catechism is the first "par excel lence" of the gifts of knowledge and understanding in the Church?

Yes, for it is the reproduction in a lesser or greater

degree of the most marvellous of these fruits, which is the *Summa Theologica* of St. Thomas Aquinas.

Has the " Summa Theologica " any special authority in the Church?

Yes, for the Church ordains that all who teach in her name should be imbued with its teaching (*Code*, Canons 589, 1366).

There is then nothing more profitable than to live in this doctrine?

There is nothing more profitable, for one is sure to live in the full light of reason and faith.

V.—OF HOPE AND ITS NATURE—OF THE VICES OPPOSED THERETO, NAMELY, OF PRE SUMPTION AND OF DESPAIR—OF THE FORMULA OF AN ACT OF HOPE, AND OF THOSE ABLE TO MAKE THIS ACT

(A)

What is the second theological virtue?

The second theological virtue is the virtue of hope.

What is the virtue of hope?

It is one of the three theological virtues, which effects that our will, relying on the help of God, is drawn towards Him revealed by faith, as towards the one who is to be some day our perfect happiness (XVII. 1, 2).

Is hope possible without faith?

No, it is impossible to have the virtue of hope without faith which is its necessary basis (XVII. 7).

Why is it impossible to have hope without faith?

Because only faith gives to hope its object and the motive upon which it relies (XVII. 7).

(B)

What is the object of hope?

First, and above all, it is God Himself according as He is Himself His own happiness, and according as He deigns to give Himself to us one day in heaven to make us happy (XVII. 1, 2).

Can there be anything else other than God which can be the object of hope?

Yes, every true good can be the object of hope, provided it be subordinated to the principal object, which is God Himself (XVII. 2, *ad* 2).

What is the motive upon which hope relies?

The motive upon which hope relies is nought but God Himself, who Himself comes to our help or uses His creatures to this end that we may one day possess Him in heaven in token of reward (XVII. 2).

Does hope then necessarily imply virtuous and meritorious actions performed with God's help that we may approach Him in the way that He desires, namely, that He might give Himself to us in heaven?

Yes, hope necessarily implies these virtuous and meritorious actions.

(c)

Is it a sin against hope to count upon the possession of God one day, and to hold that such is possible without taking the trouble to prepare ourselves by a life of supernatural virtue?

Yes, this is a sin against hope.

What is this sin called?

It is called presumption (XXI.).

Is this the only sin that can be committed against hope?

No, there is another that is called despair (XX.).

What is the sin of despair?

The sin of despair consists in this: by reason of the high excellence of God, who is to be won as He is in Himself, or by reason of the difficulties of practising supernaturally a virtuous life, one does God the injury to think it impossible to practise this life of virtue and so gain happiness; a virtuous life is therefore renounced and no longer does one seek God's help (XX. 1, 2).

Is the sin of despair a very grave sin?

In some sense it is the gravest sin of all, for of itself it makes all supernatural effort impossible, and the sinner in some sort damns himself (XX. 3).

No matter then how great are man's miseries and his sins he should never despair?

No, man ought never to despair no matter how great his sins; for the mercy of God is so great and He is so good that He will always help him by His grace.

What then should man do when he feels the weight of his troubles and of his sins?

He should turn to God immediately corresponding to the grace God always gives, and trust that God will give him strength to live a virtuous life, and so gain heaven.

(D)

What is the formula of an act of hope?

The following: " O my God, I trust that by Thy mercy and power Thou wilt grant me the grace to lead a virtuous life, so that one day I may possess Thee in the glory of heaven."

(E)

Who is able to make an act of hope?

All the faithful who are still on earth.

Can the blessed in heaven make an act of hope?

No, for they have no longer the virtue of hope since they possess God (XVIII. 2).

Have the lost in hell the virtue of hope?

No, for God, who is the object of hope, is separated from them for ever (XVIII. 2).

Have the souls in purgatory the virtue of hope?

Yes; but for them an act of hope is not quite the same as for the faithful on earth; for although they do not yet possess God they no longer have need of His grace to merit heaven since they are sure of heaven, all sin hence forth being impossible to them (XVIII. 3).

VI.—OF THE GIFT OF FEAR WHICH CORRE SPONDS TO THE VIRTUE OF HOPE—OF SERVILE FEAR, AND OF FILIAL

(A)

Only the faithful on earth then require that the virtue of hope should strengthen their will lest excessive fear prevent them from possessing God one day?

Yes (XVIII. 4).

Is there a fear attaching to the virtue of hope that is essentially good?

Yes.

What is this fear called?

This fear of God is called filial fear (XIX. 1, 2).

What is meant by filial fear?

By this is meant that one's attitude towards God is that of a holy respect because of His excellence, or of the goodness of His infinite majesty, and that one fears only what displeases Him or keeps us away from Him in such wise as to prevent us from possessing Him eternally in heaven (XIX. 2).

Is there any other fear of God beside this filial fear?

Yes; it is called servile fear (XIX. 2).

What is meant by servile fear?

By this is meant a disposition of an inferior order such as is proper to slaves whereby one fears a master because of the penalties and punishments He is able to inflict (XIX. 2).

(B)

Has the fear of the punishments which God can inflict always the nature of servile fear?

Yes, except that it need not always have a sinful character such as is proper to sin (XIX. 4).

When does servile fear have a sinful character such as is proper to sin?

It has this character when punishment, or the loss of a

created good whatsoever (which is the object of this fear) is a thing one fears as if it were the supreme evil (XIX. 4).

If then one fears this evil, not indeed as the supreme evil, but as subordinate to the loss of God loved above all, is servile fear an evil thing?

On the contrary, it is even a good thing, albeit of an inferior order and of much less worth than filial fear (XIX. 4, 6).

Why is this fear of less worth than filial fear?

Because filial fear recks not at all the loss of all created goods, provided that the possession of the Uncreated Good which is God Himself remains assured (XIX. 2, 5).

It is then only the loss of the Infinite Good which is God Himself, or of whatsoever compromises perfect possession of it, that filial fear dreads?

Yes, it is only the loss of the Infinite Good which is God Himself, or of whatsoever compromises perfect possession of it, that filial fear dreads (XIX. 2).

(c)

Has filial fear any relation to the gift of the Holy Ghost which is called the gift of fear?

Yes, filial fear is most intimately related to this gift of the Holy Ghost (XIX. 9).

Does then the gift of the Holy Ghost which is called the gift of fear, belong in a special manner to the theological virtue of hope?

Yes (XIX.).

In what precisely consists that gift of the Holy Ghost which is called the gift of fear?

It consists in this, that by its means one subjects oneself to God and to the action of the Holy Ghost, resisting Him not, but rather revering Him in all, lest one lose Him (XIX. 9).

(D)

In what precisely does the gift of fear differ from the virtue of hope?

It consists in this, that the virtue of hope views the

infinite good of God to be gained by the help which He Himself gives, whereas the gift of fear views rather the evil of being separated from Him and of losing Him in withdrawing ourselves by sin from that help which He gives in order to lead us to Him (XIX., *ad* 2).

Is the virtue of hope of a higher order than the gift of fear?

Yes, as indeed are all the theological virtues superior to the gifts; also because the virtue of hope views the good to be possessed, whilst the gift of fear views the evil which is the lack of such good.

Is the fear which is proper to the gift of the Holy Ghost inseparable from charity or the perfect love of God?

Yes, since charity or the perfect love of God is the cause of this fear (XIX. 10).

Can this fear co-exist with servile fear, such as is, of course, free from fear that is sinful?

Yes, it can exist at the commencement, together with servile fear that is not sinful, and for this reason it is called *initial* fear; but according as charity grows it also grows, until at length it has only the name of fear taking on the most pure character of filial or chaste fear which is wholly penetrated with the love of God, Who is the one and only truth, and Whose loss would be for us the greatest evil and in some sort the only evil (XIX. 8).

(E)

Will this fear still exist in heaven?

Yes, but in its highest perfection; moreover, its effect will not be entirely the same as here on earth (XIX. 11).

What will be the effect of filial fear in heaven?

In some sort its effect will be a holy trembling in the presence of the infinite greatness and majesty of God's goodness; but no longer will it be the trembling of fear as if it were possible to lose God, it will be the trembling of wonderment in so far as God is seen to be infinitely above all that is possible to nature, since for evermore the blessed will have the most intimate consciousness that their eternal happiness comes from God alone (XIX. 11).

VII.—OF THE PRECEPTS RELATING TO HOPE

(A)

Are there in God's law any precepts relating to the virtue of hope and the gift of fear?

Yes, in God's law there are certain precepts relating to the virtue of hope and the gift of fear; but like the precepts relating to faith, these precepts in their primary notion have a special character distinct from the precepts properly so-called that are contained in God's law (XXII. 1, 2).

In what consists this special character of the precepts of faith and of hope as regards what is primarily essential to them?

It consists in this: they are not given in the manner of precepts; but under the form of propositions in the case of faith; and under the form of promises or threats in the case of hope and fear (XXII. 1).

Why are these precepts given under this special form?

The reason is because of necessity they precede the precepts properly so-called such as are contained in the law (XXII. 1).

Why should these precepts attaching to faith, hope, and fear necessarily precede the precepts properly so-called that are contained in the law?

It is because the act of faith makes man's mind ready to acknowledge that the author of the law is such as to whom one is in duty bound to submit; and the hope of reward or the fear of chastisement makes man ready to observe the precepts (XXII. 1).

What are the precepts properly so-called which constitute the substance of the law?

They are those which are given to man thus subject and ready to obey, whereby he may order and regulate his life, especially in regard to the virtue of justice.

(B)

Are these latter precepts those which make up the Decalogue?

Yes, they are these very precepts.

Then the precepts relating to faith and hope are not, properly speaking, precepts in the Decalogue?

No, they are not, properly speaking, precepts of the Decalogue; for, first of all, they precede and make the latter possible; and then in the unfolding of the law of God, such as the Prophets or Jesus Christ and the Apostles have made, they take on a new form, developing in their turn the character of counsels or of complementary formal precepts (XXII. 1, *ad* 2).

Nothing then is more necessary nor more ardently desired by God and ordained by Him than that man's mind should be wholly submitted to Him by faith and by hope, which relies on His help for attaining unto Him through the means of a life altogether supernatural?

No, there is nothing more necessary nor more ardently desired and ordained by God than this.

Is there a special virtue which has precisely the role of making man lead a wholly supernatural life with a view to the possession of God?

Yes, and this virtue is called charity.

VIII.—OF CHARITY AND ITS NATURE; OF ITS PRINCIPAL ACT AND THE FORMULA OF THIS ACT

(A)

What then is charity?

Charity is a virtue which raises us to a life of intimacy with God for His own sake, in so far as He is His own happiness and has deigned to wish to communicate His happiness to us (XXIII. 1).

What does this life of intimacy with God to which the virtue of charity raises us imply in us?

This life of intimacy with God implies two things in us: first of all a participation of the divine nature which divinizes our nature and elevates us above every natural order (whether human or angelic) to the order which is proper to God, making us gods and members of His family; secondly, it implies in us principles of activity proportionate to this divine existence which enable us to act as true children of God even as God Himself acts—knowing Him as He knows Himself, loving Him as He loves Himself, and enabling us to enjoy Him as He enjoys Himself (XXIII. 2).

Are these two things indissolubly connected with the presence of charity in the soul?

Yes, and charity itself is their consummation or perfection.

Is it then true always that whoever has charity has also sanctifying grace together with the virtues and the gifts?

Yes, of necessity he must have all these (XXIII. 7).

Is charity the queen of all the virtues?

Yes, charity is the queen of all the virtues (XXIII. 6).

Why is charity the queen of all the virtues?

Because charity rules them all and causes them to act with the view of possessing God, who is the proper object of charity (XXIII. 6).

How does charity cleave and unite itself to God, its proper object?

It is by love that charity cleaves and unites itself to God (XXVII.).

In what precisely consist this cleaving and union of charity to God, its proper object?

It consists in this, that man by charity desires for God the Infinite Good which is God Himself, and for himself he desires the same good, which is God, precisely as constituting His own happiness (XXV., XXVII.).

(B)

What is the difference between these two loves?

This: one is a love of complacency in God in so far as
He is Himself happy; the other a love of complacency in
God in so far as He is our own happiness.

Are these two loves inseparable in the virtue of charity?

Yes, they are absolutely inseparable.

Why are they inseparable?

Because each rules the other, and they are reciprocally
cause and effect.

*How can it be shown that they rule each other, and are
reciprocally cause and effect?*

By this: if God were not our good we would have no
reason at all for loving Him; and if there were not in
Him, as in its fount, the good that He is for us, we would
not love Him by the love with which we love Him
(XXV. 4).

Are both these loves pure and perfect?

Yes, in very truth.

*Is each one of them a love belonging to the virtue of
charity?*

Yes.

*Is there not, however, some order between these two loves;
and which of the two holds the first place?*

Yes, there is here a certain order; and that love holds
the first place which is complacency in God, because of
the infinite good which He is to Himself.

Why does this love hold the first place?

Because the good that God is to Himself outbalances
the good that God is to us: not that this good is really
different, for it is always God Himself in so far as He is in
Himself; but because this good is in God in an infinite
manner and as it were in its source; whereas it is in us in
a finite manner and by participation.

*Does the love of charity embrace others besides God
and us?*

Yes, the love of charity reaches to all those who already

possess the happiness of God or who hope to possess it one day (XXV. 6-10).

Who are those who already possess the happiness of God?

The angels and the elect in heaven.

Who are those who hope to possess it one day?

All the souls of the just in purgatory and all living on earth.

Must one then love all men on earth with the love of charity?

Yes.

(c)

Are there degrees in this love of charity which we must have for others as well as for ourselves?

Yes, there are degrees in this love of charity; for first we must above all love ourselves, and then others accord ing as they approach in nearness to God in the super natural order, or according as they are more or less near to us in the divers relations that bring us into touch with them, such relations, for instance, as ties of blood, friend ship, life in common, etc. (XXVI.).

What is meant by saying as to the order of the love of charity that we must above all love ourselves after the love of God?

By this is meant that we must wish for ourselves the happiness of God above all things else excepting God, to whom we must wish this happiness first and in preference to all other.

Is it only the happiness of God that we must wish for ourselves and for others also by virtue of charity?

It is the happiness of God before all and above all; but we must or may also wish for ourselves and for others, by virtue of charity, all that is ordained to the happiness of God or that is dependent upon Him.

Is there anything that is directly ordained to the happiness of God?

Yes, the acts of the supernatural virtues (XXV. 2).

*Should we therefore desire for ourselves and for others the
acts of the supernatural virtues immediately after the desire
for the happiness of God and by reason of this happiness?*
Yes.
*May we also by virtue of charity desire temporal goods for
ourselves and for others?*
Yes, we may and sometimes we ought to desire for
ourselves and for others temporal goods in virtue of
charity.
When ought we to desire this kind of goods?
When they are indispensable to our life on earth, and
for the practice of virtue.
When may we desire them?
When they are not indispensable but may be useful.
*If they were hurtful to the good of virtue, would it not be
possible to desire them for ourselves and for others without
detriment to the virtue of charity?*
No, for if these temporal goods become an obstacle to
a life of virtue and are a cause of sin, we cannot desire
them neither for ourselves nor for others without preju
dicing the virtue of charity.

(D)

*How may one formulate accurately the act of love which
constitutes the principal act of the virtue of charity?*
In this wise: "My God, I love Thee with all my heart
and above all things; I desire no other happiness but
Thyself, wishing this same happiness before all and above
all to Thyself; further, I desire this happiness for all those
who already possess Thee or who, by Thy bounty, are
called to possess Thee one day."

IX.—OF THE SECONDARY ACTS, OR THE EFFECTS OF CHARITY; OF JOY, PEACE, MERCY, KINDLINESS, ALMSDEEDS AND FRATERNAL CORRECTION

(A)

When the soul has the virtue of charity and performs in truth the principal act of charity, what is the result in the soul?

The result is the first effect of charity which is called joy (XXVIII. 1).

Is this joy, which is the proper effect of charity, perfect without any trace of sadness?

Yes, this joy is perfect, without trace of sadness, when it reaches towards the infinite happiness that God is to Himself or towards the elect in heaven; but it is mingled with traces of sadness when it reaches to the happiness of God which is not as yet possessed by the souls in pur gatory, or by us and all those who are still on earth (XXVIII. 2).

In the latter case why is the joy belonging to charity mingled with sadness?

The mingling of sadness in this joy is due to the presence of physical or moral evil which affects or can affect those who are in the divers states mentioned (*ibid.*).

But then even in these cases ought not joy to predominate by the very virtue of charity?

Yes, by the very virtue of charity joy should always predominate, because this joy has for its principal object and for its first cause the infinite happiness of the Divine Friend, Who enjoys eternally the infinite good which is no other than Himself, and which He essentially possesses secure from all evil (*ibid.*).

(B)

Is there any other effect in us consequent upon the principal act of charity?

Yes; and this other effect is called peace (XXIX. 3).

What is peace?

Peace is the tranquillity of order or perfect harmony resulting in us and in all things from the fact that all our inclinations and the inclinations of all other creatures are turned towards God, who is the supreme object of our perfect happiness (XXIX. 1).

(c)

Is there any other effect which attends the principal act of charity besides these two interior effects?

Yes, there is another interior effect which follows this act which is called mercy (XXX.).

What is meant by mercy?

By mercy is meant a special virtue distinct from charity, and of which it is the fruit, whereby we sorrow for the misery of our neighbour as something possible to ourselves, or at least as if the misery in some sense were our own, and this by reason of the friendship which unites us to our neighbour (XXX. 1-3).

Is this virtue of mercy a great virtue?

Yes, for it is a virtue which belongs to God *par excellence*, not indeed in so far as there is any feeling of sorrow or of sadness (which cannot be in Him), but as regards the effects which this feeling moved by charity produces (XXX. 4).

Among men, does this feeling belong above all to the most perfect?

Yes, for the nearer one approaches to God, so much the more must mercy have root in him, inclining him to give help to all around him according to the extent of his means, whether they be spiritual or temporal (XXX. 4).

Would the practice of this virtue be a great help towards the establishment and the strengthening of social peace among men?

Yes, indeed this would be so.

(D)

Are there also any exterior acts which are the proper effect of the virtue of charity by reason of its principal act?

Yes; and one of the first is kindliness (XXXI. 1).

What then is kindliness?

Kindliness, as its very name implies, consists in doing good (*ibid.*).

Is this act always an act proper to the virtue of charity?

Yes, provided one understands it in the precise sense of doing good to others (*ibid.*).

Can it also be the act of other virtues distinct from charity that are, however, dependent upon charity?

Yes, it can also be the act of other virtues distinct from, yet dependent upon charity, when to the general reason of doing good is added some special and particular reason, as, for instance, when a thing is due, or necessary, or is a thing of which one has need (*ibid.*).

What virtue is implied in an act of well-doing when to this is added the particular reason of a thing as due?

In this case the virtue of justice is implied (XXXI. 1, *ad* 3).

And when in the same act of well-doing, there is found added to the general reason of well-doing the particular reason of something that is necessary or of which one has need, what virtue is implied?

The virtue of mercy (*ibid.*).

(E)

What is that act of charity called which consists in doing good through the means of mercy?

It is called almsdeeds (XXXII. 1).

Are there divers kinds of almsdeeds?

Yes, there are two great kinds of almsdeeds: those that are spiritual and those that are corporal (XXXII. 2).

What are corporal almsdeeds?

Corporal almsdeeds are the following: To feed the hungry; to give drink to him that thirsts; to clothe the naked; to give hospitality to the stranger; to visit him who is ailing; to set at liberty those in captivity; and to bury the dead (XXXII. 2).

And what are spiritual almsdeeds?

Spiritual almsdeeds are prayer, teaching, counsel,

consolation, correction, and the forgiving of an offence (XXXII. 2).

Are all these almsdeeds of great worth?

Yes, and indeed we see by the Gospels that at the day of judgment the sentence of eternal damnation or eternal reward will depend upon them.

When is there a strict and grave obligation of performing an almsdeed?

Always when our neighbour is in pressing need, whether spiritual or corporal, and when we only are able to help him (XXXII. 5).

Although there may be no pressing need for helping our neighbour, is there any strict and grave obligation to make use of the spiritual and temporal goods one has received in superabundance from God with the view of bettering our neighbour or society?

Yes, one who has received spiritual and temporal goods in superabundance from God is in duty bound to act in this way (XXXII. 5, 6).

(F)

Is there a certain kind of almsdeed which is in particular important and of a delicate nature?

Yes, it is called fraternal correction (XXXIII. 1).

What is meant by fraternal correction?

It is a spiritual almsdeed which is, properly speak ing, directed to the healing of sins evil in the sinner (XXXIII. 1).

Is this almsdeed an act of the virtue of charity?

Yes, it is eminently an act of charity, through the medium of mercy and the help of prudence, which should choose the proper means for this end, which is as excellent as it is delicate and difficult (XXXIII. 1).

Is fraternal correction of precept?

Yes, it is of precept and is obligatory, but only in the case when owing to circumstances it is imperative upon us to help our neighbour out of some evil which en dangers his salvation (XXXIII. 2).

Who are those bound to make use of fraternal correction?

Everybody who is animated by the spirit of charity and who, consequently, is free himself from the evil he per ceives in his neighbour, is bound to point out the fault in his neighbour whoever the latter may be, even if a superior, provided, of course, proper respect is preserved and there is hope of amendment; otherwise there is no obligation, and one should abstain therefrom (XXXIII. 3-6).

X.—OF THE VICES OPPOSED TO CHARITY AND THEIR ACTS: OF HATRED; DIS TASTE FOR SPIRITUAL THINGS AND LAZINESS; ENVY; DISCORD; STRIFE; SCHISM; WAR; QUARRELLING (THE DUEL); SEDITION; SCANDAL

(A)

What feeling, above all, should be banished from man's heart in his dealings with his fellow-men?

It is the feeling of hatred (XXXIV.).

What then is hatred?

Hatred is the greatest of all the vices opposed directly to the principal act of charity, which is an act of love of God and of one's neighbour (XXXIV. 2-4).

Is it possible that God should be hated by any one of His creatures?

Yes, it is even possible for God to be hated by one of His creatures (XXXIV. 1).

How is it possible to explain that God, who is the Infinite Good, and from whom comes all good for the benefit of His creatures, whether in the natural or the supernatural order, can be hated by one of His creatures?

It is explained by the moral depravation of some of His creatures, who no longer consider God as the Infinite Good and the source of all good things, but as the Legis lator who forbids the evil one loves, or as the judge who condemns and punishes the evil one commits, and of which one is unwilling to repent or to ask pardon (XXXIV. 1).

It is then a sort of diabolical obstinacy in doing evil which causes rational creatures to hate God?

Yes, it is a sort of diabolical obstinacy in evil.

Is hatred of God the greatest of all sins?

Yes, it is by far the greatest of all sins (XXXIV. 2).

Is it ever permitted to hate any one of our fellow-men?

No, this is never permissible (XXXIV. 3).

But has not one the right to hate men who do evil?

No, one never has the right to hate evildoers; but one should detest the evil they do, because of the love one must have towards them (XXXIV. 3).

May one never wish them evil?

No, one may never wish them evil; but in view of the good which one wishes to them, or to society, and still more to God, one may wish them to suffer certain evils to the end that they might be drawn to a good life, and thus safeguard the good of society and the glory of God (XXXIV. 3).

May one ever wish that a man on earth, no matter how bad he may be, may suffer eternal damnation?

No, one may never wish this of any man living; for this would be an act directly opposed to the virtue of charity, which makes us wish for all in the end the happiness of God, with the sole exception of the devils and the lost who are already in hell.

(B)

Is there a vice which is specially opposed to the second act of charity which is called joy?

Yes; and this is the vice of sadness touching spiritual and supernatural good which is the proper object of charity, and which we know to be God Himself, our perfect happiness (XXXV.).

How is such sadness possible?

It is possible because man by reason of his distaste for spiritual things esteems the divine good, which is the object of charity, as something not good, and as baneful and oppressing.

Is this always a mortal sin?

Yes, it is always a mortal sin when it passes from the lower or sensitive part of our nature and infects the rational and higher part of our soul (XXXV. 1).

Why is it then a mortal sin?

Because it is directly opposed to charity which makes us in duty love God above all things, and as a consequence makes us bound to seek in Him the first and ultimate peace and joy of our soul (XXXV. 3).

Is this sadness one of the capital sins?

Yes, it is a capital sin, because on its account men do many evil things and commit numerous sins either to avoid and get rid of it, or because its oppressiveness makes them take refuge in evil acts (XXXV. 4).

What is this evil sadness which is a capital sin called?

It is called spiritual laziness, or distaste for spiritual things.

What are the sins which flow from this sin, or what are the daughters of this spiritual laziness?

They are despair, pusillanimity, sluggishness as regards the precepts, spite, malice, and the wandering of the mind among unlawful things (XXXV. 4, *ad* 2).

Is this laziness the only vice opposed to the joy of charity?

No, there is another called envy (XXXVI.).

What is the difference between these two vices?

There is this difference: spiritual laziness is opposed to the joy of the divine good in so far as this good is in God and ought to be in us; whereas envy is opposed to the joy of the divine good in so far as this good belongs to our neighbour (XXXV., XXXVI.).

(c)

What then is envy?

Envy is sadness because of the good of another, not because this good is a cause of evil to us, but merely because it is another's and not ours (XXXVI. 1, 2, 3).

Is this sadness of envy a sin?

Yes, because one is sad when one ought to have cause for joy, namely, at the good of another (XXXVI. 2).

Is envy always a mortal sin?

Yes, it is always of its very nature a mortal sin, since it is essentially opposed to the joy of charity; but it may be venial if it be a question of an imperfect voluntary act (XXXVI. 3).

Is envy a capital sin?

Yes, because it carries men to numberless sins, either in the endeavour to avoid it or to follow its commands (XXXVI. 4).

What are the daughters of envy?

They are obloquy, detraction, gladness in the adversities of our neighbour, affliction at his prosperity and hatred (XXXVI. 4).

(D)

Are there any vices opposed to the peace of charity?

Yes, there are several.

What are they?

They are discord within the soul, wrangling and fighting, schism, strife, sedition, warfare (XXXVII.–XLII.). .

(E)

What precisely is discord, which is a sin against charity?

It consists in not wishing purposely what others wish when they manifestly desire the good, that is what is for the honour of God and our neighbour's good, and precisely for this very reason; or, to take part in this disagreement without a direct bad intention, except that it has reference to things that belong essentially to God's honour and our neighbour's good; or to be unduly obstinate and stubborn in disagreeing no matter what the object may be and no matter how right be our intention (XXXVII. 1).

(F)

What is wrangling?

Wrangling is to contend with another in words (XXXVIII. 1).

Is wrangling a sin?

Yes, if one thus contends with the sole desire to contradict; and the more so if one does this in order to hurt a neighbour or contaminate the truth which our neighbour defends by his words; it would also be a sin if, in defending the truth oneself, one's manner or speech wounds our neighbour's feelings (XXXVIII. 1).

(G)

What is schism?

Schism is the separating oneself intentionally from the unity of the Church, either by refusing to submit to the Sovereign Pontiff as to the head of the Church, or by refusing to have communication with the members, as such, of the Church (XXXIX. 1).

(H)

Why is war counted among the sins opposed to charity?

Because when war is unjust it is one of the greatest evils that can be inflicted on our neighbour.

Is it ever permissible to make war?

Yes, when there is a just cause, and no injustice is committed in the course of the war (XL. 1).

What is meant by a just cause?

By this is meant the hard necessity of making respected even by force of arms the essential rights among men, when these rights have been violated by a foreign nation which refuses to make reparation (XL. 1).

Is it then permitted to make war in this case only?

Yes (XL. 1).

Do those who fight in a just war, and who commit no act of injustice in the course of the war, perform an act of virtue?

Yes, they perform a great act of virtue, since they

expose themselves to the greatest of perils for the welfare of their fellow-men or for the good of God.

(I)

*What is understood by faction, the sin that is opposed to
peace?*

By faction is understood strife between individuals
without any sanction whatsoever of the public authority;
and it is always of itself a grave sin in him who is the
author thereof (XLI. 1).

(J)

Is the duel related to this sin?

Yes, but with this difference, that the duel is a thing
calculated and is in a sense not fought in the heat of
passion; and this circumstance adds to its gravity.

Is the duel, in itself, always essentially bad?

Yes, because therein one jeopardizes one's own life or
that of one's neighbour contrary to the law of God, who
alone is the master of life.

(K)

*What is sedition, a sin that is also opposed to charity
and to peace?*

Sedition is a sin whereby parties of the same people con
spire or rise up tumultuously one against the other, or
against the established and legitimate authority, whose office
it is to guard the well-being of the whole people (XLII. 1).

Is sedition a great sin?

Yes, it is always a great sin, because humanly speaking
there is nothing more excellent and more to be desired
than the maintenance of public order, hence the crime
of unjust war, and perhaps sedition even more so, is the
greatest crime against the well-being of our fellow-men
(XLII. 2).

(L)

*Is there any special kind of sin which is directly opposed to
charity as regards the external act which is called beneficence?*

Yes, and the sin is called scandal (XLIII.).

What is scandal?

Scandal is that sin which through some word or deed offers to another an occasion of sinning; or the fact of taking occasion to sin because of what is said or done by another: in the first instance one gives scandal; in the second, one is scandalized (XLIII. 1).

Is it only weak souls that are scandalized?

Yes, that is those that are not as yet proof against evil; although many sensitive souls cannot help but be painfully affected when they see or hear something that is bad (XLIII. 5).

Are good and virtuous souls incapable of giving scandal?

Yes, because in the first place they never do or say anything bad that could really scandalize; if perchance scandal is ever given to others, this is due to the malice of the latter only (XLIII. 6).

May it not sometimes happen that virtuous souls are under an obligation to forego certain things lest weaker souls be scandalized?

Yes, provided of course it is not a question of things necessary for salvation (XLIII. 7).

Is one ever bound to forego some good thing in order that the wicked may not be scandalized?

No (XLIII. 7, 8).

XI.—OF THE PRECEPTS RELATING TO CHARITY

Is there in the law of God any precept relating to the virtue of charity?

Yes (XLIV. 1).

What is this precept?

This precept is the following: "Thou shalt love the Lord thy God with thy whole heart, with thy whole mind, with thy whole soul, and with thy whole strength " (XLIV. 4).

What do these words mean precisely?

They mean that in all our actions our intention should be directed towards God; that all our thoughts should be subject to Him; and that all our affections should be regulated according to His will; and that all our external acts should be performed in fulfilment of His will (XLIV. 4, 5).

Is this precept of charity a great precept?

Yes, it is indeed the greatest of all the precepts, since it contains virtually all other precepts, for these are ordained to it (XLIII. 1-3).

Is this precept of charity one and single, or does it embrace several other precepts?

This precept taken in its fulness is both one and many; and this means that understood in its proper sense it alone is sufficient in the order of charity; for in very truth one cannot love God without loving one's neighbour whom we must love for God's sake; but in order that the precept may be properly understood by all, to this first precept is added a second, which is really not distinct from the first, viz., " Thou shalt love thy neighbour as thyself " (XLIV. 2, 3, 7).

Are these precepts of charity contained in the Decalogue?

No, for these precepts of charity precede, and as it were dominate, the Decalogue; indeed, the precepts con tained in the Decalogue were only given in order that the carrying out of the precepts of charity might be assured (XLIV. 1).

Are these precepts of charity in the supernatural order manifest of themselves without any need of their being promulgated?

Yes, for just in the same way as there is a law of nature inborn in all which commands that in the natural order God must be loved above all and all things else for His sake; so it is a law essential to the supernatural order that God, who is the fount of all in this order, must be loved with a supernatural love above all and all things else for His sake.

Then, not to love God above all, and not to love one's neighbour as oneself, is to run counter to what is essential in the order of the affections?

Yes, this is so.

XII.—OF THE GIFT OF WISDOM WHICH COR RESPONDS TO CHARITY; AND OF THE SIN TO WHICH IT IS OPPOSED

(A)

Is there a gift of the Holy Ghost that corresponds to the virtue of charity?

Yes; and it is the gift of wisdom which is the most perfect of all the gifts (XLV.).

What is the gift of wisdom?

The gift of wisdom is that gift of the Holy Ghost which effects that man, under the direct action of the Holy Spirit, judges of all things by reference to the highest and most sublime of all causes, which is the wisdom itself of God in so far as it is made manifest to us by faith (XLV. 1).

How is this gift of wisdom distinguished from the in tellectual virtue of the same name, or from the gifts of intuition or insight, of knowledge and of counsel, and in so far as these latter are distinguished from the intellectual virtues which are also called intuition or insight, knowledge and prudence?

In a few words these differences may be summed up thus: On the part of the intellect, in things of faith, there are several acts essentially distinct to which corre spond the virtues or their respective gifts which are themselves distinct from each other.

The very essence of faith is the act that assents to things revealed by God. Upon this act of assenting, which is the principal act, there ensue certain secondary or complementary acts that perfect the intellect in the same order of the things of faith; and these acts are understanding and judging. The act of understanding or perceiving is, generically speaking, one only, and to it corresponds the intellectual virtue of insight or intuition, and in a higher scale of perfection the gift of under standing. The act of judging is manifold, for it is

threefold: this act may judge of things, in general, accord
ing to divine reasons or according to human; or it may
judge of things by the application of its knowledge to
things themselves in particular. In the first case, the
intellectual virtue which corresponds to the act of
judging is called the intellectual virtue of wisdom;
and, in a higher scale, the gift of wisdom. In the second
case, it is called the intellectual virtue of knowledge; and,
in a higher scale, the gift of knowledge. In the third
case, it is called the intellectual virtue of prudence;
and, in a higher scale, the gift of counsel.

(B)

Is there anything worthy of note in this doctrine?

Yes; we owe this teaching to St. Thomas Aquinas.
He himself tells us that he did not perceive the harmony
and the beauty of this doctrine except after many years
of study and reflexion (VIII. 6).

*Among these virtues and gifts that perfect the mind in its
knowledge of the truth, is there one which, in perfection,
holds the first place?*

Yes, and it is the virtue of faith upon which all the
others depend; indeed, it is the role of the other virtues
and gifts to assist in the knowledge of this truth.

Which is the most perfect after the virtue of faith?

After the virtue of faith the most perfect is the gift of
wisdom.

*In what does this perfection of the gift of wisdom consist,
in particular with regard to the gift of knowledge?*

It consists in this, that by the gift of knowledge we judge
of things divinely by referring them to their immediate and
created causes; whereas by the gift of wisdom we judge
of all things divinely by referring them to the highest of
all causes, that, namely, which itself is independent of
all causes and from which all other causes depend.

*It is then by the gift of wisdom that one attains to the
highest degree of knowledge to be had on earth?*

Yes.

(c)

Is there any sin which is opposed to this gift that is so supreme and beautiful?

Yes, and it is that lack of wisdom which consists in judging finally of a thing without taking into account, or perhaps even by contemning, the sovereign counsels of God.

What ought this sin to be called?

There is only one fitting name for this sin: it is abject stupidity or supreme folly (XLVI. 1).

Is this sin often found among men?

Yes; for, practically speaking, it is the sin of all those who lead a life apart from or in defiance of the things of God.

Is there an insuperable opposition between the wisdom of the world and the wisdom of God?

Yes, for each regards the other as folly.

In what does the opposition consist?

It consists in this, that the world esteems those wise who arrange their life in such a way as to lack none of the things of this world, and such people seek their last end in the good things of this life in contempt of the Good of God which is promised us in another life; whereas the wisdom of the children of God consists in subordinating all the things of the present life to the possession of God in heaven.

Are these two kinds of life distinct necessarily in every way?

Yes, because the last end of each is absolutely different; and it is the last end which rules all in a life.

It is then only by practising the theological virtues of faith, hope, and charity and cultivating the corresponding gifts that man can tend towards his true final end, and is able as it behoves to view that last end in all the acts of his life?

Yes, of a truth this is so.

XIII.—OF THE MORAL VIRTUES: OF PRU DENCE, ITS NATURE AND ELEMENTS, AND OF ITS ATTENDANT VIRTUES; OF THE SPECIES OF PRUDENCE, NAMELY, INDIVIDUAL, DOMESTIC, POLITICAL, AND MILITARY

(A)

What is the first of the moral virtues?
The virtue of prudence (XLVII.).

What is prudence?
Prudence is a principle of moral action that perfects man's practical reason, so that in every action he dispose and order all things as it behoves, by commanding him self and those under him to do at each moment what is necessary for the perfect realization of every virtue (XLVII. 1-9).

Is this virtue of great importance in man's life?
Yes, for without it there could be no virtuous act in man's life at all (XLVII. 13).

If man has this virtue in its perfect state, can he lead a perfectly virtuous life?
Yes (XLVII. 14).

Why can prudence effect this?
Because in prudence all the other virtues are united, each single one being dependent upon prudence just as prudence is dependent upon them.

In order for this virtue of prudence to be perfect, are certain conditions necessary as regards its proper act?
Yes.

What are these conditions?
They are, first of all, the elements which constitute it, without which it cannot exist at all; secondly, certain other virtues which are ordained to prudence and which prepare the way for its proper act are necessary; and lastly, the division of prudence according to the diversity of objects to be governed or ruled (XLVIII.-LI.).

(B)

What are the elements which constitute prudence?

They are these: Memory of past things; insight into the principles of action whether in general or in par ticular; docility and respect for what has been determined by the wise; astuteness in order to discover a right course of action at a time when recourse to another is not possible; the healthy exercise of the reason applying, as is meet, the principles of the action to be performed to the manifold individual conditions of the action itself; foresight at the moment of acting as regards the substance of each act in particular; circumspection as regards all the accompanying circumstances of the act; precaution against obstacles or against whatsoever might endanger the happy result of the act (XLIX. 1-8).

(C)

What are the virtues ordained to prudence and which prepare the way for its proper act?

They are these: The virtue of good counsel; and the two virtues which ensure a right judgment: the one which regards the ordinary events of life and respects the established laws; the other which regards extra ordinary events, and in this case recourse must be had to the higher sources of the natural law alone (LI. 1-4).

(D)

What is the act proper to prudence called?

It is called the command (XLVII. 8).

But does it not seem that the virtue of prudence is not so much the virtue that commands but rather that counsels, since a man is called " prudent " who takes counsel before acting?

A man is called " prudent " by reason of the counsel he takes before accepting the command; but prudence proper is in the act itself of giving a command with decision at a time when one has to act (XLVII. 8, *Obj.* 2).

(E)

Are there several species of prudence?

Yes, there are as many species of prudence as there are species of commanded acts; acts, that is, that present some special difficulty in the order of virtue.

How many species are there of acts of command?

There are four: the act of command as regards oneself; the act of command in a family; in a society; and in the army (L. 1-4).

What are these different species of prudence called?

They are called individual prudence, domestic, political, and military (*ibid.*).

(F)

What is individual prudence?

It is that necessary to each individual person for the leading of a virtuous life for his own individual good.

(G)

What is domestic prudence?

It is that necessary to every member of a family, so that each, under the head of the family, concur in the common welfare of the family (L. 3).

(H)

What is political prudence?

It is that necessary to the head of a society, whether an independent city or a nation, for the governing thereof as it behoves.

Is it sufficient for the well-being of a city or of a nation that he or those that govern be prudent?

No, there must be a proportionate prudence also in the people governed (L. 2).

In what does this prudence of the governed consist?

It consists in this, that each member of a society should strive by his correspondence to the orders of the government to further the common interests of the society (L. 2).

(1)

Is the object of military prudence also for the furtherance of the interests of the common good?

Yes, military prudence is of great importance for the well-being of the society, since it is through the able commanding of the officers and the perfect discipline of the rank and file that the country defends its rights and repels the unjust invasions of an enemy (L. 4).

XIV.—OF THE GIFT OF COUNSEL WHICH CORRESPONDS TO PRUDENCE

What is the gift of the Holy Ghost that corresponds to prudence?

The gift of counsel (LII.).

What is this gift?

It is a supernatural perfection of man's practical reason that makes him docile and ready under the action of the Holy Ghost to take counsel and to sift well everything that in life relates to salvation; this gift is therefore of the greatest help to man, for even though he possess all the acquired and the infused virtues he cannot do without this gift, which helps him to make a perfect judgment and act of command, since he is for ever liable to err amidst the complexity of circumstances that accompany every human act (LII. 1, 2).

Will the gift of counsel exist also in heaven?

Yes, but in a way much more perfect (LII. 3).

In what more perfect way will it exist there?

In this way: the minds of the blessed in heaven will be wondrously enlightened by God as regards all human activity in so far as it harmonizes with the final end which is already in their possession; and this, whether there be question of those acts which, for evermore, shall be produced in virtue of the actual possession of the final end; or there be question of the help the blessed are destined to give until the last day, to those on earth that they also may gain heaven (LII. 3).

XV.—OF THE SINS THAT ARE OPPOSED TO PRUDENCE, VIZ., OF IMPRUDENCE; HASTINESS; LACK OF THOUGHT; IN CONSTANCY; NEGLIGENCE; FALSE PRU DENCE; PRUDENCE OF THE FLESH; SLYNESS ; DECEIT; FRAUD; FALSE SOLICITUDE

(A)

Are there any sins opposed to prudence?

Yes, and some of them are opposed to prudence on account of defect, whereas others are opposed on account of excess.

What are those sins called that are opposed to prudence on account of defect?

They go under the general name of imprudence (LIII.).

What is imprudence considered in this general way?

Imprudence, in general, is every act of the practical reason which runs counter to the rules of prudence (LIII. 1).

Can an act of imprudence be a mortal sin?

Yes, this can be so whenever man's reason acts contrary to the divine laws; such a one who spurns the laws of God acts with rashness (LIII. 1).

When is the sin only venial?

When man acts contrary to God's laws but without contempt and without peril to what is necessary for his salvation (*ibid.*).

Is any other sin linked up with the sin of imprudence?

Yes, indeed every other sin, for no sin would ever come to be if there were no act of imprudence; the latter sin, however, is distinct from and can exist apart from other sins (LIII. 2).

In what case does this sin of imprudence exist apart from other sins?

In every case when, without doing anything in itself bad or even when doing something that is good, one acts

with hastiness, or with lack of thought, or with inconstancy, or with negligence (LIII. 2).

(B)

What is hastiness?

Hastiness is a sin against prudence, which consists in
not making sufficient enquiry before acting as regards
when one should act and in what manner one should
act (LIII. 3).

(C)

What is lack of thought?

It is a sin against the rectitude of judgment; and it
consists in despising or in neglecting to consider what is
necessary to ensure a right judgment in conduct (LIII. 4).

(D)

What is inconstancy?

Inconstancy is a defect in the very act of commanding
which is the proper act of prudence; and in very fact
the inconstant man is he who for lack of a firm command
does not effect what he had resolved upon after enquiry
and the taking of counsel (LIII. 5).

(E)

*Is this the only defect which touches the principal act
of prudence?*

No, there is also another called negligence, which is
opposed to the principal act of prudence on the side
of solicitude which this act entails (LIV.).

What is negligence?

It is the want of readiness in putting into execution,
by way of command, the resolutions of the judgment,
made after due enquiry and counsel, as regards the
attainment of the end of virtue (LIV. 1).

Is negligence a great sin?

Yes; for it paralyzes all virtuous action; at times it
hinders a virtuous act altogether, or it effects that the act
is done only half-heartedly, in such wise that it loses most
of its worth and merit (LIV. 3).

When negligence reaches also to the external act by enervating it, what is it called?

It is called laziness or torpidity (LIV. 2, *Obj.* 1).

Are these two sins distinct from negligence properly so-called?

Yes, for strictly the sin of negligence consists in the want of readiness and energy in the act of command in so far as this defect is due to the interior weakness of the will (LIV. 2).

Is it important to keep careful watch over the sin of negligence?

Yes, it is of extreme importance, for negligence attacks the very root of virtuous action and is opposed to the principal act of the practical reason from which the realization of every virtuous act depends.

Is negligence sometimes a mortal sin?

It is always a mortal sin when it affects whatever is of precept that concerns salvation; even when it is not a mortal sin, unless one is on one's guard, it causes a spiritual sickness that leads inevitably to spiritual corrup tion and death (LIV. 3).

(F)

What are the sins that are opposed to prudence by excess?

They are called false prudence and false solicitude (LV.).

What is false prudence?

It is that complexity of sins which vitiate the true character of prudence by seeking an end that is bad, or by exceeding the limits of prudence in choosing wrong means to an end (LV. 1-5).

What is that which vitiates the true character of prudence by seeking an end that is bad?

It is called the prudence of the flesh (LV. 1).

In what does it consist?

It consists in disposing our life in the interests of the flesh which is served as an end (*ibid.*).

Is this a mortal sin?

Yes, whenever the interests of the flesh are looked upon as the last end; if, however, these interests are not looked

upon as the last end and as not ordained to the last true
end of human life, then the sin is only venial (LV. 2).

(G)

*The sins that exceed prudence as to the means employed,
what are they?*
They are the sins of slyness, with which are connected
deceit and fraud (LV. 3-5).

What is slyness?
It is that false prudence which consists in using false
and deceitful means whether it be question of a good
or of a bad end for which they are used (LV. 3).

What is deceit?
Deceit consists in effecting by words or by deeds
the projects suggested by slyness (LV. 4).
What is the difference between deceit and fraud?
The difference comes to this, that although both are
concerned with the projects suggested by slyness, deceit
puts into execution these projects whether it be by word
or by deed, whereas fraud is confined to the execution of
some project by deed only.

Are slyness, deceit, and fraud the same as lying?
No, for the lie takes falsehood as its end; whereas
the three sins above mentioned take it as a means. If
by chance the latter deceive, this is only to gain some end
in view.
What follows from this difference?
It follows that lying is a special sin in the order of the
moral virtues, a sin that is in opposition to the virtue of
telling the truth only; whereas slyness, deceit, and fraud
can be in divers genera of sins, not that they constitute any
one sin in particular in the order of the moral virtues,
but only in the order of prudence whose characteristic it
is to be included in all the other virtues.

(H)

What is the sin of false solicitude?

By this is meant that solicitude the sole object of which is the seeking after temporal things, or after some empty vanity, or that which makes one fear inordinately the loss of these things (LV. 6).

Is there a solicitude for temporal things that is good?

Yes, it is that solicitude for temporal things that seeks them in a moderate way, by ordaining them to the end of charity, and by trusting to the providence of God (LV. 6).

What is to be said of that solicitude which regards the future?

This solicitude is always bad when it usurps what should be left to the future (LV. 7).

When is solicitude for the future good?

That solicitude is good when it contents itself to provide for the future in so far as the future depends upon those things which should occupy the attention here and now; leaving alone for future consideration the things that are future (LV. 7).

XVI.—OF THE PRECEPTS RELATING TO PRUDENCE

Is there any precept among those of the Decalogue which corresponds to the virtue of prudence?

No; for the precepts of the Decalogue formulating what has reference to the natural reason should bear upon the ends of human life which are the proper object of the virtues, and not upon the means which are the proper object of the virtue of prudence. But all the precepts are related to prudence in that the latter directs all the acts of the virtues (LVI. 1).

Since then the precepts are directly related to the virtue of prudence, are they as it were complementary and of later origin?

Yes; and they are to be found in other places in the

inspired books, even in the Old Testament; and later on in the New Testament (LVI. 1).

Are there not even in the Old Testament certain precepts of particular consequence that forbid certain sins opposed to the virtue of prudence?

Yes; they are the precepts relating to slyness, deceit, and fraud (LVI. 2).

Why are these sins particularly prohibited?

Because in their external application they militate against justice, which all the precepts of the Decalogue safeguard (LVI. 2).

XVII.—OF JUSTICE AND ITS NATURE; OF LAW; OF NATURAL LAW; OF POSITIVE, PRIVATE, PUBLIC, NATIONAL, INTER NATIONAL, CIVIL, AND ECCLESIASTI CAL LAW—OF LEGAL JUSTICE AND OF PARTICULAR—OF THE SINS OPPOSED THERETO

(A)

After the virtue of prudence, is the virtue of justice the most important of the other virtues?

Yes, after the virtue of prudence, which occupies a place apart in the order of the moral virtues and without which no one single virtue can exist, the most important among the other virtues is the virtue of justice (LVII.–CXXI.).

What is the virtue of justice?

It is that virtue which has for its object right or the just (LVII. 1).

What is meant by this?

By this is meant that the object of justice is to make respected among men those relations which are founded upon the respect due to existence and possession, which are legitimately the privilege of every human being (LVII. 1).

*But how does one know that the existence or the possession
of any one particular person is legitimately of such a nature
or should be of such a nature?*

One knows this by what natural reason tells con
cerning each man; also by that which, by common
consent, is determined by the reason of different men;
and also by the reason of those who are in authority
whose office it is to regulate such matters (LVII. 2-4).

*What is that law called which is founded upon what the
natural reason dictates?*

It is called the natural law (LVII. 2).

*And that law which is determined by the common accord
of different men, or that which is determined by those in
authority whose duty it is to make regulations concerning
the relations between men?*

It is called positive law, which is divided into private
law and public law; the latter is further divided into
national and international according as there is question
of private conventions or of the laws of a country, or of
the laws agreed upon and established between different
nations (LVII. 2).

What is the civil law and ecclesiastical law?

Civil law treats of the relations between men in so far
as they are determined by the civil authority; ecclesiastical
law in so far as they are determined by the ecclesiastical
authority.

(B)

*Does the right upon which the virtue of justice bears
confine itself only to the relations of individuals of a society
among themselves; or does it refer also to the relations of
individuals with the society?*

It embraces both species of relations (LVIII. 5-7).

What law is the first called?

It is called particular justice (LVIII. 7).

And the second?

Legal justice (LVIII. 5).

(c)

What is precisely the virtue of justice?

It is that perfection of man's will which inclines him to desire in all things, spontaneously and unceasingly, the good of the society of which he is a part; and also to desire that each should have what is his due (LVIII. 1).

What is the sin that is opposed to this virtue called?

It is called injustice; which, now, is in opposition to legal justice, spurning the common good which legal justice seeks to promote; and, now, is in opposition to particular justice which seeks to maintain what is right and just among individuals (LIX.).

In what does the sin of injustice precisely consist?

It consists in this, that with full knowledge one attacks the right of another; that is to say, that one acts contrary to what a rational will should naturally desire (LIX. 3).

XVIII.—OF THE ACT OF PARTICULAR JUSTICE, VIZ., JUDGMENT

Has the virtue of justice an act which is particularly proper to it, especially in so far as it is particular justice?

Yes, and this act is called the judgment, which consists in determining precisely what is due to each person; whether this judgment be given in an official capacity between two parties at law, or whether for love of right in itself the judgment be given for all and for all time in the desire to appreciate even within the soul the rights of everyone to existence and possession (LX.).

Ought this judgment, which is the act of the virtue of justice, to interpret doubtful things in a good sense?

Yes, whenever it has reference to our neighbour and nis acts justice should never either internally or externally judge in a bad sense so long as there remains any doubt about the motives of our neighbour and his acts (LX. 4).

But if, however, there is doubt with regard to things that might be hurtful to oneself or to others, may not one be suspicious and take precautions?

Yes, legal justice, and prudence, and charity demand that when there is question of some evil to ourselves or to others we should be on our guard even though our suspicions may arise from conjecture only (LX. 4, *Obj.* 3).

But even in this case is no reservation to be made?

Yes, even when it is right to take precautions one must not either in words or in thought pronounce a formal judgment which is prejudicial to another (*ibid.*).

XIX.—OF PARTICULAR JUSTICE, AND OF ITS SPECIES: OF DISTRIBUTIVE AND OF COMMUTATIVE JUSTICE

Does particular justice comprise several species?

Yes, it comprises two species: distributive justice and commutative justice (LXI. 1).

What is distributive justice?

It is that species of particular justice which safeguards fairness in the relations that exist between the society and the individuals of which the society is composed (LXI. 1).

What is commutative justice?

It is that species of particular justice which safeguards fairness in the relations of men with each other in the same society (*ibid.*).

If one considers the individual members of a society as parts ordained to the whole, what kind of justice safeguards fairness between the individuals and the society?

This is the great virtue called legal justice (LXI. 1, *Obj.* 4).

XX.—OF THE ACT OF COMMUTATIVE JUSTICE, VIZ., OF RESTITUTION

(A)

What is the proper act of commutative justice?

It is called restitution (LXII. 1).

What is restitution?

It is that act whereby the right relation between one man and another is re-established, whenever this relation has been broken by the fact that one of the two has not received his due (LXI. 1).

Restitution then does not always imply an act of injustice?

No, for also the virtuous man may make restitution, by restoring what belongs to another immediately and with scrupulousness when such thing ought to be restored.

(B)

What are the essential rules of restitution?

The following, and they are those which natural equity dictates. By restitution, that which another lacks or might lack unfairly is given to him or restored to him. That which is restored must be the thing itself or its exact equivalent, neither more nor less, in so far as the person possessed it previously, whether actually or virtually: further, one must take into account whatever change may have taken place in the thing restored and make proper restitution as the case may be; and further, one must take into account the consequences that are or were prejudicial to the owner of the object due to the detention thereof. An object to be restored must be given back to the owner and not to any other person unless the latter be acting for the owner. He, whosoever he may be, who is in possession of an object to be restored is the one who must make restitution thereof, or whosoever is the one who is responsible for the act which was an offence against justice. Restitution must be made without delay, except in the case when the immediate restoration of an object is impossible (LXII. 2-8).

XXI.—OF THE SINS OPPOSED TO DISTRIBU TIVE JUSTICE: OF THE RESPECT OF PERSONS; OF THE SINS OPPOSED TO COMMUTATIVE JUSTICE; OF HOMI CIDE; OF CAPITAL PUNISHMENT; OF MUTILATION; OF FLOGGING; AND OF IMPRISONMENT

(A)

What is the sin opposed to distributive justice?
It is the sin of the respect of persons (LXIII.).
What is meant by this sin?
It is the fact of giving something or of refusing to give to a person what is for his good, or to impose something on a person that is burdensome or difficult, and this not by a consideration of his merits or demerits but merely because the person is such and such a one (LXIII. 1).

(B)

What sins are opposed to commutative justice?
These sins are divided into two groups (LXIV – LXXVIII.).
What are those of the first group?
They are those which touch our neighbour in which his own will has no part (LXIV.–LXXVI.).
What is the first of these sins?
It is homicide, which affects our neighbour by deed, as regards his greatest good, viz., by taking his life (LXIV.).
Is this a great sin?
It is the greatest sin against our neighbour.
Is it ever permitted to attempt our neighbour's life?
No, never.
Is it never permitted to take away a man's life?
It is never permitted to take away a man's life, unless through some crime, he has merited death (LXIV. 2, 6).

When a man through crime merits to lose his life, who alone has the right to deprive him of life?

Only the public authority has the right to do this (LXIV. 2).

Whence does the public authority derive this right?

It derives this right from the duty incumbent upon it of guarding over the common good of the society (*ibid.*).

Does the common good of the society sometimes demand that a man be put to death?

Yes, because there may be no other efficient way of putting a stop to the crimes committed within the society; or because the public feeling demands such satisfaction for the expiation of certain crimes that are hateful and revolting (LXIV. 2).

Is it only for crime that a man can be put to death by the public authority?

Yes, for this reason only (LXIV. 6).

May public interest sometimes justify the putting to death of an innocent person?

No, never, because the supreme good in a society is always the good of virtue (LXIV. 6).

(c)

Has an individual, in order to defend himself, or his belongings, the right to take the life of the one who attacks him?

No, an individual has never the right to do this unless there be question of losing his own life or the life of those in his charge, and there be absolutely no defence other than that which entails the death of his assailant; further, in thus defending himself he must in no way whatever intend the death of his assailant, but only intend to defend his life or that of others in his charge (LXIV. 7).

What are the other sins against our neighbour that touch his person?

They are mutilation, which attacks the integrity of his person; flogging, which inflicts pain on his body; and imprisonment, which deprives him of the freedom of his person (LXV. 1-3).

When are these acts sinful?

Whenever they are done by those who have no authority, or who, having authority, exceed the just bounds (*ibid.*).

XXII.—OF THE RIGHT OF PROPERTY, AND OF THE DUTIES IT ENTAILS—OF THE VIOLATION OF THIS RIGHT, VIZ., OF THEFT AND ROBBERY

(A)

Besides the sins that attack the person of our neighbour, what is the greatest sin that can be committed against him by deed?

It is the sin which touches what belongs to him (LXVI.).

Has man the right to possess anything?

Yes, and to use it as he wills, without the interference of anyone else (LXVI. 2).

Whence comes this right?

It comes from the very nature of man himself; for since he is a rational being and made to live in society, his own good, the good of his family, and the good of society absolutely demand that the right of property be safeguarded (LXVI. 1, 2).

But why do these divers goods demand the safeguarding of the right of property?

It is because the right to possess is a condition of man's liberty, it is, moreover, for the family, the way *par excellence* whereby it is upheld in all its rights and is the guarantee of its existence in the society; further, this right of property effects that in the society itself more care is taken of things to the exclusion in a great measure of disagreements and litigations (LXVI. 2).

(B)

Does the right of property entail certain duties?

Yes, it entails certain grave duties.

What are these duties?

They are, first of all, the duty of taking care of one's belongings and of doing one's best to promote their productiveness. Then, according to the productiveness of these things, one must in due measure, after supplying one's own wants, use these things for the good of others who are in the society. There is indeed a duty in social justice of giving to those who are in need the superfluity of one's possessions, or of employing the labour of others, or of giving facilities for such labour to those who by this means earn their livelihood, and this one must do for the love of the public good generally. The state in the interests of the public good has the right to make levies on the goods of individuals as regards whatever it judges necessary or useful for the good of the society, and individual members are bound to conform to the laws made by the state for this end; there is indeed for them an obligation to comply therewith in strict justice. But the good of individuals and the need of supplying their necessities does not oblige with the same rigour, for there is no positive human law constraining one to this. On the other hand, the natural law demands this in all rigour. Not to succour the needy with the superfluity of one's possessions is to act in direct opposition to the natural law; this obligation enforced by the natural law takes on a sacred character through divine positive law, especially through the law contained in the Gospels. God Himself preached this personally in order to impress more on the minds of men what He had already graven on their hearts (LXVI. 2-7; XXXII. 5, 6).

If such are the duties of those who possess towards their fellow-men, what are the duties of the latter in relation to the former?

They must respect the property of those who possess and never take anything against their owner's will (LXVI. 5, 8).

(c)

What is that act called which consists in taking the property of another against his will?

It is called theft or robbery (LXVI. 3, 4). ··

What is theft?

Theft is to appropriate the property of another secretly (LXVI. 3).

And what is robbery?

Robbery is the appropriation of another's property by violence (LXVI. 4).

Which is the graver of these two sins?

Robbery is more grave than theft; but theft, in itself, is always a mortal sin unless the thing taken is of small consequence (LXVI. 9).

XXIII.—OF THE SINS AGAINST JUSTICE BY WORDS; OF THE JUDGMENT PRO NOUNCED BY A JUDGE; OF THE SINS ON THE PART OF THE ACCUSED AND OF THE ACCUSER; AND ON THE PART OF THE WITNESS AND OF THE ADVOCATE

(A)

Are there any sins against justice that are committed by words?

Yes, and these are twofold: those that are committed in the solemn act of judgment; and those that are committed in the ordinary course of life (LXVII.–LXXVI.).

What is the first sin that can be committed in the solemn act of judgment?

It is the sin of the judge who judges unjustly (LXVII.).

What is required of a judge that he may judge justly?

He should consider himself as it were a living justice, whose duty it is to restore in the name of the society which he represents the injured right to whosoever has recourse to his authority (LXVII. 1).

(B)

What then is the duty of a judge in the fulfilment of his office?

It is his duty to judge those only who come under his jurisdiction: moreover, in drawing up his judgment he must take as his basis the facts of the case as set forth by the parties in litigation, it being allowable for him to interfere only if one of the parties lodges a complaint; but he must always dispense justice in its integrity, not show ing to the culprit pity falsely so-called, whatever be the penalty in the name of the law established by God or by men he may have to pronounce against him (LXVII. 2-4.).

(C)

What is the second sin which may be committed against justice in the solemn act of judgment?

It is the sin of those who are wanting in their duty as accusers, or who accuse unjustly (LXVIII.).

What is meant by the duty of accusing?

By this is meant that duty incumbent upon every man living in a society who knows of some evil that assails the society itself; he is thereby bound to bring to the notice of the judge the author of the evil so that justice may be done; he is free from this obligation only if he is unable to establish the truth of the fact juridically (LXVIII. 1).

When is an accusation unjust?

Accusation is unjust when from simple malice one falsely imputes crimes to another; or if when one is called upon to give evidence one does not follow up the accusa tion according as justice demands, either by making over tures to the opposite party or by unreasonably declining to follow up the accusation (LXVIII. 3).

(D)

What is the third sin committed against justice in the act of judgment?

It is the sin of the accused who refuses to conform to the rules of the law (LXIX.).

What are these rules to which the accused must conform, under pain of sin against justice?

They are that he is bound to tell the truth to the judge when the latter, in virtue of his authority as judge, in terrogates him; and that he must never defend himself by fraudulent means (LXIX. 1, 2).

If he is condemned, may not the accused decline to accept the judgment by making an appeal?

The accused, who is not allowed to defend himself by fraudulent means, has no right to make an appeal from a just judgment with the sole object of retarding the putting into execution of the judgment. He may make an appeal only when he is the victim of manifest injustice. Even then he must use his right within the limits established by the law (LXIX. 3).

Has one who is condemned to death the right to resist the sentence of condemnation?

The man who is unjustly condemned to death can resist even by violence provided no scandal is given. But if he be justly condemned, he is bound to submit to the penalty without resistance whatsoever; it is, however, permissible to make good his escape should he find the means, for no one is bound to concur in one's own punishment (LXIX. 4).

(E)

What is the fourth sin that is opposed to justice in the act of judgment?

It is the sin of the witness who is wanting in his duty (LXX.).

How may a witness be wanting in his duty?

He may be wanting in his duty either by abstaining from giving evidence when he is required to do so by the public authority, which he is bound to obey in things that belong to justice; or whenever his evidence may prevent loss to someone; or by adducing false testimony (LXX. 1, 4).

Is false testimony always a mortal sin?

Yes, it is always a mortal sin, if not always on account

of the lie, which may be venial, it always is mortal by reason of perjury, and also by reason of injustice if one give such testimony against a just cause (CXX. 4).

(F)

What is the last sin against justice in the act of judgment?

It is the sin of the advocate who refuses to defend a just cause such as can be defended by him only; or who defends an unjust cause particularly in civil causes; or who demands an exorbitant sum for his fee (LXXI. 1, 3, 4).

XXIV.—OF THE SINS OF SPEECH COMMITTED IN THE ORDINARY COURSE OF LIFE, VIZ., OF INVECTIVE, OF DETRACTION (AND CALUMNY), OF WHISPERINGS, OF MOCKERY, OF THE CURSE

(A)

What are the sins of injustice committed against our neighbour by speech in the ordinary course of life?

They are invective, detraction, whisperings, mockery, and the curse (LXXII.–LXXVI.).

What is understood by invective?

Invective is that sin which wounds another, in the honour or in the respect due to him, by words (LXXII. 1).

Is it a mortal sin?

Yes, whenever such words attack the honour of another in a grave way. The sin is venial only if our neighbour's honour is not seriously injured, or if one has no intention of seriously injuring another (LXXII. 2).

Is one bound in justice to treat others with the reverence due to them?

Yes, one is strictly bound in justice to do this, for the harmony of all living in a society is dependent upon this (LXXII. 1-3).

Upon what is this duty founded and what is its im-portance?

It is founded upon this, that the honour of each one is a thing which men cherish most. Even the least among men has a right to be treated with the respect due to his own particular status in life: to be lacking towards him in respect, whether by word or deed, is to wound him in what he holds most dear (*ibid.*).

One ought then with the greatest care to avoid saying or doing anything whatsoever which may bring disconsolation or humiliation upon our fellow-men?

Yes, one must do this at all cost (*ibid.*).

Is it ever permitted to act otherwise?

This is only permitted in the case of a superior whose duty it may be to correct one under his charge when the latter merits such correction; with this condition, however, that a superior do not do this in the heat of passion, or in a manner that is indiscreet or uncalled for (LXXII. 2, Obj. 2).

What should be done with regard to those who are lacking in respect?

With such as these charity, and sometimes justice, demands that their boldness be punished. But in this case it is necessary to be on one's guard lest, in punishing them, one exceed the right bounds imposed by the law and so bring injury to oneself (LXXII. 3).

(B)

What is understood by detraction?

Detraction, in its strict sense, implies the intention of attacking the reputation of our neighbour, or of taking away wholly or in part the esteem in which he is held by others, whensoever there is no just cause for so doing (LXXIII. 1).

Is this a great sin?

Yes, since it is to take away unjustly from our neighbour a good that is more precious than riches which are taken from him by theft (LXXIII. 2, 3).

In how many ways may one commit the sin of detraction?

In four ways: in imputing to our neighbour things that are false or in exaggerating his defects; or in making known things unknown about him and which prejudice him in the eyes of others; or in attributing to him inten tions that are of a doubtful and perhaps of an evil character, whereby all that he does with the best intention becomes vitiated (LXXIII. 1, *Obj.* 3).

Is there any other sin of detraction that is hurtful to our neighbour?

Yes, in an indirect way, by refusing to acknowledge the good in him, or by keeping silence maliciously concerning his good points, or by lessening their worth (LXXIII. 1, *Obj.* 3).

(c)

What is the sin called whispering?

It is that sin which attacks our neighbour by seeking directly through dishonest and insidious speech, to sow discord and create misunderstanding between those who are united by the bonds of friendship (LXXIV. 1).

Is this a grave sin?

This is a most odious sin against our neighbour, and merits perhaps more than other sins that can be committed against our neighbour the just reproval both of God and men (LXXIV. 2).

(D)

What is mockery?

Mockery is a sin of the tongue against justice which consists in reviling our neighbour by bringing to his notice his defects and shortcomings, which fact makes him lose confidence in himself as regards his relations with others (LXXV. 1).

Is this a grave sin?

Yes, of a truth, for it implies contempt for the person of our neighbour; and this is a most detestable thing and well merits chastisement (LXXV. 2).

Is irony also a kind of mockery and is it also a grave sin?

Irony may be only slightly culpable if it touch only the

small faults or defects of our neighbour, and it may exist without contempt for our neighbour's person. Some times irony may be no sin at all, whenever, for instance, one taunts another for the sake of innocent amusement and no risk be run of bringing depression or humiliation upon him who is the object. This manner of amuse ment is, however, of a delicate nature and should be used with much prudence (LXXV. 1, *Obj.* 1).

May not irony sometimes be an act of virtue?

Yes, if one employ it as it behoves, by way of correc tion. A superior may advantageously correct an inferior in this manner, or even those on an equal footing may employ it with advantage and with charity by way of fraternal correction.

In such case what does the use of irony demand?

It demands that it be used with great discretion. For if it is good for those who have too good an opinion of themselves to be brought to acknowledge in a truer measure their proper worth, one has to take care lest, by exceeding the bounds of irony, a person become so depressed as wholly to lose confidence in himself; and without this praiseworthy self-confidence all spontaneity of action would be paralyzed.

(E)

What relation is there between the sin called the curse, and the four sins of invective, detraction, whispering, and mockery?

All these sins have in common this, that they are sins of the tongue which attack the good of our neighbour; but whereas the four latter do this by the words of a proposi tion which formulate evil, or deny the good of our neighbour, the curse attacks our neighbour's good by wishing him evil (LXXVI. 1, 4).

Is the curse then essentially bad?

Yes, whenever one wishes evil to another for evil's sake; and such a wish is, of itself, always a grave sin (LXXVI. 3).

XXV.—OF THE SINS THAT DECEIVE OUR NEIGHBOUR, AND OF THOSE THAT TAKE ADVANTAGE OF HIM, VIZ., OF FRAUD AND OF USURY

What is the last kind of sins which are committed against commutative justice?

They are those sins whereby our neighbour is induced to agree to things that are prejudicial to him (LXXVII., *Prologue*).

What are these sins called?

They are called fraud and usury (LXXVII., LXXVIII.).

(A)

What is fraud?

It is an act of injustice, which is committed in buying and selling whereby our neighbour is deceived and is led to will what is to his loss (LXXVII.).

In how many ways can one commit the sin of fraud?

This sin may be committed: by reason of the price which is more than the thing is worth; by reason of the thing sold in so far as it is not what it appears to be, the seller knowing this and the buyer ignoring it; by reason of the seller who conceals a defect in the object sold; and by reason of the end in view (LXXVII. 1-4).

Is it never permitted knowingly to sell a thing for more than it is worth or to buy a thing for less than it is worth?

No, for the price of a thing bought or sold must always correspond to the worth of the thing itself; to ask more or to give less knowingly is of itself essentially unjust, and obliges to restitution (LXXVII. 1).

Is it against justice to sell a thing for what it is not, or to buy a thing which is other than what the seller believes it to be?

Yes, to sell or to buy a thing which is other than it appears to be, whether there be question of its substance, or its quantity or quality, is contrary to justice, and is a sin if one do this knowingly; moreover, one is bound to make restitution. Further, this obligation of making restitution exists even when there has been no sin, as soon as ever one discovers the disproportion between the price and the thing sold or bought (LXXVII. 2).

Is the seller always bound to bring to the notice of the buyer the defects of his wares in so far as he knows them?

Yes, he is bound to do this whenever the defects are hidden, and might be a cause of danger or loss to the buyer (LXXVII. 3).

Is it allowable to take up buying and selling as a form of trade for the sake of gaining money?

Trading for the sake of trading is a shameful thing and is contrary to justice; because of itself it promotes the love of lucre, which knows no limits, but seeks to acquire without end (LXXVII. 4).

What then is necessary that trading may become licit and honest?

Lucre should not be sought after for its own sake but for some good end. In this way one may seek a moderate gain by trading in order to maintain one's household, or to give help to the needy, or one may do this for the public benefit to the end that one's fellow-men may not lack the things necessary for daily life, and one may seek such gain not as an end in itself but as the recompense for one's work (LXXVII. 4).

(B)

What is usury?

Usury is an act of injustice which consists in taking advantage of the need of our neighbour by lending him money, or any other thing that has a money value (whose only use is the consumption thereof which is destined to meet present necessities), and in return obliging him to give back the money or the thing lent by a fixed date with an addition as the price of the use (LXXVIII. 1, 2, 3).

Is usury the same thing as lending out at interest?

No; for although all usury is lending out at interest, all lending out at interest is not usury.

In what does lending out at interest differ from usury?

It differs from usury in so far as money is considered as productive, by reason of the social and economic circumstances in which we live to-day.

What is necessary in order that lending out at interest may be allowable and may not run the risk of becoming usury?

Two things are necessary: first, the amount of interest charged must not exceed the legal charge, or the charge fixed by reasonable custom; and second, those who are well off should not be exacting towards the poor who have need of borrowing, not in order to trade in money but with the object of immediate consumption and the succouring of their needs.

XXVI.—OF THE ELEMENTS OF THE VIRTUE OF JUSTICE: OF DOING GOOD AND AVOIDING EVIL—OF THE SINS OPPOSED THERETO: OF OMISSION, AND OF TRANS GRESSION

In speaking of the virtue of justice, apart from its divers species, may not one consider the elements which constitute the virtue, just in the same way as was said of prudence?

Yes; and these elements are none other than what are described as doing good and avoiding evil (LXXIX. 1).

Why are these two elements proper to the virtue of justice?

Because in the other moral virtues, as, for instance, in fortitude and temperance, *not to do evil* is identified with *to do good;* whereas in the virtue of justice, *to do good* consists in so acting that fairness in the relations between us and our neighbour be maintained; and *not to do evil* consists in avoiding anything which upsets the justness of these relations (LXXIX. 1).

What is that sin called which is contrary to "doing good?"

It is called the sin of omission (LXXIX. 3).

And what is that sin called which is opposed to "avoiding evil"?

It is called the sin of transgression (LXXIX. 2).

Of these two sins which is the more grave?

Considered in itself the graver sin is that of trans gression; although a particular kind of omission may be more grave than a particular kind of transgression. For instance, it is more grave to insult someone than not to pay him the respect due to him; but if it be question of a high superior, to be lacking in due respect to him by not paying him the homage that such respect demands, particularly in public, would be more grave than a slight sign of contempt for, or a resentful word that may wound, a person in a lower scale of society (LXXXIX. 4).

XXVII.—OF THE VIRTUES ATTACHING TO JUSTICE: OF RELIGION; OF FILIAL RESPECT; OF REVERENCE; OF GRATI TUDE; OF RETRIBUTIVE JUSTICE; OF TRUTHFULNESS; OF FRIENDSHIP; OF LIBERALITY; OF NATURAL EQUITY

Are there also certain virtues that refer to justice and are, as it were, parts attaching thereto?

Yes (LXXX. 1).

In what are these other virtues distinct from justice properly so-called?

They are distinct in this, that the object of justice properly so-called is to render to another exactly what is his due; whereas the object of these other virtues, although having reference to one's neighbour (and this they have in common with justice) is: to give to another something which is not due to him strictly but in a wide sense only, but such as could be exacted in the name of the law before a tribunal; or only to give a thing which is strictly due in a way that falls short of the strict justness demanded (LXXX. 1).

How many virtues attach to justice, and what are they?

There are nine, and they are religion, filial respect, reverence, gratitude, retributive justice, truth, friendship, liberality, and natural equity (LXXX. 1).

Is it possible to justify the above order among these virtues?

Yes, in this wise. The first eight refer to particular justice, the ninth to general or legal justice. Of the first eight, three—religion, filial respect, and reverence—have something in common, for they are outside the domain of strict justice, not because there is no debt to be paid, but because of the impossibility of attaining justness in the acquittance of the debt: religion with regard to God, filial respect with regard to parents and one's country, reverence with regard to the good and to those in high places. The other five virtues are defective on the part of the debt; for they do not refer to something which is legally due to another, such as could be exacted in justice before a tribunal, but only to something which is morally due, the payment of which is left to the good will of each; such payment is, however, necessary for the well-being of human life and the harmony of the relations between men, either necessarily as truthfulness, gratitude, and retribu tive justice, or for the betterment of human relations as friendship and liberality (LXXX. 1).

XXVIII.—OF RELIGION AND ITS NATURE

What is the virtue of religion?

The virtue of religion (so-called because it constitutes the bond *par excellence* which unites man to God, who is the source of all man's good) is a perfection of the will inclining man to acknowledge as it behoves his absolute dependence upon God, who is the first beginning and last end of all (LXXXI. 1-5).

What are the acts of religion?

Every act which, of itself, makes man recognize his dependence upon God is the proper object of the virtue of religion. But this virtue also may ordain to this same end all the acts of the other virtues; and in this case it makes the whole of man's life an act of the worship of God (LXXXI. 7, 8).

In the latter case what is it called?

It is called sanctity. For the saint is precisely he whose whole life is transformed into an act of religion (LXXXI. 8).

Is the virtue of religion most excellent?

Yes, for after the theological virtues it is the most excellent of all the virtues (LXXXI. 6).

Whence does the virtue of religion derive this excellence?

It comes from this, that among all the moral virtues whose object is to perfect man in every order of conscious activity in his striving after heaven, such as faith, hope, and charity, there is no other virtue whose object approaches so nigh to this end. The other virtues direct man, either in regard to his own conduct or in regard to other creatures, whilst religion directs him towards God: it effects that he look to God, as it behoves, by recognizing His Sovereign Majesty, serving and honouring Him by his acts as the one whose excellence infinitely surpasses every created thing (LXXXI. 6).

XXIX.—OF RELIGION AND ITS INTERIOR ACTS: OF DEVOTION; OF PRAYER, ITS NATURE AND NECESSITY; OF THE " OUR FATHER " OR THE LORD'S PRAYER, AND ITS EFFICACIOUSNESS

(A)

What is the first act of religion?

It is that interior act which is called devotion (LXXXII. 1, 2).

What is devotion?

Devotion is a certain movement of the will whereby it gives itself and all dependent on it to the service of God, and this always and with a holy zeal (LXXXII. 1, 2).

After devotion, what is man's first act in the service of God?
It is the act of prayer.

(B)

What is prayer?

Prayer, understood in its widest sense and in so far as
it is addressed to God, is an act of the practical reason by
which, under the form of supplication, we desire to lead
God to grant what we ask (LXXXIII. 1).

But is this a reasonable thing?

Yes, of a truth it is; for there is nothing more reasonable
and more in harmony with our nature than to do this
(LXXXIII. 2).

How can this be shown?

By the following considerations: since we are by nature
rational beings, we have need of considering in the
greatest degree what God is and what we are. But we are
filled with miseries; and He is the source of all good.
The more intimately we know then our own misery in
all its details, and that God only is capable of succouring
our needs, the more we shall come to know what we ought
to be, that is to know what our very nature has need of;
and this is precisely what prayer effects. It is, moreover,
the more perfect when it makes us the more conscious
of our misery and of the goodness of God, which is the
remedy of that misery. It is for this reason that God
in His mercy wishes us to pray, and He has even deter
mined that certain boons shall not be conferred upon us
unless we ask Him for them (LXXXIII. 2).

*It is then God's will that we are fulfilling when we
endeavour by prayer to lead Him to grant what we ask?*

Yes, it is God's will that we should do this; that is of
course whenever what we ask of Him is for our own true
good.

(c)

Does God always hear our prayers then?

Yes, God always hears our prayers when we ask of
Him, under the very impulse of the Holy Ghost, what is
for our true good (LXXXIII. 15).

Is there a form of prayer whereby we may be assured of asking always for what is for our good?

Yes, there is a form of prayer *par excellence* of this kind which is called the " Our Father " or the Lord's Prayer (LXXXIII. 9).

What is meant by the words: the Lord's Prayer?

It is that prayer which was taught us by Jesus Christ Himself in the Gospel.

What are the words of this prayer?

The following:

Our Father, who art in heaven;

Hallowed be Thy name;

Thy Kingdom come;

Thy will be done on earth as it is in heaven;

Give us this day our daily bread;

Forgive us our offences as we forgive them that trespass
      against us;

And lead us not into temptation;

But deliver us from evil.   Amen.

(D)

Does this prayer contain all the requests we may ask and ought to ask of God?

Yes; for whatever we ask of God can be reduced to one or other of the petitions expressed in the " Our Father," provided, of course, that our request is for some good (LXXXIII. 9).

Has this prayer any other excellence which is proper to it alone?

Yes; and this excellence consists in this, that this prayer puts upon our lips in the very order that they should be in our hearts, all the desires that ought to be ours (LXXXIII. 9).

Can this order of the petitions in the " Our Father " be shown?

Yes, in a few words thus.   Of all our desires the first must be that God should be glorified, since the glory of God is the end of all things; and in order that we ourselves might co-operate in the best way towards this glory, we must desire to be admitted one day to a participation of that glory in heaven. Such is the sense of the first two petitions of the " Our Father " when we say: " Hallowed be Thy name; Thy Kingdom come." This glorification of God in Himself and of us in Him will one day be the final term of our life. On earth and during the present life we have to strive to be admitted to the glory of God in heaven. To attain this end there is only one thing to be done: to accomplish in all things the will of God as perfectly as possible. And this we ask when we say: ' Thy will be done on earth as it is in heaven." But in order to fulfil the will of God in the most perfect way possible, we have need of God's life to strengthen our weakness whether as regards temporal needs or spiritual. We ask for this help when we say: " Give us this day our daily bread." This indeed would be sufficient were it not necessary to avoid or get rid of evil which can be an obstacle either as regards our attainment of the Kingdom of God, or the accomplishment of His will, or the sufficiency of things of which we have need in the present life. Against this threefold evil we say: " Forgive us our offences as we forgive them that trespass against us; and lead us not into temptation; but deliver us from evil " (LXXXIII. 9).

Why do we say at the beginning of this prayer: " Our Father, who art in heaven " ?

We say these words in order that we may inspire our hearts with the liveliest confidence, since He to whom we address our prayer is our Father whose kingdom is heaven itself (LXXXIII. 9, *Obj.* 5).

Ought we to recite the " Our Father " frequently?

We should live continually in its spirit, reciting it from time to time, and indeed as often as we can according as the conditions of our life permit (LXXXIII. 14).

No matter what our condition of life be, is it not the least we can do to recite this prayer once every day?

Yes, this is the only fitting thing to do.

(E)

Should we address our prayers to God only?

Yes, to God alone must we pray, from whom all good things come; but we may also pray to certain creatures that they may intercede for us before God (LXXXIII. 4).

To what creatures may we pray for such end?

To the angels and saints in heaven; and the good who are still on earth (LXXXIII. 11).

Is it good to recommend oneself to the prayers of souls that are saintly?

Yes, it is an excellent thing to do this.

(F)

Of all creatures is there not one in particular to whom we should have recourse in our prayers?

Yes, and this one is Mary, ever a virgin and the Mother of the incarnate Son of God, our Lord Jesus Christ.

What name has been given to our Blessed Lady by reason of the special mission she has of interceding for us?

She has been called the All-Powerful.

What is meant by these words?

By these words is meant that all those for whom she has interceded before God have been heard by Him in their prayers.

Is there any special form of prayer for soliciting our Blessed Lady to intercede for us before God?

Yes, it is called the " Hail Mary."

What are the words of this prayer?

The following:

Hail Mary, full of grace;
The Lord is with Thee;
Blessed art Thou among women;
And blessed is the fruit of Thy womb, Jesus:
Holy Mary, Mother of God, pray for us sinners,
Now, and at the hour of our death.   Amen.

When is it a good thing to recite this prayer?

It is a good thing to recite it as often as possible, and especially to recite it after saying the " Our Father."

(G)

Is there any excellent manner of prayer in which these prayers are united together?

Yes, in that form of prayer known as the Rosary.

What is the Rosary?

It is a prayer which consists in bringing to mind the fifteen mysteries of our redemption, and of reciting with the memory of each mystery the " Our Father " followed by ten " Hail Marys," after which is added: " Glory be to the Father, and to the Son, and to the Holy Ghost, as it was in the beginning, is now, and ever shall be, world without end.   Amen."

XXX.—OF THE EXTERNAL ACTS OF RELIGION: OF ADORATION; OF SACRIFICE; OF OBLATION; OF TITHES; OF VOWS; OF OATHS; OF CALLING ON THE NAME OF GOD

(A)

After the internal acts of devotion and prayer, what are the other acts of the virtue of religion?

They are all those external acts which, of themselves, are directed to the honouring of God (LXXXIV.–XCI.).

What are these acts?

They are, first of all, certain movements of the body, such as the inclination of the head, genuflexion, and prostration, and all those acts which are comprised under the general name of adoration (LXXXIV.).

In what does the excellence of these acts consist?

It consists in this, that even the body is made to con tribute towards the honouring of God; and when these acts are performed in a fitting manner they help much towards the better performance of the internal acts (LXXXIV. 2).

Is it only the body we should make use of to honour God in the virtue of religion?

No, for there are also certain things we can offer to God in homage under the form of sacrifice or of pious con tribution (LXXXV.-LXXXVII.).

(B)

Is there in the New Law only one kind of sacrifice, understood in its strict sense, which implies the immolation of a victim?

Yes, it is the Holy Sacrifice of the Mass, in which is immolated under the sacramental species of bread and wine He who since His sacrifice on the Cross is the only victim offered to God, and the only one that is agreeable to Him (LXXX. 4).

Is it an act of religion pleasing to God to contribute according to one's means towards the upkeep of His external worship by giving the wherewithal for the maintenance of its ministers?

Yes, this is an act of religion and is especially pleasing to God (LXXXVI.-LXXXVII.).

(c)

Is it only thus in giving to God for the upkeep of His worship and His ministers that one performs an act of religion?

No, for one can also perform an act of religion by promising to God something which of its nature is pleasing to Him (LXXXVIII.).

What is such a promise called?

It is called the vow (LXXXIII. 1, 2).

If one makes a vow is one obliged to keep it?

Yes, if one makes a vow one is bound to keep it except in the case of impossibility or dispensation (LXXXIII. 3, 10).

(D)

Is there any other kind of acts of religion?

Yes; there are those acts performed in order to honoui

God by using something that touches God Himself
(LXXXIX.).

*What are those things touching God which we can utilize
for His honour and homage?*

They are holy things; and also the holy name of God.

What is understood by holy things?

By holy things is meant whatsoever has received from
God through the medium of His Church some consecra
tion or particular blessing: as, for instance, persons con
secrated to God; the sacraments; and the sacramentals,
such as holy water or objects of piety; and also places of
worship (LXXXIX., *Prologue*).

(E)

*In what way may one use the Holy Name of God as a
homage rendered to Him?*

One may use the Holy Name of God for this purpose by
calling it as witness to the truth of what one says, or by
invoking it in praise (LXXXIX.-XCI.).

*If one calls on the Holy Name as witness to the truth of
what one says or of what one promises, what is this invoca
tion called?*

It is called the oath (LXXXIX. 1).

Is an oath a good thing in itself, and to be commended?

The oath is good only when grave necessity de
mands it; and it should be used with extreme reserve
(LXXXIX. 2).

And to adjure or to swear, what is that?

To adjure or to swear is an act which consists in calling
on the name of God or upon some holy thing in order to
induce someone to act or not to act in the way we wish
(XC. 1).

Is this act allowable?

Yes, provided it be done with respect and according
to the condition of those whom we adjure (*ibid.*).

Is it good to invoke often the name of God?

Yes, provided one do this with the greatest respect
and in the form of praise (XCI. 1).

XXXI.—OF THE SINS OPPOSED TO RELIGION: OP SUPERSTITION, AND OF DIVINATION; OF IRRELIGION: OF TEMPTING GOD, OF PERJURY, AND OF SACRILEGE

(A)

What are the sins opposed to the virtue of religion?

They are of two kinds: those of excess, which come under the name of superstition; and those of defect, which are comprised under the name of irreligion (XCII., *Prologue*).

What is meant by superstition?

By superstition is understood that complexity of sins which consists in paying worship to God such as cannot be pleasing to Him; or to pay to things other than God the worship that belongs to Him alone (XCII., XCIII., XCIV.).

Is there not some form of the latter which is particularly prevalent?

Yes, it is the inordinate desire to learn the future or to bring to light things that are hidden, which effects the giving up of oneself to the manifold kinds of divination, or to what are called superstitious practices (XCV., XCVI.).

(B)

What does the sin of irreligion comprise?

It comprises two things: the fact of not treating with due respect things that belong to the service and worship of God; or the fact of abstaining altogether from acts of religion.

Is the last sin particularly grave?

Yes, it is of extreme gravity, because it implies con tempt or the scornful disregard of Him whom we are bound in the strictest sense to honour and to serve.

Under what special form does the latter exist at the present day?

Under the form of what may be called secularism.

What is understood by secularism?

It is that system in which God is put out of one's life completely: whether in a positive manner, in getting rid of Him in every way and in persecuting both Him and everything that has to do with Him; or in a negative way, in taking no account of Him at all in our life, individual, domestic, or social.

Whence arises this sin of secularism both in its positive and negative form?

In its positive form it arises from hatred or from some fanatic sectarianism; in its negative form it arises from a sort of intellectual and moral obtuseness, particularly with regard to the supernatural order.

Ought one to combat secularism with all one's strength?

There is no more pressing duty than to do this by all the means in one's power.

(c)

What are the other sins of irreligion?

They are to tempt God and perjury, which are committed against God Himself and His Holy Name; also sacrilege and simony, which are committed against things holy (XCVII.-XCIX.).

What is understood by tempting God?

It is that sin against the virtue of religion which consists in want of respect towards God in making appeal to His intervention; or to make appeal to Him in circumstances that forbid His intervention (XCVII. 1).

Is it tempting God to count upon some special help from Him when one does not do oneself all that is possible to be done?

Yes, to do this is to tempt God; and this one should avoid with the utmost care (XCVII. 1, 2).

(D)

What is understood by perjury?

By this is understood a sin against the virtue of religion that consists in calling on God to witness a thing that is false, or calling on God as witness to a promise which we do not fulfil (XCVIII. 1).

(E)

Is it also a sin, akin to perjury, to call on God by the invocation of His Holy Name at every turn?

Yes, for although this is not properly speaking perjury, it shows a great lack of respect towards the Holy Name of God; and such disrespect one must scrupulously avoid.

(F)

What is sacrilege?

Sacrilege is the violation of person, thing, or place consecrated to God, which are dedicated to His service and worship (XCIX. 1).

Is sacrilege a great sin?

Yes, it is a great sin; for to touch things that belong to God is in some sort to touch God Himself; and even on this earth God sometimes severely punishes this sin (XCIX. 2-4).

(G)

What is simony?

Simony is a sin of irreligion which consists in imitating the impiousness of Simon the Magician by offering insult to things holy in treating them as ordinary material things, of which men dispose as though they belonged to them, and which they buy or sell for a sum of money (C. 1).

Is simony a great sin?

Yes, and the Church punishes this sin with the most severe penalties (C. 6).

XXXII.—OF FILIAL RESPECT TOWARDS ONE'S PARENTS, AND TOWARDS ONE'S COUNTRY

After the virtue of religion, which is the greatest of the other virtues relating to the virtue of justice?

It is the virtue of filial respect (CI.).

What is filial respect?

It is that virtue whose object is to give to parents and to the fatherland the honour and the respect that is due to them; and this because of the existence that, together with all the benefits thereto attached, they have bestowed upon us (CI. 1-3).

Are these duties towards our parents and country par-ticularly sacred?

Yes, after our duties towards God there are none more sacred than these (CI. 1).

What are the duties of filial respect towards our parents?

They are: always respect and deference; obedience when living under their authority; and assisting them in case of need (CI. 2).

What are the duties of filial respect towards one's country?

They are respect and reverence towards those who represent it; obedience to its laws; and one's service even to the sacrifice of one's life in the case of just war against enemies.

XXXIII.—OF REVERENCE TOWARDS SUPERIORS

Is there any virtue other than the virtues of religion and filial respect which demands obedience?

Yes, it is the virtue of reverence towards superiors (CII.).

What is understood by this reverence?

By reverence is understood that virtue whose object it is to regulate the relations of inferiors with regard to superiors, which is over and above the reverence due to God, to parents, and to authorities representing our country (CII., CIII.).

Is it the virtue of reverence which safeguards the right relations between pupil and master, between apprentice and master, and, in short, between all inferiors and superiors?

Yes (CIII. 3).

Does reverence always imply the virtue of obedience?

No, except when it is a question of superiors having authority over inferiors.

Is there any order of superiority beside the orders that imply authority over inferiors?

Yes, as, for instance, a superiority in talent, in riches, in age, in virtue, and so forth (CIII. 2).

Do all these orders lend themselves to the practice of the virtue of reverence?

Yes, for this virtue effects that man pays to every kind of superiority the honour due to it; and he does this in such order that first of all he pays honour to superiors that are in authority (*ibid.*).

Is this important for the good of society?

Yes, it is most important, for every society implies a certain multiplicity and in some sort a certain subordination, and every subordinate should practise the virtue of reverence, without which the harmony of the relations between men is impossible.

Is it possible for everybody without exception to practise the virtue of reverence?

Yes, for there is no one, in whatsoever order he himself may be superior, that is not in some other order inferior to some other person (CIII. 2, *Obj.* 3).

XXXIV.—OF GRATITUDE

What is the first of the other virtues annexed to justice that has for its object, not indeed a strict debt that it is impossible to acquit fully, but a certain debt of the moral order such as one is able to pay, and the payment of which is necessarily ordained to the well-being of society?

It is the virtue of gratitude (CVI.).

What is the role of this virtue?

The role of this virtue is to make us recognize rightly as it behoves, and to give payment as it were in return for, all the boons we have received from another (CVI. 1).

Is this an important virtue?

Yes, for the opposite sin, which is ingratitude, is extremely odious and well merits reproof from all (CVII.).

In gratitude ought one to strive to give in return even more than one has received?

Yes, so as to imitate oneself the goodness of a benefactor (CVI. 6).

XXXV.—OF REVENGE OR OF RETRIBUTIVE JUSTICE

From the point of view of virtue can anything be done against evildoers?

Yes, there is a special virtue called retributive justice, whose office it is to see that an evildoer does not go unpunished whenever justice demands such retribution (CVIII.).

XXXVI.—OF TRUTHFULNESS—AND OF THE SINS OPPOSED THERETO: OF LYING; OF PRETENCE; AND OF HYPOCRISY

(A)

What other virtue of the same order is necessary (not indeed for the sake of others precisely, but for the sake of him who acts) for the well-being of society?

It is the virtue of truthfulness (CIX.).

What is meant by truthfulness?

By this is meant that virtue which inclines us to manifest ourselves in all things both in words and in deeds, such as we really are (CIX. 1-4).

What are the sins opposed to this virtue?

They are lying, pretence, and hypocrisy (CX.–CXIII.).

What is lying?

It is the fact of speaking or of acting in such wise that knowingly one expresses or signifies what is not (CX. 1).

Is it evil to do this?

Yes, for it is essentially bad, and under no pretext whatsoever can it become good (CX. 3).

But is one always bound in word and deed to say or to signify what is the truth?

No, one is not always bound to say or to signify what is the truth; but one may never knowingly say or signify what is not the truth (CX. 3).

(B)

How many kinds of lies are there?

There are three kinds: the jocose lie, the officious, and the pernicious (CX. 2).

In what are these three distinguished?

In this: the jocose lie is told for amusement's sake; the officious lie in order to help another; and the pernicious lie in order to do another harm (*ibid.*).

Is the last kind of lie the worst of all?

Yes; for whereas the first two kinds may be only venial sins, the third is of itself always a mortal sin, unless the injury done is only slight (CX. 4).

What is understood by pretence and hypocrisy?

Pretence consists in showing oneself externally in one's life what one is not interiorly; and hypocrisy is pretending to be holy when one is not (CXI. 1, 2).

Is one bound, so as not to commit these sins, to show forth exteriorly the bad that is in one?

In no wise; on the contrary, it is a duty to let nothing that is bad in us appear externally so as to avoid harming oneself in the opinion of others, or so as to avoid dis-edification and scandal. What the virtue of truthfulness demands is that we let nothing appear externally, whether good or bad, which does not correspond to our inner life (CXI. 3, 4).

Is one bound by the virtue of truthfulness to abstain from word or deed which might lend itself to a false interpretation?

No; one would not be bound to do this except in the

case when such false interpretation might cause some evil which it is our duty to prevent (CXI. 1).

Is it possible to commit the sins of lying, pretence, and hypocrisy in several ways so that they constitute sins that are specifically distinct?

Yes; one can sin by exceeding the truth, and this is called boasting; or by deficiency, that is in falling short of the truth, when, for instance, a person makes out that he is lacking in some good which he really has, and this sin is called the belittling of oneself unduly (CXII., CXIII.).

XXXVII.—OF FRIENDSHIP; AND OF THE OPPO SITE SINS, NAMELY, OF DISPUTE AND FLATTERY

Is there any other debt that binds only morally, the acquittance of which helps in a great degree towards the welfare of society, although not with the same rigour as that of gratitude, retributive justice, and truthfulness?

Yes; and this is the debt of friendship (CXIV. 2).

What is friendship?

It is that virtue which makes man endeavour by the whole of his exterior, both in word and deed, to treat his fellow-beings as it behoves in order to bring mutual pleasantness and charm to their lives (CXIV. 1).

Is this a virtue of great price?

Yes, this is a social virtue of great worth; and it might fittingly be called the flower of the virtues of justice and of charity.

In what way is it possible to sin against this virtue?

In two ways: by defect, in troubling ourselves little or not at all with what may bring pleasure or annoyance to others; or by excess, and this is the sin of flattery, which fails in disapproving externally the words or deeds of those with whom we live that deserve reproval (CXV.-CXVI.).

XXXVIII.—OF LIBERALITY; AND OF THE SINS OPPOSED THERETO, VIZ., OF AVARICE, AND OF PRODIGALITY

(A)

What is the last virtue relating to particular justice that acquits a debt, such as binds only morally, as regards the relations between men?

The last virtue is that of liberality (CXVII. 5).

What is liberality?

Liberality is a disposition of soul which effects that man is attached to external goods only in such ordered measure as ever to be ready to give them and especially to give money for the well-being of others (CXVII. 1-4).

Is this a great virtue?

If one considers the immediate object of this virtue, which is riches, it is the least of the virtues; but considered in its consequences it is lifted up to the perfection of the others, for liberality is able to help and sustain each of the other virtues (CXVII. 6).

(B)

What are the sins opposed to this virtue?

They are avarice and prodigality (CXVIII.–CXIX.).

What is avarice?

Avarice is the inordinate love of riches (CXVIII. 1, 2).

Is this a grave sin?

If one considers this sin as regards its object, namely, money, it is the least of sins, for it vitiates man's love with regard to exterior goods only, namely, riches; but if one considers the disproportion between the soul, which is spiritual, and riches, to which it is inordinately attached, it is the most degrading of all sins; since therein the soul subjects itself to what is beneath it (CXVIII. 4, 5).

Is this sin particularly dangerous?

Yes, because there is no end to this inordinate love of riches; for to gain riches one may be induced to commit all sorts of crime against God, one's neighbour, and oneself (CXVIII. 5).

Is avarice a capital sin?

Yes, it is one of the capital sins, because it carries with it one of the conditions necessary for happiness which everyone desires, namely, the abundance of goods to which everything is subservient (CXVIII. 7).

What are the daughters of avarice?

They are hardness of heart which knows no pity, disquietude, violence, deceit, perjury, fraud, and treach ery; for the inordinate love of riches may lead to excess: as regards the effort to retain them; or as regards the effort to acquire them: on the part of the desire to have riches; or on the part of the endeavour to obtain them: by violence, or by guile: or in words expressed under oath or otherwise; or by deed: as regards things; and as regards persons (CXVIII. 8).

(c)

Is prodigality, which is the other sin opposed to liberality, also opposed to avarice?

Yes; for whereas avarice exceeds in the love of riches without being drawn to make good use of them by giving to others, prodigality does not properly estimate riches and distributes them with too ready a hand (CXIX. 1, 2)

Of these two sins which is the more grave?

Avarice, because it is more opposed to the virtue of liberality, which gives rather than retains (CXIX. 3).

(D)

Is it possible by a consideration of their objects to sum up and to show the order between the virtues that are related to particular justice?

Yes, in a few words thus. In the first place comes religion, which refers to God as regards the service and worship due to Him by reason of His being the Creator and Lord of all things; then comes filial respect, which refers to parents and country to whom we owe our life and benefits; then reverence, which refers to superiors in authority, dignity, and excellence in no matter what order this be; then gratitude, which refers to benefactors; then retributive justice with regard to evildoers or those who do us harm, who merit the punishment meted out to them; and lastly come truthfulness, friendship, and liberality, which we owe to all for our own sakes.

XXXIX.—OF NATURAL EQUITY (OR EPIKEIA)

Is there not also a virtue annexed to legal justice?

Yes, it is that virtue which may be called natural equity or fairness, and which also goes under the name of epikeia (CXX.).

What is the role of this virtue?

Its role is to incline the will to seek justice in all things and in all orders, as it were, outside of and above the established laws among men, whenever the natural reason in virtue of its very first principles shows that in a given case the established laws cannot and should not be applied (CXX. 1).

Is this a virtue of great worth?

In the order of justice and indeed among all the virtues which regulate man's relations with his neighbour, this virtue is the most important, dominating all in some sort and aiding them towards the betterment of the social good as regards its very essentials (CXX. 2).

XL.—OF THE GIFT OF PIETY WHICH CORRESPONDS TO JUSTICE AND ITS PARTS

Which is the gift of the Holy Ghost which corresponds to the virtue of justice?

It is the gift of piety (CXXXI.).

In what does the gift of piety exactly consist?

It consists in an habitual disposition of the will which makes man ready to receive the direct and personal action of the Holy Ghost, inclining him to treat God,

considered in the highest mysteries of His divine life, as a
Father tenderly and filially revered, served, and obeyed;
and to treat all men in the way the divine and super
natural good demands which unites all to God as to the
Father of one great divine family (CXXI. 1).

*Must one say that the gift of piety is as it were the seal
that sanctifies the relations that should exist between men,
and between them and God?*

Yes, the gift of piety is as it were the seal of this sanctification; it is the crowning of the virtue of justice and of
all the virtues thereto annexed; and if by means of this
gift everyone corresponded perfectly to the impulses of
the Holy Spirit, men's life on earth would be the life of a
divine family, and as it were a foretaste of the life of the
blessed in heaven.

XLI.—OF THE PRECEPTS RELATING TO JUSTICE WHICH ARE THOSE OF THE DECALOGUE: OF THE THREE FIRST; AND OF THE LAST FOUR

(A)

*Are there any precepts that relate to the virtue of justice
and the virtues thereto annexed together with the gift of
piety which crowns them?*

Yes; they are the precepts of the Decalogue (CXXII. 1).

Do the precepts of the Decalogue relate only to these virtues?

Yes; for those precepts which relate to other virtues
are of later origin and are determinations or unfoldings
of the former precepts (CXXII. 1).

Why is this so?

This is so because the precepts of the Decalogue, in so
far as they are the first precepts of the moral law, should
refer to what for all and at first sight manifestly has the
nature of a thing that is due; and further, this perception
of a thing as due should include relations towards others
such as the virtue of justice with its virtues annexed
demand (*ibid.*).

(B)

How are the precepts of the Decalogue divided?

They are divided into two parts, which are called the two tables of the law.

What do the precepts of the first table comprise?

They comprise the first three precepts relating to the virtue of religion which regulates man's dealings with God.

·What order is there between these three precepts?

The order among them is of such sort that the first two put aside the two principal obstacles to the worship of God, viz., superstition or the worship of false gods, and irreligion or the lack of respect towards the true God; then the third precept determines positively the worship of the true God (CXXII. 2, 3).

What does the third precept of the Decalogue comprise?

It comprises two things: abstaining from servile works; and the occupying oneself with the things of God (CXXII. 4, *Obj.* 3).

What is meant by abstaining from servile works?

By this is meant the obligation of putting aside for one day in the week (which is now Sunday) and on days of obligation (which are for the entire Church the feast of Christmas, the Circumcision, the Epiphany, the Ascension, Corpus Christi, the Immaculate Conception, the Assumption, the feast of St. Joseph, of St. Peter and St. Paul, and All Saints) manual work which is not necessary for the maintenance or welfare of our material life, or which urgent necessity does not demand (CXXII. 3, *Obj.* 3; *Code,* 1247).

And what does the occupying ourselves with the things of God comprise?

It comprises in a most express way and under penalty of grave sin, the obligation to assist at the Holy Sacrifice of the Mass on Sundays and on the feast days above mentioned (CXXII. 3, *Obj.* 4).

If one is unable to assist at Mass on the above days is one bound to perform some exercise of piety?

One is not bound to any exercise of piety that is in any way determined; but one would be certainly wanting in the positive obligation of keeping holy the above days if one let them go by without any act of religion at all.

(c)

What do the precepts of the second table comprise?

They comprise the precepts relative to the virtue of filial respect towards parents and to the virtue of strict justice towards our neighbour whoever he may be (CXXII. 5, 6).

XLII.—OF THE VIRTUE OF FORTITUDE AND ITS ACT; OF MARTYRDOM; OF THE SINS OPPOSED THERETO: OF FEAR; OF INSENSIBILITY TO FEAR; OF RASHNESS

(A)

What is the virtue that comes after justice and holds the third place among the cardinal virtues?

It is the virtue of fortitude (CXXIII.–CXL.).

What is fortitude?

It is that perfection in the moral order of the sensitive appetite whose object is to make man hold firm in the presence of the greatest fear, or to keep within bounds the most daring boldness as regards peril of death that presents itself in the course of just war, in order that man might never fail in his duty (CXXIII. 1-6).

(B)

Is there any special act of this virtue in which all its excellence is shown forth?

Yes, it is martyrdom (CXXIV.).

What is martyrdom?

It is that act of the virtue of fortitude which sustains

man in accepting death in testimony of the truth from the hands of those who persecute the name of Christian and all that pertains thereto (CXXIV. 1-5).

(c)

What are the sins opposed to the virtue of fortitude?

They are, on the one hand, fear, which lacks courage in the presence of dangers of death, or insensibility to fear in the presence of peril, which is the lack of shunning peril when one ought to; and on the other hand, rashness which rushes towards danger imprudently (CXXV.– CXXVII.).

Can then one sin by excess of bravery?

One never sins by excess of bravery; but one may, under the impulse of excessive courage which is unre strained by reason, be so carried away as to perform acts that are not really acts of true courage, but have only the semblance of bravery (CXXVII. 1, *Obj.* 2).

XLIII.—OF THE VIRTUES ANNEXED TO FOR TITUDE; OF MAGNANIMITY; OF THE SINS OPPOSED TO MAGNANIMITY; VIZ., OF PRESUMPTION; OF AMBITION; OF VAINGLORY; AND OF PUSILLANIMITY

(a)

Are there any virtues relating to the virtue of fortitude in that they imitate the act or manner of acting of this virtue, but in matters of less difficulty?

Yes, and they are, on the one hand, magnanimity and magnificence; and on the other, patience and perse verance (CXXVIII.).

In what are these two kinds of virtue distinguished?

In this, that the two first relate to fortitude by reason of an act which attacks what is most difficult and arduous; whereas the two others relate thereto by reason of an act which stands firm in presence of the greatest fear (CXXVIII.).

What is the proper object of magnanimity?

It is to strengthen one's soul in its effort to accomplish great acts in so far as great honours or great glory result therefrom (CXXIX. 1, 2).

Everything then that pertains to magnanimity is great?

Yes, all is great in this virtue; and it is the virtue *par excellence* of great souls.

(B)

Are there any sins opposed to this virtue?

Yes, there are a number of sins which are opposed thereto either by excess or defect.

What are the sins opposed to magnanimity by excess?

They are presumption, ambition, and vainglory (CXXX.–CXXXII.).

How are these different sins distinguished from each other?

In this, that presumption inclines one to the perform ance of acts that are too much for one's capabilities; ambition seeks honours greater than one deserves; and vainglory seeks some glory that has either no object, or that has an object of little worth, or which is not directed to the one true end which is the honour of God and the welfare of men (*ibid.*).

Is vainglory a capital sin?

Yes, for it implies the showing off of one's own ex cellence which one seeks in everything, and which may lead one to commit all manner of sins (CXXXII. 4).

What are the daughters of vainglory?

They are boasting, hypocrisy, stubbornness, discord, strife, and disobedience (CXXXII. 5).

(c)

What sin is opposed to magnanimity by defect?

It is the sin of pusillanimity (CXXXIII.).

Why is pusillanimity a sin?

Because it is contrary to the natural law which inclines every being to act according to its capabilities (CXXXIII. 1).

It is then indeed blameworthy not to make use of the powers and the means God has given us by the mistrust of oneself, or by taking up an unseemly attitude with regard to honours and glory?

Yes, this is indeed blameworthy and should not be confounded with true humility, about which we shall speak later (*ibid.*).

XLIV.—OF MAGNIFICENCE; AND OF THE SINS THERETO OPPOSED, VIZ., OF STINGINESS AND OF EXTRAVAGANCE

In what does the virtue of magnificence consist?

It consists in a disposition of the sensitive appetite, which strengthens the soul in its effort to fulfil what is arduous as regards the expenses demanded by the undertaking of great works (CXXXIV. 1, 2).

Does this virtue presuppose great riches and great opportunities of dispensing them for the public welfare?

Yes, this virtue presupposes great riches and the opportunity to dispense them, especially as regards the worship of God or the public welfare of a city or state (CXXXIV. 3).

Is it then a virtue belonging, properly speaking, to the rich and the great?

Yes.

What are the sins opposed to this virtue?

The sin of stinginess, which makes man begrudge and be unwilling to give even what is necessary for the undertaking of some work; and the sin of extravagance, which inclines one to expend unreasonably over and above what is necessary for some work undertaken (CXXXV. 1, 2).

XLV.—OF PATIENCE—OF LONGANIMITY AND OF CONSTANCY

What is the essence of the virtue of patience?

The essence of patience consists in supporting, for the sake of the future life, all the troubles that come to us unceasingly in the present life, whether they be caused by life's own whims or by the actions of others in their dealings with us (CXXXVI. 1-3).

Is patience the same as longanimity and constancy?

No; for although all three help us to bear the miseries of this life, patience helps us to bear especially the troubles which come about daily in our dealings with others; whereas longanimity bears us up against those troubles which arise from the delay of the realization of something for which we have to wait; and constancy buoys us up against the troubles which we encounter in the struggle to do good (CXXXVI. 5).

XLVI.—OF PERSEVERANCE; AND OF THE SINS OPPOSED THERETO, VIZ., OF EFFEMINACY AND OF OBSTINACY

What relation has perseverance to the virtues afore-mentioned?

Perseverance does not refer to the bearing up under troubles; it refers rather to the fatigue occasioned by the sustained effort of practising a virtuous life (CXXXVII. 1-3).

Are there any sins opposed to this virtue?

Yes, they are the lack of resistance or effeminacy, which makes one give way to the least difficulty or to the least fatigue; and obstinacy, which makes one persist in not giving way when it is reasonable to do so (CXXXVIII. 1, 2).

XLVII.—OF THE GIFT OF FORTITUDE WHICH CORRESPONDS TO THE VIRTUE OF FORTITUDE

Is there a gift of fortitude which corresponds to the virtue of fortitude?

Yes, it is the gift which bears the same name and is called the gift of fortitude (CXXXIX.).

In what precisely does the gift of fortitude differ from the virtue of fortitude?

In a few words it differs in this wise: Like the virtue, the gift has to do with fear and in some sort with courage. But whilst fear and courage, which the virtue of fortitude regulates, only refer to dangers which it is in the power of man to overcome, fear and courage, which the gift of fortitude excites, refer to perils or evils which it is absolutely impossible for man to overcome; death separates us from all the goods of the present life without it itself being able to give the only one good superior to all and, indeed, such as is infinitely above them all, carrying with it all good to the exclusion of all evil, viz., the actual possession of eternal life. This substitution of eternal life for all the miseries of the present life, in spite of all its difficulties and dangers and even of death itself, which is the complement of them all, is exclusively due to the action of the Holy Spirit Himself. This is the reason why it belongs to Him only to move the soul of man effectively towards this supreme acquisition, in such way that a strong and unfailing confidence takes hold of man, making him steadfast in the presence of the greatest fear and even to approach death itself fearlessly, not indeed to be conquered thereby, but to triumph: and it is by the gift of fortitude that man is thus moved by the Holy Ghost. In truth one may describe the proper effect of this gift as the victory over death (CXXXIX. 1).

XLVIII.—OF THE PRECEPTS RELATING TO FORTITUDE

Are there any precepts in the divine law that refer to the virtue of fortitude?

Yes, there are precepts of this kind as is meet. For especially in the New Law, in which everything is done in order to make man fix his mind on God, man is forbidden under the form of a negative precept to fear temporal evils; and under the form of a positive precept he is commanded to fight unintermittingly his worst enemy, who is the Devil (CXL. 1).

Are the precepts relating to the other virtues which are annexed to fortitude equally given in the divine law?

Yes; with regard to the other virtues only precepts (and these positive) are given that have reference to patience and perseverance that bear upon the ordinary occurrences of life; but as regards magnificence and magnanimity which bear upon things that belong rather to the order of perfection, no precepts are given but only counsels (CXL. 2).

XLIX.—OF TEMPERANCE; OF ABSTINENCE, AND OF FASTING: AND OF THE SIN OPPOSED THERETO, VIZ., OF GLUTTONY

(A)

What is the last of the great moral virtues which perfects man's life in his journey towards God?

It is the virtue of temperance (CXLI.–CLXX.).

What is understood by the virtue of temperance?

It is that virtue which keeps man's sensitive appetite within the bounds of reason so that it may not be carried away by pleasures, particularly those that refer to the sense of touch in those acts that are necessary for the conservation of bodily life (CXL. 1-5).

Of what kind of pleasures is there question?

Of the pleasures of the table and of marriage (CXLI. 4).

What name is given to the virtue of temperance when it refers to the pleasures of the table?

It is called abstinence or sobriety (CXLVI., CXLIX.).

What precisely is abstinence?

It is that which regulates the sensitive appetite with regard to eating and drinking so that this be done in con formity with what reason demands (CXLVI. 1).

Under what special form may one practise the virtue of abstinence?

Under the form that is called fasting (CXLVII.).

What is fasting?

Fasting is doing without a part of what is normally required for each day's food (CXLVII. 1, 2).

But is it not wrong to do this?

No; on the contrary to fast may be a most excellent thing, for it serves to keep concupiscence under control; to make the mind more free to occupy itself with the things of God; and to make satisfaction for sin (CXLVII. 1).

What conditions are required for fasting to be a good and excellent thing?

In this matter one must always be ruled by discretion and prudence, and there must be no danger to health, and it must not prove an obstacle to duty (CXLVII. 1, Obj. 2).

Is everyone who has attained the use of reason bound to fast?

Yes, everyone who has attained the use of reason is bound to some sort of fasting or of some privation pro portionate to the demand of the virtue; but not to the fasting prescribed by the Church (CXLVII. 3, 4).

What is understood by the fasting that is prescribed by the Church?

It is a form of fasting specially fixed by the Church for those who have attained a certain age that has to be under taken on certain days of the year (CXLVII. 5-8).

In what does this special form of fasting consist?

It consists in this, that only one full meal is allowed during the day (CXLVII. 6).

Is the time or the hour of this meal absolutely fixed?

No; for this repast may be taken at midday or in the evening.

May one take anything outside this repast?

Yes; in the morning one may take some little food, and in the evening also by way of collation (*Code*, 1251).

Who are bound to the fast prescribed by the Church?

All baptized Christians who have attained their twenty-first year until they have attained the fifty-ninth year completed (*Code*, 1254).

Given these conditions may one yet have the right not to fast?

Yes, whenever health or work manifestly forbid that one should fast; or if there be doubt on this point whenever legitimate authority dispenses from fasting (CLXVII. 4).

Who may give such dispensation?

In practice it is sufficient to ask for it from our immediate ecclesiastical superior.

What are the days on which one is bound to the Church fast?

They are all the days of Lent except Sundays; Wednesdays, Fridays, and Saturdays of the Ember weeks; the vigils of Pentecost, of the Assumption, of All Saints, and of Christmas. If these vigils fall on Sunday one is not bound to anticipate them (*Code*, 1252).

Is there a law of the Church concerning abstinence distinct from the law of fasting?

Yes; and the law obliges abstaining from flesh meat and its products on all Fridays of the year, and during Lent on Ash Wednesday, and on all Saturdays to the midday of Holy Saturday inclusively; and lastly, on the Wednesdays and Saturdays of the Ember weeks (*Code*, 1250, 1252).

Who are bound to the law of abstinence?

All the faithful who have reached the age of seven years (*Code*, 1254).

(B)

What is the sin opposed to the virtue of abstinence?

It is gluttony (CXLVIII. 1).

Are there several species of this sin?

Yes; for the inordinate desire to eat and drink may bear upon the nature and the quality of food, or upon its quantity, or upon its preparation, or upon the actual consumption of the food by not waiting for the proper time of eating, or by eating with greediness (CXLVIII. 4).

Is gluttony a capital sin?

Yes, because it bears upon one of those pleasures which of its nature incites man to desire things of sense and to act in accordance with them (CXLVIII. 5).

What are the daughters of gluttony?

They are dulness of mind with regard to things intellectual, inept mirth, immoderate speech, buffoonery and impurity (CXLVIII. 6).

Are these sins particularly gross?

Yes; for they imply more than other sins the absence and almost total lack of reason; and these sins are the outcome of gluttony because thereby the reason becomes sluggish and almost paralyzed, and can no longer guide man in the way he should go (*ibid.*).

L.—OF SOBRIETY AND OF THE SIN OPPOSED TO IT, VIZ., DRUNKENNESS

(A)

Is there in addition to abstinence any other virtue which helps man to avoid such sins?

Yes, it is the virtue of sobriety (CXLIX.).

What is the virtue of sobriety?

It is that virtue the object of which is only to take intoxicating drink as it behoves (CXLIX. 1, 2).

(B)

What sin is opposed to this virtue?

It is the sin by which man passes the just measure in drinking and becomes drunk (CL.).

Is drunkenness always a sin?

Yes, whenever it comes about through one's own fault by not ceasing to drink when one should and not taking into account the intoxicating character of the drink one takes (CL. 1).

What is necessary for this sin to be mortal?

One should be able to foresee that an excess of such drink may lead to the state of drunkenness, and that one has chosen this consequence rather than be deprived of the pleasure that the drink offers (CL. 2).

Is drunkenness a particularly gross and debasing sin?

Yes, because by it man knowingly deprives himself of the use of his reason and puts himself lower than brute beasts, for these at least always keep their instinct to guide them (CL. 3).

LI.—OF CHASTITY AND OF VIRGINITY; AND OF THE SIN OPPOSED THERETO, VIZ., OF VOLUPTUOUSNESS

(A)

Is there any other great virtue besides abstinence and sobriety that is a species of temperance?

Yes; and it is the virtue of chastity (CLI.).

What is meant by the virtue of chastity?

It is that perfection of the sensitive appetite which makes man master of all the impulses that bear him towards the things of marriage (CLI. 1).

Is there in the order of chastity any special virtue which is its crowning and highest perfection?

Yes; and this virtue is called virginity (CLII.).

What is virginity?

It is the firm and absolute purpose, made holy by a vow, of renouncing for ever the pleasures of marriage (CLII. 1-3).

(B)

What is the sin opposed to the virtue of chastity?

It is the sin called voluptuousness (CLIII.).

In what does the sin of voluptuousness consist?

It consists in using things on account of the pleasure attached thereunto which nature has ordained for the conservation of the human species, whether this be by deed, or desire, or thought willed, in which pleasure is taken; for this is contrary to the natural order whose office it is to control the use of such things (CLIV.).

Are there several species of voluptuousness?

Yes, there are as many species as there are distinct subversions of order in the things concerned with voluptuousness (CLIII. 1-3).

What are these distinct subversions of order in the matter of voluptuousness?

They are simple fornication, which is directly opposed to the good order of the things of marriage as regards the end of marriage, which is the welfare and the education of offspring; or, and this is the most grave of all, the sin against nature which is opposed directly and wholly to the first and essential end of marriage, which is the birth of offspring; or incest, adultery, the ravishing of a ward, and rape, which relate to the sexual abuse of those near to us by blood ties, or of those married, or of those in the guardianship of their protector, or of those against whom violence is performed; and lastly, sacrilege, which is the abuse of persons consecrated to God (CLIV. 1-12).

(C)

Is voluptuousness a capital sin?

Yes; and this on account of the extraordinary attraction of these matters which carries men away by its extreme vehemence (CLIII. 4).

What are the daughters of voluptuousness?

They are blindness of mind, rashness, unmindfulness, inconstancy, self-love, hatred of God, cleaving to the present life, and horror of the world to come (CLIII. 5).

Have all these sins a character in common such as is particularly grave?

Yes, they have this in common, although in different degrees, that the mind is absorbed by the flesh; moreover, there is a special gravity attaching to each of these sins and to voluptuousness, which is the mother of them all, for man falls from his high estate even below the estate of the brute beast which is without reason (CLIII. 5, 6).

LII.—OF THE VIRTUES ANNEXED TO TEM PERANCE, VIZ., OF CONTINENCE, AND OF INCONTINENCE WHICH IS THE SIN OPPOSED THERETO

(A)

Besides these virtues which are species of temperance, are there not other virtues which are annexed to temperance?

Yes; and they are those virtues which imitate its act or manner of acting (which is the controlling of what by its nature carries us away) but in matters that are of less difficulty; or which do not attain to the perfection of the act of temperance (CLV.).

What are these other virtues?

They are continence, clemency and meekness, and modesty (CLV.–CLXX.).

(B)

What is continence?

It is that virtue, in some sort imperfect in the order of virtue, which consists in choosing not to follow the violent movements of passion, and this for some motive of reason (CLV. 1).

Why is there in continence something imperfect in the order of virtue?

Because perfect virtue presupposes that the movements of passion are held in check, whereas continence does no more than resist them (*ibid.*).

(c)

Is there a sin opposed to continence?

Yes; and it is called incontinence (CLVI.).

In what does it consist?

It consists in this, that man gives way to the violence of passion and becomes its slave (CLVI. 1).

Which is the more grave sin, that of intemperance or that of incontinence?

Intemperance; for just as continence is less perfect than temperance in the order of virtue, so, in the order of sin, incontinence is less evil than intemperance (CLVI. 3).

LIII.—OF CLEMENCY AND OF MEEKNESS; AND OF THE SINS OPPOSED THERETO, VIZ., OF ANGER, AND OF CRUELTY OR SAVAGENESS

(A)

What are clemency and meekness?

They are two virtues: the first of which moderates the degree of external punishment to be meted out to some one so that it does not exceed the right limits of reason; the second virtue controls the interior movement of the passion which is called anger (CLVII. 1).

Are clemency and severity opposed to each other, and are meekness and retributive justice also opposed?

In no wise, for they are all different in motive, and in some sense they are the same in that they all seek what is in accordance with right reason (CLVII. 2, *Obj.* 1).

(B)

What sins are opposed to clemency and meekness?

Anger in the bad sense of the word, and cruelty or savagery (CLVIII.-CLIX.).

What is anger?

It is a movement of the irascible appetite which seeks unjust avengement, or an avengement which is just but which is sought with too much temper (CLVIII. 2).

Are there several kinds of anger?

Yes, there are three species of anger: the anger of those who are fretful and who become angry at the slightest cause; the anger of those who are bitter, who forget with difficulty an injury done to them; and the anger of those who are revengeful, who without ceasing seek the punishment of those by whom they have been wronged (CLVIII. 5).

Is anger a capital sin?

Yes, because men are particularly borne towards the seeking of revenge in satisfaction for an injury done them (CLVIII. 6).

What are the daughters of anger?

They are indignation, excitement of the mind, contumely, clamour, blasphemy, and quarrelling (CLVIII. 7).

Is there any sin opposed to the sin of anger?

Yes, it consists in the lack of anger when reason demands it, for there is a just anger which is the result of the right will to punish when punishment is due (CLVIII. 8).

(c)

What is understood by cruelty which is opposed to clemency?

It is a kind of crudity or rawness of soul owing to which one seeks to increase punishment beyond the just limits fixed by reason (CLXI. 1).

And what is savageness?

It is something absolutely inhuman which delights in the infliction of punishment, taking pleasure therein merely because it is an evil. Savageness is directly opposed to the gift of piety (CLIX. 2).

Is such a thing possible?

Yes, of a truth, for depraved human nature can reach even to this excess; in former times there were whole nations apparently in the highest degree of civilization which took supreme delight in the spectacles of the amphitheatres.

LIV.—OF MODESTY: OF HUMILITY AND OF ITS OPPOSITE SIN PRIDE; OF THE SIN OF ADAM AND EVE; OF SECULARISM

(A)

What is the last of the virtues annexed to temperance?

It is modesty (CLX.–CLXX.).

What is modesty?

Modesty is that virtue which restrains the sensitive appetite in things that are less difficult to regulate than those which are the object of temperance, continence, clemency, and meekness (CLX. 1, 2).

What are these things of less difficulty which are kept under control by the virtue of modesty?

They are the desire of one's own excellence; the desire to know; the exterior actions of the body; and lastly, one's exterior as regards the manner of dress (CLX. 2).

What are those virtues called which regulate the sensitive appetite with regard to these divers things?

They are called humility, the virtue of the studious, and modesty in its strict sense (CLX. 2).

(B)

What is humility?

It is that virtue which makes man repress or regulate whatever touches his own worth in such wise that he does not seek more than is in accordance with the degree of his excellence as fixed by God (CLXI. 1, 2).

What follows from this as regards man's dealings with others?

It follows that man does not esteem anything as due to him considered in himself, but that all he has and is comes from God; for of himself he has nothing at all, except sin; as regards his neighbours, he esteems that their worth is due to them according to the state of perfection in which God has placed them; and as regards the rest of creation, he wishes only that things should have the place and order such as God has disposed (CLXI. 3).

Humility then seeks always the strict truth?

Yes, humility seeks always and acknowledges the exact truth (*ibid.*).

(c)

What is the sin opposed to humility?

It is pride (CLXII.).

What is pride?

It is that special and in some sort general sin which, in despisal of God and of the order He has established in His work, strives to dominate all and to make one place oneself before all others by esteeming oneself superior to all (CLXII. 1, 2).

Why is it said that pride is a special and in some sort a general sin also?

Because this esteeming of oneself and one's worth in despisal of God and the rules established by Him, leads man to commit all manner of sins (*ibid.*).

Is this a grave sin?

It is the gravest of all sins by reason of the contempt of God which it directly implies; and owing to this it aggravates the gravity of all other sins no matter how grave these may be in themselves (CLXII. 6).

Is pride the first of all sins?

Yes; for there can be no grave sin that does not presuppose the sin of pride, although such sin in itself, or by reason of the motive which makes it a specific sin, is not itself a sin of pride; for it is pride, by reason of the contempt it implies for God, that completes as it were the

essence of other sins in so far as they make man turn away
from God (CLXII. 7).

Is pride a capital sin?

Yes, and it is even more than this, for it is the head
and the king as it were of every sin and vice (CLXII. 8).

(D)

Was the first sin of Adam and Eve a sin of pride?

Yes, their first sin was a sin of pride; and the sin of the
bad angels was also a sin of pride (CLXIII. 1).

*But was not the first sin of Adam and Eve rather a sin
of gluttony, or of disobedience, or an empty curiosity with
regard to knowledge, or a lack of faith in the word of God?*

All these sins here mentioned were the consequence of
the sin of pride, without which no other sin could exist
at all (CLXIII. 1).

*Why could no other sin be committed by Adam and Eve
without the sin of pride?*

Because their state of integrity made all within them to
be perfectly under control so long as their mind remained
subjected to God; but their mind could only turn away
from God for some motive of pride by wishing themselves
some excellence which was not their due (CLXIII. 1, 2).

*Is not the sin of secularism which is so prevalent in these
days also a sin of pride?*

Yes, and it is of exceptional gravity; for it is an imita
tion of the contempt and of the revolt of Satan and of the
bad angels, and afterwards of our first parents.

LV.—OF THE VIRTUE OF THE STUDIOUS; AND OF ITS OPPOSITE SIN, VIZ., OF CURIOSITY

*What is understood by the virtue of the studious, which
is the second of those virtues annexed to temperance?*

It is that virtue which makes man control in con
formity with right reason the desire to know and to learn
(CLXVI. 1).

What is the sin opposed to this virtue?

It is called curiosity (CLXVII.).

What is curiosity?

It is the inordinate desire to know what one has no right to know, or to know what may prove a source of danger to virtue owing to one's weakness (CLXVII. 1, 2).

Does one easily commit the sin of curiosity?

Yes; it is frequently committed, whether this be as regards knowledge in general, or as regards that knowledge which effects the senses and the passions (CLXVII. 1, 2).

Does the inordinate desire to read daily papers and novels also belong to this sin; or further, to be present at spectacles of all sorts, such as the theatre, the cinematograph, and other such things?

Yes; all these things belong to the sin of curiosity, and perhaps also to the sin of sensuality or of voluptuousness; indeed, one cannot do too much to overcome the inordinate desire for such things.

LVI.—OF EXTERNAL MODESTY

What is the last of the virtues annexed to temperance under the general name of modesty?

It is the special virtue of modesty understood in the strict sense (CLXVII.-CLXX.).

What is this virtue?

It is that perfection in the sensitive appetite which makes everything in a person's exterior as regards his movements, gestures, words, the tone of his voice, and of his general attitude, to be what it ought to be according to the status of the person, and this in such way that nothing whatever is offensive in his conduct; and on this head modesty is akin to friendship and truthfulness (CLXVIII. 1).

Must one attribute to the virtue of modesty whatever has reference to games and recreation which are part of the economy of human life?

Yes; and this virtue then goes by another name, which

is that of *eutrapelia;* and this virtue effects that a person plays, amuses, or recreates himself as it behoves, avoiding both excess and defect (CLXVIII. 2-4).

Does modesty also have reference to one's manner of dress?

Yes; and this is what is implied by modesty understood in its strictest sense (CLXIX.).

What does modesty do with regard to dress?

It effects that the sensitive appetite is exactly what it ought to be with regard to dress to the exclusion of unseemly fashion or disorderly negligence (CLXIX. 1).

Is it against this virtue of modesty that many sin in that they do not keep a just measure as regards the excesses of what is called fashion, and which may prove an occasion of sin to others?

Yes, to exceed in this way is against the virtue of modesty and at the same time against the virtue of chastity; and indeed such excess cannot be sufficiently reproved (CLXIX. 2).

LVII.—OF THE GIFT THAT CORRESPONDS TO THE VIRTUE OF TEMPERANCE

Is there a gift of the Holy Ghost that corresponds to the virtue of temperance?

Yes, the gift of fear (CXLI. 1, *Obj.* 3).

But was it not said above that the gift of fear corresponds to the theological virtue of hope?

Yes, but the gift of fear corresponds also to the cardinal virtue of temperance, not, however, under the same aspect (*ibid.*).

In what does this difference consist?

In this, that the gift of fear corresponds to the theological virtue of hope in so far as man reveres God directly by reason of His infinite greatness and avoids offending Him; and it corresponds to the virtue of temperance in so far as the respect that it inspires with regard to God's greatness makes man avoid those things which are more offensive to God, and these are the pleasures of the senses (*ibid.*).

But does not the virtue of temperance make one avoid those things already?

Yes, but in a way that is in every sense less perfect; for temperance puts these things aside only in that measure of which man is able of himself by the light of reason or of faith; whereas the gift of fear makes him avoid them according to the personal action of the Holy Ghost, moving him and leading him by reason of the reverence which the infinite majesty of God inspires to hold the pleasures of the senses as so much rottenness.

LVIII.—OF THE PRECEPTS RELATING TO TEMPERANCE AND ITS PARTS

(A)

Is there any precept in the divine law referring to temperance?

Yes, there are two precepts in the Decalogue that refer to temperance (CLXX.).

What are these two precepts?

They are the sixth and the ninth precepts: " Thou shalt not commit adultery," and " Thou shalt not covet thy neighbour's wife."

Why is only adultery spoken of? and why in the matter of adultery are there two distinct precepts in the Decalogue?

Because of the things that have to do with temperance, adultery brings man more into relation with his neighbour especially from the point of view of justice, which is precisely that of the precepts of the Decalogue; and the reason of the two distinct precepts with regard to this matter is due to the importance of preventing at its very source the great evil of adultery (CLXX. 1).

(B)

Are there any precepts among those of the Decalogue that have reference to the parts of temperance?

No, there is no precept which refers directly to the

parts of temperance, because these of themselves do not refer to man's dealings with God or his neighbour. Nevertheless these divers parts are referred to indirectly by reason of their effects, and this either by the precepts of the first table or by those of the second table. It is for instance through pride that man does not give to God or his neighbour the respect due to them; and it is through anger that man assails the person of his neighbour even to the attempting of his life (CLXX. 2).

Would it not have been fitting to speak in the Decalogue of the positive side of the precepts that relate to temperance and its parts?

No, because the Decalogue should contain only the first precepts of the divine law such as are applicable to all men and to all times; but whatever belongs to the positive side of these virtues, as abstinence, the manner of speaking, acting, etc., can vary with different peoples, in different places, in different times, etc. (CLXX. 1, *Obj.* 3).

To what particular authority in the New Law does it belong to determine such things?

It belongs to the Church to determine these things for the right behaviour of the faithful.

LIX.—OF THE TWO KINDS OF LIFE, VIZ., OF THE ACTIVE AND THE CONTEMPLATIVE; OF THE STATE OF PERFECTION—OF THE RELIGIOUS LIFE; AND OF THE RELIGIOUS COMMUNITIES IN THE CHURCH

(A)

Have we now a sufficient knowledge of all the virtues that man must practise in order to get to heaven, and of the sins he must avoid so as not to lose heaven and gain hell?

Yes. For we have learnt about the three great virtues of faith, hope, and charity, whereby man can attain his last supernatural end in the way that he must attain it in

this life, so that it might direct his steps aright and com
mand as it were his life of virtue. We have learnt also
about the four great moral or cardinal virtues, which are
prudence, justice, fortitude, and temperance, with all the
virtues annexed to them; and we have considered them
not only in the natural order in so far as they are called
the acquired virtues, but also in the supernatural order in
which they are called the infused virtues, and on this head
they are on a level with the theological virtues. We have
seen that these virtues effect that man is able to direct
his moral life with regard both to himself and his neigh
bour as it behoves in order that his life may be in harmony
in all things with his supernatural end. If man practises
all these virtues, connected as they are with the corre
sponding gifts of the Holy Ghost, they are sufficient for
the attainment of the vision of God which we know
must be his eternal happiness in heaven. If, however, man
sins against any one of the above virtues he must by means
of another virtue which is called penance (and of which
we shall speak in the Third Part) make satisfaction for his
sin in union with the satisfaction of our Lord Jesus Christ.

*Can such a thing be found anywhere on earth as the
putting into practice of the whole of the virtues and the
coming into play of all the gifts which truly constitute man's
life on earth?*

Yes, such a life is found under two forms which are
distinct, and in some sense separate; these two forms are
called the contemplative and the active life (CLXXIX.–
CLXXXII.).

(B)

What is meant by the contemplative life?

It is that kind of life, in which man finds peace in his
soul as a result of the subjection of his sinful passions,
and of his withdrawal from the external affairs of life;
under the impulse of the love of God, he passes his time
in the contemplation of God in Himself and in His works
in so far as this is possible on earth; rejoicing in the vision
of God whom he loves, and finding in this enjoyment of

God his highest perfection, such as makes him live a life detached from all things on earth and to cleave to God alone (CLXXX. 1-8).

Does the contemplative life presuppose all the virtues?

Yes, it presupposes all the virtues, and it helps to make them perfect; but in itself it consists in a certain activity wherein all the intellectual and theological virtues come into play, remaining always and entirely subject to the personal action of the Holy Ghost through the instru mentality of the gifts (CLXXX. 2).

(c)

What does the active life entail?

The active life entails all the acts of the moral virtues, and most especially the acts of the virtue of prudence; and the reason is because the precise object of the active ie i o regulate, as it behoves, all things of the present life (CLXXXI. 1-4).

Of these two lives which is the more perfect?

Incontestably the contemplative life is the more perfect be aus ven on earth it brings with it a foretaste of heaven (CLXXXII. 1).

Is it possible for anyone to live both these kinds of lives at the same time?

Yes, it is possible to lead both the contemplative and active life in what is called a state of perfection.

What is understood by a state of perfection?

It is a certain condition of life in which man lives in a fixed and permanent way, apart from the ties which make him a slave to the necessities of the present life, making him free to occupy himself exclusively with the things of God (CLXXXIII. 1, 4).

(D)

Is this state of perfection the same thing as perfection itself?

No, for perfection consists in something that is internal; whereas the state of perfection, of which we are speaking,

14

consists in a condition of life which should be considered rather as the assemblage of external acts (CLXXXIV. 1).

Can one have the perfection of the virtues and gifts, or the perfection of the life of charity, without being in a state of perfection; and, conversely, can one be in a state of perfection without having the perfection of charity?

Yes, both these are possible (CLXXXIV. 4).

Why then should one enter a state of perfection?

Because, of itself, it facilitates in a great degree the acquisition of perfection itself; and generally speaking it is in a state of perfection that perfection is found.

What then constitutes a state of perfection?

It is the fact of obliging oneself for ever, under a certain solemn form, to things which are of perfection in so far as they relate to the external organization of one's life (CLXXXIV. 4).

(E)

Who are they who live in a state of perfection?

Those who are bishops and those who are religious (CLXXXIV. 5).

Why are bishops in a state of perfection?

Because bishops at the moment when they take upon themselves the pastoral office, oblige themselves to give their lives to the service of their flocks; and this assumption of office is attended with the solemnity of consecration (CLXXXIV. 6).

What makes religious to be in a state of perfection?

The fact that under the form of perpetual vows they oblige themselves to give up the things of the world of which they might lawfully have made use, in order to occupy themselves more freely with the things of God; and they make these vows with a certain solemnity of profession or of blessing (CLXXXIV. 5).

Of these two states of perfection which is the more perfect?

That of bishops (CLXXXIV. 7).

Why is the state of bishops more perfect than that of religious?

Because bishops in virtue of their state must possess

the perfection which religious by their state strive to acquire (CLXXXIV. 7).

How do religious by their state tend toward perfection?

Religious by their state tend to acquire perfection in so far as by the three vows of poverty, chastity, and obedience, they are placed outside the danger of com mitting sin and are happily constrained to act virtuously in all things (CLXXXVI. 1-10).

Are the three vows essential to the religious state?

Yes; and in such way that without them there could be no religious state at all (CLXXXVI. 2-7).

(F)

Can there be a diversity of religious communities, all having the essential conditions of the religious state?

Yes (CLXXXVIII.).

In what does this diversity consist?

It is according to the diversity of things as regards which man may devote himself wholly to the service of God; and according as one may attain this in different ways and by different exercises (CLXXXVIII. 1).

What are the two great species of religious communities?

They are the contemplative and the active (CLXXXVIII. 2-6).

What is understood by the community which devotes itself to the active life?

It is that religious community which devotes itself for love of God to the service of man in order to bring him to God (CLXXXVIII. 2).

And what is the religious community which devotes itself to the contemplative life?

It is that which devotes itself wholly to the service of God in Himself (CLXXXIII. 2, *Obj.* 2).

Of these two kinds of religious communities which is the more perfect?

The contemplative; but the most perfect of all are those religious communities the principal part of whose life is given up to the contemplation of divine things or to the worship and service of God in Himself, but with the object in view of giving to others the benefit of their contemplation in the endeavour to lead them to the service and the greater love of God (CLXXXVIII. 6).

Is not the existence of the divers religious communities in the Church a very great blessing?

Yes, for apart from the fact they are the chosen homes of those who seek to practise virtue in all its perfection, they contribute towards the greatest good of society by their works of charity or the apostolate, and by their life of immolation to God.

Whence arises this excellence of religious communities?

This excellence arises from the fact that they seek openly and by their very vocation to walk in the way in which every man whosoever he be should walk in order to practise the same virtues and reach the happiness of heaven.

What is this way without which it is impossible to practise the virtues and reach to the happiness of God?

This way is no other than Jesus Christ or the mystery of the Word made flesh. It is of Jesus Christ now that we must speak; and the consideration of Him will form the subject-matter of the Third Part of this work.

THE THIRD PART

OF JESUS CHRIST

THE WAY WHEREBY MAN RETURNS TO GOD)

The Incarnation; Christ's life on earth; the part taken therein by Our Blessed Lady.

The Sacraments: Baptism; Confirmation; Holy Eucharist; Penance; Extreme Unction; Holy Orders; Matrimony.

The Last Things. Purgatory; Heaven; Hell. The Resurrection; the Last Judgment.

I.—OF THE MYSTERY OF THE INCARNATION OR OF THE WORD MADE FLESH

What is meant by the mystery of the Incarnation or of the Word made flesh?

It is that truth, absolutely incomprehensible for us on earth, according to which the second Person of the Most Holy Trinity, viz., the Word or the only Son of God, existing from all eternity together with the Father and the Holy Ghost, the same, one, and only true God, the Creator and Sovereign Master of all things, came, in time, upon this earth by His Incarnation in the womb of the Virgin Mary of whom He was born: lived moreover our mortal life and evangelized the Jewish race in Palestine to whom He was personally sent by His Father; was rejected by this people, was betrayed and delivered up to Pontius Pilate, the Roman governor; was condemned and put to death on a cross; was buried, and descended into hell, and rose again from the dead the third day; ascended into heaven forty days afterwards; sits at the right hand of God the Father, from whence He governs the Church established by Him on earth, and to which He sent the Holy Ghost, who is His as well as the Father's; sanctified this Church by the sacraments of His grace, so preparing it for His second coming at the end of time; at the last day He will judge the living and the dead, having made the latter rise from their tombs; and this in order to make the final separation of the good from the bad; the good He will take with Him into the Kingdom of His Father, and the bad He will curse and condemn to everlasting punishments.

II.—OF THE FITTINGNESS AND NECESSITY OF THE INCARNATION

(A)

Is this coming on earth of the Son of God by His Incarnation in harmony with what we know of God?

Yes. For we know that God is goodness itself; on the other hand, we know that goodness endeavours to com municate some of its perfection to others. Now God could not communicate Himself to His creatures in a way more marvellous than by His Incarnation (I. 1).

Was the Incarnation of the Son of God necessary?

No; considered in itself the Incarnation was in no way necessary; but given the fall of the human race by the sin of Adam, and that God wished to reinstate the human race in the most perfect way, and that above all He desired to exact the most complete satisfaction for the first sin, then it was necessary that a God-Man should take upon Himself this sin and make reparation for it (I. 2).

It is then by reason of man's sin and for the reparation thereof that the Son of God became incarnate?

Yes, it was for this precise reason (I. 3, 4).

Why then did not the Son of God become incarnate immediately after the fall of Adam?

The reason was because God wished the human race to know fully its misery, and the need it had of a God-Saviour; and also as was meet for so great a coming in order that a great line of prophets might precede and foretell the advent of the Saviour (I. 5, 6).

(B)

In what does the Incarnation of the Son of God consist, considered in itself?

It consists in this, that the divine nature and a human nature, each preserving what was proper to each, were substantially and indissolubly united in the unity of the one and same divine Person, which is the Person of the Son of God (II. 1-6).

Why did this union take place in the Person of the Son rather than in that of the Father or the Holy Ghost?

The reason is because the properties of the Son, who in God, has the nature of the Word, and to whom belongs by way of appropriation all that refers to *wisdom* through which God created all things, make the Son to be especially fitting for the restoration of the fallen human race; and also because proceeding from the Father, He could be *sent* by the Father, and He, in His turn, could *send* us His Spirit as the fruit of His Redemption (III. 8).

III.—CONCERNING THAT WHICH THE SON OF GOD TOOK OF US AND WHICH HE UNITED TO HIMSELF IN HIS INCARNATION

(A)

When it is said that the Son of God was incarnated, or that the Word was made flesh, or that He was made man, what do these different expressions signify?

All these expressions signify that the Word, or the Son of God, took, in order to unite it to Himself in His Passion, our human nature such as it is to be found in every indi vidual human being descended from Adam (IV. 1-6).

Does it then follow that in the incarnate Word or Son of God made man there is a human individual?

Absolutely no. There is in Him an individual human nature, but not a human individual or a human person; for the nature He took was united to His divine Person, so that in the Incarnation there is only one person, and that is the Person of the Word or of God the Son (IV. 3).

Is this human nature which is united to the Person of God the Son, as regards its two essential parts, exactly the same as the human nature in each of us?

Yes (V. 1-4).

The incarnate Son of God has then a body like to ours, of flesh and bone, with the same members, senses, and organs?

Yes (V. 1, 2).

Has He also a soul like to ours, with the same parts and faculties, and with an intellect and a will like to ours?

Yes, He has a soul with the same parts and powers like to ours exactly (V. 3, 4).

Were all the parts which constitute an individual human nature in its essence and integrity united to the Person of the Son of God at the same time?

Yes, but He united them to Himself in a certain order (VI. 1-6).

(B)

In what order did God the Son unite to Himself the human nature and its parts?

In such wise that He took the body and all its parts by reason of the soul; and the soul and its other powers by reason of the intellect; and the body, soul, and intellect by reason of the human nature which all the above con stitutes in its essence and integrity (VI. 1-5).

Was this union of the human nature and all its parts with the Person of God the Son made directly and immediately without the intermediary of any created reality whatsoever?

Yes, and this precisely because the term of this union is the very being of the Person of God the Son which is com municated to this human nature and all its parts (VI. 6).

IV.—OF THE PRIVILEGES OR PREROGATIVES OF THE HUMAN NATURE UNITED TO GOD THE SON, VIZ., OF HABITUAL OR SANCTIFYING GRACE; OF THE VIR TUES AND GIFTS OF THE HOLY GHOST; AND OF THE GRACES GRATUITOUSLY GIVEN

(A)

Are there not, however, in the human nature united to the person of God the Son and in the faculties of its soul certain created realities of the gratuitous order which unite it to God?

Yes, but it is not by these that it is united to the Person of God the Son; they are, on the contrary, consequences of this union such as the transcendency of the union demands (VI. 6).

What are these created realities?

They are, first of all, habitual grace in the essence of the soul; then in the faculties all the virtues with the exception of faith and hope; and all the gifts of the Holy Ghost; also all graces gratuitously given, the object of which was the manifestation of the divine truth to the world, not excepting prophecy in so far as it implies the prophetic state properly so-called (VII. 1-8).

What was and what is the role of the habitual grace in the essence of Christ's soul?

The role was, and will be through all eternity, to make this soul, by participation, to be what the divine nature is in itself, by essence; and to impart to the soul through its faculties the principles of divine activity which are the virtues and the gifts (VII. 1).

Why did Christ's human nature have all the virtues except faith and hope?

Because these two virtues imply an imperfection such as was incompatible with the perfection of the soul united to the Person of God the Son (VII. 3, 4).

In what does this imperfection consist?

In this, that faith implies that one does not see what one believes, and that hope bears one towards God not yet possessed in the beatific vision (*ibid.*).

(B)

What are understood by graces gratuitously given?

They are those privileges enumerated by St. Paul in the First Epistle to the Corinthians, chap. xii., ver. 8 *et seq.*, viz., faith, wisdom, knowledge, the grace of healing, work ing of miracles, prophecy, discerning of spirits, diverse kinds of tongues, and interpretation of speeches (VII. 7).

Is faith here mentioned the same as the virtue of faith?

No, for it implies a certain supereminent certainty with regard to divine truths which makes one fit to explain these truths to others (I.–II., CXI. 4, *Obj.* 2).

And the wisdom and knowledge aforementioned, are they distinct from the intellectual virtues and the gifts of the Holy Ghost which are called by the same name?

Yes, for they signify a certain abundance of knowledge and wisdom whereby man obtains a just appreciation of divine things, and is able to instruct others therein and to refute adversaries (I.–II., CXI., *Obj.* 4).

Did Christ ever use while on earth the spiritual privilege which is called diversity of tongues?

No, for the ministry of His Apostolate was exercised among the Jews only or among those who used the same language as the Jews; but He possessed this gift and could have made use of it had occasion offered (VII. 7, *Obj.* 3).

What is meant by saying that Christ had the grace of prophecy in so far as it implies the prophetic state properly so-called?

By this is meant that Christ during His life on earth lived the life we live, and was hence separated from heavenly things of which he spoke to men; although as regards the higher part of His soul He lived in the very centre as it were of the mysteries of God of which He had always perfect knowledge and the perfect joy resulting therefrom. In fact it is of the essence of a prophet to speak of things that are afar off and not within the sight of those to whom he announces them, and among whom He lives (VII. 8).

(c)

What relation is there between the above-mentioned spiritual gifts and habitual or sanctifying grace and the accompanying gifts and virtues?

Sanctifying grace together with the accompanying virtues and gifts sanctify him in whom they are; whereas the spiritual gifts are given solely for the apostolate and the benefit of others (I.–II., CXI. 1, 4).

Can these two kinds of graces exist apart?

Yes, since all holy souls have habitual or sanctifying grace together with the accompanying virtues and gifts; whereas the graces gratuitously given are only given to those who have to minister to others. Further, although as regards these latter the two kinds of graces are ordinarily speaking together, they can be separated as was the case with Judas, who was bad, but who nevertheless had all the graces gratuitously given which were conferred on the Apostles.

Were both these kinds of graces in the human nature of Christ, and were they present in the highest perfection?

Yes (VII. 1, 8).

Why was this so in the case of Christ?

Because His personal excellence was infinite; and because He was the supreme doctor of the things of faith (VII. 7).

V.—OF THE FULNESS OF GRACE IN THE HUMAN NATURE OF THE INCARNATE SON OF GOD

Must it be said that in the human nature of Christ there was the fulness of grace?

Yes; and in this sense, that there was nothing that relates to the order of grace that was not there; and that this fulness of grace was present in its highest possible perfection (VII. 9).

Was this superexcellent fulness of grace proper to the human nature of Christ?

Yes, it was absolutely proper to Christ's human nature; and the reason is because of the nearness of this nature to the divine nature in the same Person of God the Son which is the source of grace; and because of the mission of our Lord on earth, which consisted in the diffusion of this superabundance of grace to all men (VII. 10).

May one say that this grace of our Lord was infinite?

Yes, in a certain sense. For if it be question of the grace of union it is infinite because it means the union of the human to the divine nature itself in the Person of the Son of God; and if it be question of habitual grace with all that accompanies it, it has no limit in the actual order of grace as regards others who participate therein, although of itself it is created and finite (VII. 11).

Could this grace thus understood be increased in the human nature of our Lord?

If one considers the omnipotence of God, which is infinite, this grace could be increased; but considered in the actual order of grace as established by God this grace could not be increased (VII. 12).

What is the relation between this grace and the grace of union?

It is a consequence of the grace of union, and is proportionate to this grace of union (VII. 13).

What is the grace of union called which is the principle of all other grace in our Lord?

It is called the *hypostatic* union from a Greek word which signifies *person;* for it is owing to the action of the Person of God the Son, in concert with the Father and the Holy Ghost, that this superexcellent dignity and honour is bestowed upon the human nature by the fact that it is united immediately to the divine nature in the Person of God the Son.

VI.—OF THE GRACE OF CHRIST IN SO FAR AS HE IS HEAD OF THE CHURCH

(A)

Apart from the graces above mentioned which belong to Christ in so far as He is a particular man distinct from other men, is there not another grace belonging to Him in so far as He is the head of His mystical Body the Church?

Yes, and it is our duty now to speak of this grace (VIII.).

What is meant by saying that Christ is head of the Church?

It means that Christ occupies in the order of nearness to God the first place, and possesses in its highest perfec tion and fulness whatsoever relates to the order of grace; and, further, Christ possesses the power to communicate all things in the order of grace to men (VIII. 1).

Is it only by reason of the soul of Christ or by reason of His Body also that Christ is the head of the Church?

Christ is head of the Church by reason of His Body also; this means to say that the whole humanity of Christ, Body and Soul, is the instrument of divinity, whereby He bestows upon the souls of men and upon their bodies also the goods of the supernatural order: He acts thus towards those on earth so that the body may help the soul in the practice of virtue; and to those holy ones who shall rise at the last day that their bodies might receive from the glorified soul their share of immortality and glory (VIII. 2).

Is Christ the head, in the sense explained, of all men?

Yes; but those who no longer live on earth, and who died in the state of final impenitence, belong to Him no longer, and are separated from Him for evermore. But those who are already in heaven belong to Him and He is their head in a special manner. Further, He is the head of all who are united to Him by grace whether they be on earth or in purgatory; and of all those who are united to Him by faith even though they have not charity; and of all those who are not yet united to Him by faith, but who will one day be united to Him thus according to the decrees of divine Providence; and lastly, of all those living on earth who could be united to Him, but who in fact will never be (VIII. 3).

Is Christ also the head of the angels?

Yes; for Christ occupies the first place with regard to the whole multitude of those who are ordained to the same end, which is the enjoyment of heaven (VIII. 4).

Is that grace whereby Christ is the head of the whole Church in the sense explained, the same grace as that which belongs to Him personally as a determinate human being in so far as He is distinct from all other human beings, and " a fortiori " from the angels?

Yes, in its essence it is the same grace, but it is desig nated by these two different names, personal grace and capital grace, by reason of its double function, viz., in so far as it adorns the human nature of Christ, and in so far as it is communicated to others (VIII. 5).

Is it proper to Christ to be the head of the Church?

Yes; for only the humanity of Christ can justify man interiorly by reason of its union to the divinity in the Person of the Word. But as regards the external govern ment of the Church others may be called, and are in fact, heads in different degrees; as, for instance, bishops in their dioceses, and the Sovereign Pontiff in the universal Church as long as his Pontificate lasts; but these heads only take the place of the one true head, Jesus Christ Himself, from whom they depend, for they are Christ's vicars and act only in His Name (VIII. 6).

(B)

Is there a head in the order of evil that leads men to their loss just as Christ in the order of good leads men to salvation?

Yes; and this head of the wicked is Satan, the Prince of the devils (VIII. 7).

In what sense is Satan the head of the wicked?

Not in the sense that he can communicate evil to man interiorly, as Christ communicates good; but in the order of external government he strives to turn men away from God, whereas Christ leads men to God; and all those who sin imitate his rebellion and his pride, whereas the good by their works imitate the submission and obedience of Jesus Christ (VIII. 7).

Is there then on account of this opposition as it were a personal struggle between Christ and Satan?

Yes.

What will be the end of this struggle?

This struggle will rise to such a pitch that Satan will con - centrate the whole of his power and malice in some indi - vidual human being who will be called Antichrist.

Will Antichrist in a special way be the head of the wicked?

Yes, for there will be more malice in him than there ever was in any other man; he will be Satan's vicar, whose object will be to strive his utmost in order to lead men to damnation and so ruin the Kingdom of Jesus Christ (VIII. 8).

VII.—OF THE KNOWLEDGE OF CHRIST: OF HIS BEATIFIC KNOWLEDGE; OF HIS INFUSED KNOWLEDGE; AND OF HIS ACQUIRED KNOWLEDGE

(A)

Besides grace are there any other prerogatives belonging to our Lord?

Yes; they are those that have reference to knowledge (IX.–XII.).

What knowledge did Jesus Christ have as man?

It was threefold: the knowledge which the blessed have in heaven through the vision of the divine essence; infused knowledge which is the infusion of all ideas by God into the soul at its birth; and lastly, acquired knowledge which is gained in the ordinary way by the human faculties with the aid of the senses (IX. 2, 3, 4).

(B)

Was the beatific knowledge of Christ as man in a very high scale of perfection?

Yes; in perfection it surpasses that of all the blessed, whether angels or men. From the first instant of con ception, by the beatific knowledge Christ was able to see everything in the divine Word, which is Himself as God, in such wise that there is absolutely nothing in the past, present, or future which Christ as man does not know; and He had this knowledge from the moment of the Incarnation (X. 2-4).

(C)

Was Christ's infused knowledge in a high scale of per-fection?

Yes; for by this knowledge He knew all that which the

15

human mind can know by its natural power, and also what soever revelation can make known to a created intelligence whether it have reference to what can be known by the gift of wisdom or the gift of prophecy, or any other such gift of the Holy Ghost; and Christ had this knowledge in a supereminent degree above angels and men (XI. 1, 3, 4).

(D)

What sort of acquired knowledge did Christ have?

By this knowledge He knew whatsoever the human mind can know by reasoning upon the data given by the senses; in this knowledge it was possible for Him to make progress according as His human mind had occasion to reason about new data attained by His senses; but He never learnt from any master, having already acquired what a master was able to teach in the various stages of progress of His life (XII. 1-3).

Did Christ as man ever receive any knowledge from the angels?

No. The whole of our Lord's knowledge came to Him only in the three ways just explained (XII. 4).

VIII.—OF THE POWER OF OUR LORD JESUS CHRIST AS MAN

Are there any other prerogatives in the human nature of Christ besides the foregoing?

Yes, there are those that refer to His power (XIII.).

What power was in Christ's Soul?

All the power that is connatural to a human soul which is the substantial form of the body; further, all the power that can belong to a human soul in the order of grace in so far as out of its fulness it had to communicate grace to others dependent upon it. Further, in Christ's Soul there was the instrumental participation of the divine power through which the Word of God performed all the marvels of transformation that were in accord with the end of the Incarnation, which is to re-establish all things in heaven and earth according to the plan of restoration determined by God (XIII. 1-4).

IX.—OF THE DEFECTS OF CHRIST'S HUMAN NATURE; OF THOSE OF THE BODY· AND OF THOSE OF THE SOUL

(A)

Were there certain defects both in the Body and the Soul of Christ?

Yes; and such were necessary for the end of the Incarnation, which was to make satisfaction for our sins to come on earth as one of us—to be for us an example by the practice of the highest virtues of patience and immolation (XIV., XV.).

What were the defects Christ took upon Himself in His Body?

They were all those defects or miseries and infirmities which are to be found in the whole of human nature as a result of Adam's sin, such as hunger, thirst, death, and so on; but in Christ there were none of those defects that are the result of personal sin or of heredity (XIV. 1).

Was the Body of our Lord, putting aside the above-mentioned defects, of great perfection and beauty?

Yes, for such belonged to the dignity of the Word of God, who was hypostatically united to this Body; and such was due also to the action of the Holy Ghost, by whom this Body was formed directly in the womb of our Blessed Lady; but of this we shall speak shortly.

(B)

What were the defects Christ took upon Himself in His Soul?

They were the capability of feeling pain, especially the sufferings inflicted upon His Body during the course of His Passion; all the interior affective motions, whether of the sensitive or intellectual order; in other words, Christ had the passions such as sadness, fear, anger, etc., except that all these passions were in perfect accord with His reason to which they were always perfectly subjected (XV. 1-9).

(c)

Can it be said that whilst living on earth our Lord was both in heaven and yet on the way to heaven?

Yes; for as regards the function that is proper to the soul in heaven, this our Lord had, since He enjoyed fully this beatitude by the vision of the divine essence; but as regards the effect of this beatitude in His Body, this He had not as yet by a sort of miraculous suspension in view of our redemption; and this redundancy of the Soul's glory in the Body did not come about until after His Resurrection and Ascension into heaven (XV. 10).

X.—OF THE CONSEQUENCES OF THE INCARNATION OF THE SON OF GOD; AND OF THE MANNER OF EXPRESSING IN WORDS THE TRUTHS THEREOF

What follows from the Incarnation of the Son of God considered in Himself, and in what manner can we rightly express the truths concerning Him?

We may and must say in all truth, "God is man," for one and the same Person who is God is man also; "Man is God," for a Person who is truly man is a Person who is God; all that is proper to and belongs to human nature can be said of God, for all such belongs to a Person who is God, and all that is proper to the divine nature can be said of man who is the Son of God, for this man is a Person who is God.   But we may not say of the divinity what is said of the humanity, or conversely, because these two natures remain distinct and each has its own properties (XVI. 1, 2).

May one say " God was made man "?

Yes, because the Person who is God began to be truly man at a particular time before which It was not man (XVI. 6).

May one also say "Man was made God"?

No, for this presupposes that there was a person who was a man first of all without being God, and that after wards he became God (XVI. 7).

May one say "Christ is a creature"?

One may not say this altogether; but it may be said pro vided one adds, " by reason of the human nature which is united hypostatically to Him," for it is true that this human nature is something created (XVI. 8).

May one say " This man " meaning Jesus Christ, " began to exist "?

No, for the sense would be that the Person of God the Son began to exist. But it may be said provided one adds, " in so far as He is man," or " by reason of His human nature " (XVI. 9).

XI.—OF THE UNITY AND MULTIPLICITY IN JESUS CHRIST: AS REGARDS HIS BEING; AS REGARDS HIS WILL; AND AS REGARDS HIS OPERATIONS

(A)

Does Jesus Christ constitute only one being or several?

He is one being only, God and man together; and this by reason of the unity of Person which subsists in both the human and the divine natures (XVII. 1, 2).

May one speak of more than one will in Christ?

Yes; for in Him there is the divine will in so far as He is God; and the human will in so far as He is man (XVIII. 1).

Is there in Him as man a multiplicity of wills?

Yes, understanding the word "will" in a wide sense and in so far as it comprises the sensitive as well as the intel lective appetite; or again in so far as the word sometimes signifies different acts of these faculties (XVIII. 2, 3).

Had the human nature in Christ a free will?

Yes. Although it was absolutely impossible for Him to sin, His will being always and in every sense conformed to the divine will (XVIII. 4).

(B)

Is there a multiplicity of operations in Christ?

Yes. For although on the part of the Person or the principle to which all operations are attributed there is absolute and perfect unity, on the part of the immediate principles of operation there were as many different operations as there were principles or faculties of operating in His human nature; and, further, the diversity of actions proper to the divine nature and the diversity of those proper to the human nature (XIX. 1, 2).

(c)

In what sense does one speak of theandric operations in Christ, and what does this expression mean?

This expression means that since Jesus Christ is both God and man there is in Him a kind of subordination between all the principles of operation in Him, particu larly between those principles proper to the human nature and those proper to the divine; so that the human operations were divinely perfected and superexalted owing to the nearness and the influence of the divine nature; and, on the other hand, the divine operations in some sort were humanized by the concurrence of the human operations (XIX. 1, *Obj.* 1).

Were the human operations in Christ meritorious as regards Himself?

Yes. It was meet He should merit for Himself all that from which He was separated only temporarily, and such as was not contrary to the excellence and dignity which was His; as, for instance, the glory of the Body and all that referred to His external exaltation in heaven and on earth (XIX. 3).

(D)

Was Christ able to merit for others also?

Yes, and by merit that was perfect or *de condigno;* and this by reason of the mystical unity between Him and all the members of His Church of which He is the head; and this merit was of such a kind that all His actions were meritorious not only for Himself, but for all those who form part of His Church in general, according to the sense already explained (XIX. 4).

What is necessary that other men might share in the merit of our Lord?

They must be united to Him by the grace of baptism, which is the grace whereby they are incorporated into Christ's Church; but of this we shall speak later (XIX. 4, *Obj.* 3).

XII.—OF THE CONSEQUENCES OF THE INCAR NATION OF GOD THE SON IN RELATION TO HIS FATHER; OF HIS SUBJECTION TO THE FATHER; OF HIS PRAYER, AND OF HIS PRIESTHOOD

(A)

As a result of the Incarnation, what were the relations between Christ and God the Father, and conversely?

The consequences of the Incarnation were that Christ was subject to the Father; that He prayed; that He served God the Father by His priesthood; and that, although He was the Son of the Father by nature, not by adoption, He was predestined by the Father (XX.–XXIV.).

How was Christ subject to the Father?

He was subject to the Father by reason of His human nature because this had only participated goodness, where as the Father is goodness by essence; hence whatever was related to Christ's human life was ruled, disposed, and ordered by the Father.

In Christ there was the most perfect and absolute obedience in respect of the Father (XX. 1).

Was not the human part of Christ also entirely subject to Himself by reason of His divine nature?

Yes, for the divine nature, by reason of which the Father was superior to the Son in His human nature, is common to the Father and the Son (XX. 2).

(B)

In what sense was Christ able and is still able to pray?

In this sense, that the human will being incapable of attaining the fulfilment of its desires independently of the divine will, Christ as man had perforce to address the Father in order that the Father by His all-powerful will might accomplish what the human will was unable to realize of itself (XXI. 1).

Did Christ pray for Himself?

Yes; He prayed for the external glorification of His Body which He had not so long as He was on earth; also in order to give thanks to the Father for all the gifts and privileges bestowed upon His human nature; and in the latter way Christ will pray through all eternity (XXI. 3).

Whilst Christ was on earth were His prayers always heard?

Yes, if by prayer one understands a petition made deliberately by the will; for Christ, who knew perfectly the will of His Father, never wished anything deliberately except what He knew to be in conformity with His Father's will (XXI. 4).

(c)

What is meant by the priesthood of Christ?

By this is meant that it belonged to Him, *par excel lence*, to bring to men the gifts of God; and to stand before God in the name of men to offer their prayers to God to appease Him and to re-establish them in His favour (XXII. 1).

Was Christ both priest and victim?

Yes; because in accepting death for our sakes he became a victim in the threefold sense of sacrifice as established by the Old Law, viz., a victim of sin, a victim of peace, and a holocaust. He has, in fact, made satis faction for our sins and has blotted them out; He has obtained for us the grace of God which is our peace and salvation; and He has opened for us the gates of heaven (XXII. 2).

Did Christ need to be priest for His own sake?

No, for He Himself could approach God without need of a mediator; further, in Him there was no sin and hence no need of a victim of expiation (XXII. 4).

Will the priesthood of Christ last for ever?

Yes, in the sense that the effect of His priesthood which is the possession of heaven, will remain always, for the attainment of heaven by the blessed is the consummation of Christ's sacrifice (XXII. 5).

Why was Christ a priest according to the order of Melchisedech?

In order to show the superiority of this priesthood over the levitical priesthood of the Old Law, which was only a figure of the former (XXII. 6).

XIII.—OF CHRIST'S DIVINE SONSHIP; AND OF HIS PREDESTINATION

(A)

When one speaks of adoption on the part of God, what does it mean?

It means that God out of His infinite goodness has deigned to give to men a participation of the glory of His beatitude; both angels and men who participate in this glory become the sons or the children of God by adoption, since the second Person of the Blessed Trinity is the only son by nature (XXIII. 1).

Is Christ as regards His human nature also a Son of God by adoption?

No; for since sonship is a personal property, wherever there is natural sonship there cannot be sonship by adoption, which is only a figure of the former (XXIII. 4).

(B)

Was Jesus Christ predestined?

Yes; for predestination is nothing else but a pre ordination fixed by God from all eternity of what is ful filled in time in the order of grace. But that a human being was God in person and this being as man came from

God was realized in time; and such event belonged in the highest degree to the order of grace. Hence it is true that Jesus Christ was predestined by God (XXIV. 1).

Is this predestination of Christ the cause of our own predestination?

Yes, God ordained that our salvation should be accomplished by Jesus Christ Himself, who is the author thereof; further, by predestination we become by adoption what Jesus Christ is by nature (XXIV. 3, 4).

XIV.—OF THE CONSEQUENCES OF THE IN CARNATION IN RELATION TO US, VIZ., THAT WE MUST ADORE CHRIST; OF CHRIST AS THE MEDIATOR

(A)

What are the consequences of the Incarnation of God the Son in relation to us?

It follows that we must adore Jesus Christ, and that He is our Mediator (XXV.–XXVI.).

What is meant by saying that we must adore Jesus Christ?

This means that we must pay to the Person of God the Son, whether as God or as man, the worship that is proper to God alone, viz., *latria;* but if we consider the human nature of Christ as the reason of the honour we pay Him then we must pay to Him what is called *dulia* (XXV. 1, 2).

(B)

Must we adore the Sacred Heart of Jesus with the adoration of "latria"?

Yes, for the Sacred Heart is part of the Person of our Lord; and of all that belongs to the Person of our Lord in His human nature His Heart should be worshipped with the adoration of *latria* in an especial manner, because it is the symbol of His great love for us.

Must we honour with the adoration of " latria " the images and pictures of Christ?

Yes, because that movement whereby the soul is

drawn towards an image precisely as an image (that is, in so far as it represents something), is the same as that movement whereby the soul is drawn towards the thing represented (XXV. 3).

(c)

Must we also honour the cross of our Lord with the adoration of "latria"?

Yes, because for us it represents our Lord nailed upon the cross and dying for us; and if it be question of the true cross upon which our Lord was nailed we adore it for this other reason, viz., because it was touched by our Lord's Body, and was saturated with His Blood (XXV. 4).

(d)

Must we honour our Blessed Lady, the Mother of Jesus, with the adoration of "latria"?

No; for the reason why we honour her is not only because she is our Lord's Mother, but because of her own worth; but since she is a creature only we do not honour her with the adoration of *latria*, which is exclusively proper to God. We pay her, however, in a supereminent way an honour in the order of *dulia* that is due to those who are united to God; but since no other creature is so intimately united to God as she is we pay her that honour which is called *hyperdulia* (XXV. 5).

(e)

Must we honour the relics of the saints and especially their bodies?

Yes, because the saints are friends of God and our intercessors before Him; we honour their bodies in particular because they were temples of the Holy Ghost, and because they will be glorified after the Resurrection, at the last day (XXV. 6).

(f)

What is meant by saying that Jesus Christ is the Mediator between God and men?

By this is meant that by reason of the hypostatic union

between the human nature and God the Son, Christ is midway between God and men; owing to this it is proper to Him to communicate to men the commands and the gifts of God, standing before God in the name of men, in order to make satisfaction for their sins and to intercede for them (XXVI. 1, 2).

XV.—OF THE MANNER ACCORDING TO WHICH THE INCARNATION TOOK PLACE, AND OF CHRIST'S DOINGS IN THE WORLD

In what manner did the Incarnation of the Son of God take place, and what were the doings of Christ in the world?

The answer to this question will be given by consider ing four things: (1) The coming into the world of God the Son; (2) His life in the world; (3) His leaving the world; (4) His exaltation after leaving the world (XXVII., *Prologue*).

XVI.—OF CHRIST'S ENTRY INTO THE WORLD, VIZ., OF HIS BIRTH OF THE BLESSED MARY EVER A VIRGIN

(A)

How did Jesus Christ come into the world?

Jesus Christ came into the world by being born of the Blessed Virgin Mary by the all-powerful and supernatural action of the Holy Ghost.

Was our Blessed Lady prepared in any special manner that she might become the Mother of our Lord?

Yes, she was immaculately conceived (XXVII.).

What is understood by the Immaculate Conception?

By this is understood that unique privilege bestowed upon our Blessed Lady whereby God, in view of and owing to the foreseen merits of Jesus Christ, preserved her from all stain of original sin, which she would other wise have contracted as a descendant of Adam; and that from the first instant of creation our Lady's soul was adorned with the supernatural gifts of grace in their fulness (Pius IX., *Definition of the Dogma of the Imma culate Conception*).

(B)

What is meant by saying that Jesus Christ was born of the Virgin Mary?

By this is meant that the Mother of Jesus, far from losing her virginity by becoming our Lord's Mother, rendered her virginity holy and doubly pleasing in the sight of God by becoming the Mother of our Lord; and this in such wise that, being a virgin before the conception of our Lord, she remained a virgin in the conception and during the birth, and for ever after the birth of our Lord (XXVIII. 1, 2, 3).

Were this conception and birth wholly miraculous?

Yes, it was wholly supernatural and miraculous that our Blessed Lady conceived and gave birth to our Lord in this manner; it must be remembered also that our Lady performed for her babe all such as any other mother performs with regard to her child born in the natural way (XXXI. 5; XXXII.).

Did God the Son unite the human nature to Himself in the womb of Mary together with all the gifts of grace, of which we have spoken, in an instant?

Yes, as soon as our Lady consented on the day of the Annunciation to become the Mother of God, immediately and in an instant by the action of the Holy Ghost she con ceived in her virginal womb all the wonders that constitute the mystery of the Incarnation (XXXIII.–XXXIV.).

Must we say that from the first instant of conception our Lord had the use of His human free will, and that He began to merit already?

Yes, from the instant of His conception our Lord had in all their perfection both the beatific and infused knowledge of which we have already spoken; and He had the full use of His free will, and also began to merit by perfect merit such as is called *de condigno* (XXXIV. 1-3).

Was the birth of our Lord a true birth in the sense that His Person was born, and how is this birth distinguished from that according to which we say He was born of the Father?

When it is said that God the Son was born of our Lady, by this is meant that the birth was a true birth affecting the Person of God the Son; but this birth is only spoken of in reference to Christ's human nature; whereas with regard to the Father He was born from all eternity, and this birth has reference to His divine nature (CXXV. 1, 2).

(c)

Owing to our Lord's birth of our Blessed Lady is she His Mother?

Yes, in every sense, for all that a mother gives to a son was given by our Blessed Lady to God the Son (XXXV. 3).

Does it follow that Mary is the Mother of God?

Yes, since she was truly the mother of the human nature assumed by Him who is God (XXXV. 4).

XVII.—OF THE NAME JESUS CHRIST GIVEN TO GOD THE SON INCARNATE

When was the name Jesus given to God the Son Incarnate?

It was given to Him on the eighth day after His birth in accordance with the command given to Mary and to Joseph by an angel of God (XXXVII. 2).

What does the name Jesus signify?

It signifies His mission to men, namely, that He is the Saviour of all men.

Why is the name Christ added?

Because this word signifies "anointed," and our Lord received the divine anointing whereby He was Saint, Priest, and King (XXII. 1, *Obj.* 3).

XVIII.—OF THE BAPTISM OF JESUS CHRIST

Why was our Lord baptized with the baptism of St. John?

In order to begin His mission which was the work of our salvation; now this consists in the remission of sins which was to be effected by the baptism that He Himself was going to inaugurate. This new kind of baptism was to be given with water in the name of the Father, Son, and Holy Ghost; and all men had to receive this baptism, since all are sinners. For this reason, wishing to point out to all this necessity, He asked to receive the baptism of John, which was only a figure of the new baptism. He received this baptism in water in order to sanctify the water and so prepare it for the matter of the Sacrament. During His baptism the whole Trinity deigned to make Itself manifested—He Himself in His human nature, the Holy Ghost under the form of a dove, and the Father in the voice that was heard—in order to make known what would be the form of the Sacrament. He also made known the effect of this new baptism by the fact that the heavens opened above His head; this was to show that by His baptism the gates of heaven were opened for men (XXXIX. 1-8).

XIX.—OF OUR BLESSED LORD'S LIFE ON EARTH: OF HIS TEMPTATION; OF HIS PREACHING; OF HIS MIRACLES; AND OF HIS TRANSFIGURATION

What kind of life did our Lord lead among men?

He led a life of the utmost simplicity and poverty; further, He fulfilled all the commands of the Old Law in order to prepare the way for the New Law which was His own (XL. 1-4).

Why did our Lord suffer to be tempted?

In order that He might instruct us and show us how to resist our temptations; and also by His victory over Satan to make good the defeat of our first parents who succumbed to Satan's temptation in the Garden of Eden (XLI. 1).

Why did our Lord preach to others?

During the three years of His public life He en
deavoured by His preaching to make men listen to His
voice that they might hear the mysteries of the kingdom
of heaven (XLII. 1-4).

Why did our Lord perform miracles?

In order that He might show to men that He was
almighty and had power over spiritual creatures, over
the heavenly bodies, over the miseries of men, and over
inanimate things. By miracles He proved to men Who
He was, and gave them an infallible testimony of His
divinity (XLIII., XLIV.).

*Is there not a miracle of our Lord which is of special
importance by reason of its character and of the circum
stances in which it was performed?*

Yes; it is that of the Transfiguration (XLV.).

What was remarkable in this miracle?

This; that after having made known to His disciples
the mysteries of His Passion and Death on the Cross, and
telling them that all had to follow Him in the way of
sorrow, our Blessed Lord wished to show to the three
privileged ones, in His own Person, the glorious end to
which the way of sorrow would lead all who followed it
courageously. Since this is the culminating point of our
Lord's teaching His authority among men was proclaimed
in a solemn way; on the one hand, the Law personified in
Moses, and the prophets personified in Elias, gave homage
to Him; and on the other hand, the voice of the Father
Himself declared our Lord to be His well-beloved Son
and to be the one to whose voice men should listen
(XLV. 1-4).

*Why was the voice of the Father proclaiming the divine
sonship of Jesus Christ heard at the baptism and at the
Transfiguration of Jesus?*

Because the divine sonship of Jesus Christ is the reason
and the end of our sonship by adoption which begins with
the grace of baptism and ends with the glory of heaven
(XLV. 4, *Obj.* 2).

Of what did Moses and Elias speak with our Lord during the glory of the Transfiguration?

Of His Passion and Death, for St. Luke says (chap. ix., ver. 31): " And they spoke of His decease which He should accomplish in Jerusalem " (XLV. 3).

XX.—OF OUR BLESSED LORD'S LEAVING THIS WORLD: OF HIS PASSION AND HIS DEATH· OF HIS BURIAL

(A)

What does the consideration of our Lord's leaving the world entail?

It entails four things: the Passion, the death, the burial, and the descent into hell (XLVI.-LII.).

Why did our Lord suffer His Passion and death on the Cross?

First of all to obey His Father, who had thus determined in His divine plans; and because, knowing intimately these divine plans, He knew that the Passion was to be the masterpiece of the wisdom and love of God, whereby salvation was secured to men (XLVI. 1).

Did the sufferings of our Lord Jesus Christ surpass all other conceivable sufferings?

Yes, because the human nature of our Lord in its sensibility and sensitiveness was exquisite and the most perfect possible; and although in the heights of His soul He possessed and enjoyed for ever the beatific vision, no ray of this splendour was allowed to enter the darkness of His sufferings to bring light and consolation to Him; further, He bore all the sins of men upon His shoulders which His sufferings were to wipe out (XLVI. 5, 6).

(B)

In what manner did our Lord's Passion work out our salvation?

The Passion of our Lord considered as an instrument of the divinity was the " efficient cause " of our salvation, itself accomplishing our salvation: in so far as it was accepted by His human will it " merited " our salvation; in so far as it was suffering in the sensitive part of our Lord's human nature it worked our salvation by " satisfy ing " for the penalties merited by our sins; in so far as it delivered us from the bondage of sin and the devil, it " redeemed " us; and in so far as it brought grace to us and reconciled us to God it worked out our salvation by way of " sacrifice " (XLVIII. 1-4).

Is it proper to Jesus Christ alone to be the redeemer of the human race?

Yes; for the price of this redemption was the Passion and Death of our Lord offered to God the Father and to the whole Trinity in order that we might be delivered from sin and the devil. Although it must be remembered that the whole Trinity is the primary cause of our redemption, and that God the Son, as man, is the immediate cause thereof (XLVIII. 5).

Did our Lord's Passion deliver us from the bondage of Satan in any special way?

Yes, because it wiped out the sin which put us in the devil's power; it reconciled us with God, Whom we had offended; and it exhausted the tyranny of Satan in that through his malice Christ who was innocent was put to death (XLIX. 1-4).

Was the opening to men of the gates of heaven a special effect of the Passion?

Yes; for the twofold obstacle of original sin and of the personal sins of men shut the gates of heaven to the whole of the human race; and it was our Lord's Passion that took away these obstacles entirely (XLIX. 5)

(c)

Was it necessary that Christ should suffer the particular death that He actually suffered?

Yes; for it was according to the wisdom of the divine counsels and of His love for us that He suffered such a death. By His death we were delivered from the spiritual

death of sin and from the death which is inflicted on us as
a penalty of sin.   In dying for us our Lord conquered
death, and He made it possible for us to triumph over
death by not fearing it, knowing that we shall come to life
again (L. 1).

(D)

Why was our Lord buried after His death?

First of all to show to men that He was really dead;
secondly, to make us know by His resurrection from the
tomb that we also shall rise some day; and thirdly, to
teach us that by dying to sin we must set ourselves apart
from this sinful life and hide ourselves in Him (LI. 1).

XXI.—OF OUR LORD'S DESCENT INTO HELL

Why did our Lord descend into hell?

He descended into hell that He might deliver us from
the obligation of descending there; also to triumph over
Satan by liberating those who were detained there; and
lastly, in order to manifest His power in visiting the dark
ness of hell and shedding the rays of His splendour there
(LII. 1).

What is this hell to which Christ descended?

He descended to that part of hell which was for the
time being the dwelling-place of the just who, having no
further penalty to pay for their sins, were detained there
only by reason of the debt due to original sin.   Our Lord
descended there to give to the holy Patriarchs the joy of
His presence.   But even in the hell of the lost the effect
of His descent was felt confounding them for their
unbelief and for their malice.   In a special way His descent
was felt in purgatory consoling the souls detained there by
the hope of being admitted into the glory of heaven as soon
as they had expiated their sins (LII. 2).

How long did our Lord remain in hell?

As long as His body remained in the tomb (LII. 4).

When our Lord came up from hell did He bring the souls of the just with Him?

Yes; for as soon as He arrived among them He com municated to them immediately the glory of the beatific vision; and when our Lord's soul left hell in order to be reunited to His body at the moment of the resurrection, He brought with Him all the souls of the just who were never again separated from Him (LII. 5).

XXII.—OF THE EXALTATION OF JESUS CHRIST: OF HIS RESURRECTION

Was it necessary that our Lord should rise from the dead by a glorious resurrection?

Yes; this was necessary. For God had need of mani festing His justice towards Him who had been humiliated even to the death on the Cross. This supreme testimony to the divinity of our Lord was also necessary in order to confirm our faith; also to strengthen our hope; and lastly, in order to manifest in our Lord's Person the marvels of the glorious life to which He has destined us (LIII. 1).

What was our Lord's risen body like?

It was absolutely the same as that which was nailed to the Cross and was laid in the tomb; but in a state of glory with the qualities of impassibility, subtlety, agility, and clarity which derived from the fulness of the soul's per fection that was henceforth free to communicate to the body its own fulness of perfection (LIV. 1-3).

Did our Lord's body retain the marks of the wounds He received in the crucifixion?

Yes, this was necessary: He retained the marks of the wounds in His hands and feet and side; and this as a sign of His victory over death; also to convince His disciples of the truth of His resurrection; also that He might show them to His Father when interceding for us; and lastly, that He might confound His enemies at the day of judg ment (LIV. 4).

XXIII.—OF HIS ASCENSION; AND OF HIS AUTHORITY AT THE RIGHT HAND OF THE FATHER

Where is the Body of our Blessed Lord now?

It is now in heaven where our Lord ascended forty days after His resurrection (LVII. 1).

In what sense is it said that our Lord ascended into heaven and sitteth at the right hand of God the Father?

In this sense, that He now enjoys the eternal peace of the blessedness of the Father, and that with the Father He has now the same royal and judiciary power over all things, a privilege which belongs to Jesus Christ alone (LVII., LVIII.).

Why, and in what sense, is judiciary power attributed to Jesus Christ?

Because Jesus Christ, as God, is the Wisdom of the Father, and the act of judging is an act of wisdom and of truth; also because as man, Jesus Christ is a Divine Person; and because He has in His human nature the dignity of being the head of the whole Church, and consequently He is the head of all men who must be judged; further, because there resides in Him sanctifying grace in its fulness which makes Him capable of judging; and lastly, it is fitting that He who was judged unjustly should vindi cate the rights of divine justice (LIX. 1-4).

Did our Lord commence to use this prerogative from the time of His Ascension into heaven?

Yes; and there is nothing that happens in the world which is not the effect of His government as He sits at the right hand of the Father. It is our Lord Jesus Christ, as God and as man, who ordains all things, whether it be question of human beings or of inanimate creatures, of angels good or bad (LIX. 5).

Will this power of our Lord over all extend also to the final and supreme judgment on the last day?

Yes; it is only then that He will exercise His power in all its fulness and perfection. It is only then that we shall appreciate the wisdom of His government of all things which are subjected to His royal and judiciary power; and by His judgment of men at the last day, each will receive fully what is his due (LIX. 5).

Does our Lord exercise His authority over both men and angels in the same way?

No; for although the good angels have received from God the Son their eternal happiness, and the bad angels their damnation, neither have received their deserts from the Son of God as man but as God. Whereas all men have received from Him, as man, the wherewith to reach eternal happiness. Moreover, God the Son, in so far as He is man, will pronounce the last sentence which will send the lost to their eternal sufferings on the last day. But both good and bad angels for ever are subject to His authority as man first of all from the day of His Incarnation, and more so from the day of His Ascension, all that they do to help man or to tempt him comes under the power and authority of Jesus Christ; and the good angels for their services will receive from Him, even according as He is man, their reward, and the bad angels the chastisement due to their wickedness (LIX. 6).

XXIV.—OF THE SACRAMENTS OF JESUS CHRIST: OF THEIR NATURE AND NUMBER; OF THEIR NECESSITY; AND OF THEIR EFFICACY

(A)

In what way did our Lord give to men the fruit of the mysteries accomplished in His person with a view to their salvation?

By instituting the sacraments (LX., *Prologue*).

What is meant by the sacraments?

They are certain outward signs or acts accompanied by certain words, which signify and produce certain graces in the soul (LX.–LXIII.).

How many sacraments are there?

There are seven: Baptism, Confirmation, the Holy Eucharist, Penance, Extreme Unction, Holy Orders, and Matrimony (LXV. 1).

Is there any reason why our Lord instituted seven sacraments?

Yes. The reason is derived from the analogy between our spiritual life of grace and our natural corporal life. Our corporal life comprises two perfections according as one considers the life of the individual or the life of the society in which he lives. As regards the individual, his life is perfected both directly and indirectly: directly by the fact that he comes into life, that he is nourished and that he grows; indirectly by the fact that he recovers health if he has lost it, and is completely restored if he has been seriously ill. In like manner in the spiritual life of grace, there is a sacrament which gives us that life, and this is " Baptism "; there is another which makes us grow strong therein, and this is " Confirmation "; another which nourishes us in this life, and this is the " Holy Eucharist." If we have lost this life by sin after Baptism the sacrament of " Penance " gives us back this life; and " Extreme Unction " wipes out the last traces of sin. As regards the society in which this life is lived there are two sacraments that assure its well-being and its continuance: for the spiritual side of the society there is the sacrament of " Holy Orders"; and for its material and corporal side the sacrament of " Matrimony " (LXV. 1).

(B)

Which is the greatest and the most important of all these sacraments, and the one to which the rest are directed and whereby they are in some sort perfected?

It is the sacrament of the Holy Eucharist. For in this sacrament, as we shall see later, our Lord Himself is present substantially, whereas in all the other sacraments there is only a power or a virtue which comes from Him. Further all the other sacraments would seem to be directed to the Holy Eucharist, as Holy Orders which effect the sacrament; or as Baptism, Confirmation, Penance, and Extreme Unction, which make one worthy or more worthy to receive the Holy Eucharist; or as Marriage which signifies it, in so far as it is a union. Lastly, one ends other ceremonies that refer to the reception of the other sacraments, almost always, by the reception of the Holy Eucharist; even after Baptism, if the one baptized be an adult (LXV. 3).

(c)

Are the sacraments instituted by our Blessed Lord necessary for obtaining the grace which corresponds to each one in particular, or is the receiving of these sacraments of counsel only?

These sacraments are absolutely necessary, in this sense, that if through one's own fault one neglects to receive them, one will not receive the grace corresponding there to; and there are three of them which produce a certain effect such as can never come to be unless the sacrament be received (LXV. 4).

What are these three, and what is this certain effect dependent upon them?

They are Baptism, Confirmation, and Holy Orders; and the effect spoken of is the character which each of these sacraments impresses on the soul (LXIII. 6).

What is this character?

It is a certain quality of the spiritual order, constituting in the higher and intellectual part of the soul a sort of power or faculty which effects that he who receives it participates in the priesthood of Jesus Christ (LXIII. 1-4).

Is this character impressed on the soul indelible?

Yes, it will remain for ever once it is received, to the glory of those who reach heaven who have therefore shown themselves worthy to bear it; and to the confusion of those in hell who have misused it (LXIII. 5).

Which character marks men according to the likeness of our Lord and makes them able to participate in His priesthood?

The sacrament of Baptism (LXIII. 6).

XXV.—OF THE SACRAMENT OF BAPTISM: OF ITS NATURE; OF THE MINISTER OF THIS SACRAMENT

(A)

What is the sacrament of Baptism?

It consists in an ablution, made with natural water, during which are pronounced over the person being baptized, by the person administering the sacrament, these words: " I baptize thee, in the name of the Father, and of the Son, and of the Holy Ghost " (LXVI. 1-5).

Can the same person receive the sacrament of Baptism more than once?

No; this sacrament can be received only once, by reason of the indelible character impressed on the soul (LXVI. 9).

Can the Baptism of blood, or the Baptism of desire, take the place of the Baptism of water?

Yes, the Baptism of blood, which is martyrdom and figures the Passion of our Blessed Lord, and the Baptism of desire, which consists in an act of the love of God through the action of the Holy Ghost, can both take the place of the Baptism of water; but in this sense, that the grace of Baptism can be obtained without the reception of the sacrament itself when this reception is impossible; but not in the sense that the character of the sacrament can be received apart from the sacrament itself (LXVI. 11).

(B)

Who can administer the sacrament of Baptism?

It can be administered validly by every human being having the use of reason and performing the rite correctly with the intention of doing what the Church intends when the Church administers it (LXVII.).

For Baptism to be administered licitly what is required on the part of the person who administers it?

The person who administers Baptism must be in the conditions determined by the Catholic Church (LXVII.).

What are these conditions?

For Baptism to be administered licitly in the case when ordinary conditions are absent (in which ordinary conditions the priest himself administers it in conformity with the rules laid down by canon law and the ritual), or when in extraordinary circumstances it is administered by a deacon, there must be an urgent necessity for the administering thereof, that is there must be danger of death; and in such case anyone can licitly administer Baptism whether he be priest, or cleric, or layman, man or woman, or child who has attained the use of reason, or even a person who is himself not baptized, provided the correct rite be used and the person have the proper intention: always the order among the persons above mentioned should be followed, and it is only in the case of the absence of the preceding person that the following one may baptize (LXVII. 1-5).

(c)

Whenever Baptism is administered under normal condi tions in the Church, or whenever the ceremonies of Baptism have to be supplemented, must there always be a godfather or a godmother for the newly baptized?

Yes, the Church ordains this by virtue of an ancient custom; and because it is fitting that there should be someone whose duty it is to watch over the newly baptized and instruct him in the things of faith and to see that he is faithful to the promises made at Baptism (LXVII. 7).

The duty of godfather or godmother is not then simply a formality but is a grave and important matter?

Yes, there is a strict obligation on the part of god father or godmother to watch over their charge during life and to see that the things promised in Baptism are kept (LXVII. 8).

XXVI.—OF THOSE WHO CAN RECEIVE THE SACRAMENT OF BAPTISM; AND OF ITS NECESSITY FOR ALL

(A)

Are all men bound to receive Baptism?

Yes, they are absolutely bound to receive Baptism; for if an adult is able to receive it and yet does not, through his own fault, he cannot be saved. The reason is because by Baptism we are incorporated with Jesus Christ; but since Adam's sin no man can be saved unless he be incorporated with Jesus Christ (LXVIII. 1-2).

But do not faith and charity suffice to be incorporated with Jesus Christ by grace in order to be saved?

Without doubt, except that faith cannot be sincere, and charity or grace cannot be in the soul if a man separate them from Baptism through his own fault, for Baptism is the sacrament of faith and produces the first grace in the soul which unites us to Jesus Christ (LXVIII. 2).

Can then one receive Baptism in the state of sin, whether it be question of original sin which is the case for all or of personal grave sins in addition?

Yes; and for this reason Baptism is called the sacrament of the dead, for it does not presuppose grace in the soul as do the sacraments of the living; indeed its proper effect is to give the life of grace to those who have it not. If, however, it be question of adults who have committed mortal sins, in order for them to receive Baptism with fruit, they should renounce all affection for sin (LXVIII. 4).

(B)

In the case of adults must there be intention to receive Baptism?

Yes, otherwise the sacrament is null and void (LXVIII. 7).

Must they also have true faith?

Yes, if they would receive the grace of the sacrament;

but not if they would receive the sacrament itself and its character only (LXVIII. 8).

In the case of infants, who can have neither faith nor intention, can they be baptized?

Yes, for the Church or those who bring them for Baptism supply both faith and intention in their case (LXVIII. 9).

May one bring infants to Church for Baptism against the will of the parents when these parents are Jews or pagans?

No, one may not do this; and if one do this one commits sin, for to act thus is to run counter to the dictates of the natural law in virtue of which a child, until able to look after itself, is in the custody of its parents. But if the child in spite of the parents be baptized, the Baptism is valid; and the Church has over this child all the rights in the supernatural order which are the consequence of Baptism (LXVIII. 10).

(c)

May one baptize the babe that is in danger of death in the mother's womb?

No, for until the babe is born it is not part of the society of men, in such wise that it comes under their action as regards the reception of the sacraments; one should in such a case recommend the babe to God and leave it to His care (LXVIII. 11, *Obj.* 1).

Infants that are born and die, and who do not receive Baptism, will they be saved?

No, they cannot be saved; for there is only one means of being incorporated with Jesus Christ and of receiving His grace, without which there is no salvation among men (LXVIII. 3).

(D)

May one baptize adults who are deprived of the use of their reason, such as idiots and those that are mad?

If they have never had the use of reason they must be treated as infants, and consequently can be baptized. But if they have had the use of reason, they cannot be baptized whilst they are in the state of insanity unless they shall have manifested some desire to be baptized in the past when they were in their right mind (LXVIII. 12).

XXVII.—OF THE EFFECTS OF THE SACRAMENT OF BAPTISM

When Baptism is received in such wise that there be no obstacle to prevent its action, are there any great effects produced in the soul?

Yes; for it unites man to the Passion of Jesus Christ, the fruits of which enter man's soul. Further, no trace of sin is left in him who is baptized, and there is no obligation of making satisfaction for past sins. By right, all the penalties of the present life are taken away by Baptism; but God leaves these with man until the day of the resurrection in order that he might be likened to Jesus Christ, and might gain much merit and show that He came to receive Baptism not for any good of the present life, but with a view to the attainment of the eternal boons in heaven (LXIX. 1-3).

Does Baptism also produce grace and the virtues in the soul?

Yes, because he who is baptized is united to Jesus Christ as to the head, from Whom all the members participate in the fulness of His grace and virtue; more over there is received in a special way a grace of light for the knowledge of the truth, and a grace of the divine fecundity for the production of good works proper to the Christian life (LXIX. 4, 5).

Are these last effects of Baptism also produced in the souls of infants?

Yes, except that these effects are in a state of embryo, as it were, or in a habitual state waiting to manifest them selves actually (LXIX. 6).

Is the opening of the gates of heaven a proper effect of Baptism?

Yes, because no trace of sin is left, and there is no

penalty due to sin; for such are the only things that shut the gates of heaven since they were opened by the Passion of our Lord (LXIX. 7).

If an adult who is badly disposed were to receive Baptism, would he receive the above-mentioned effects?

No, he would receive only the character of Baptism; but by reason of this character which remains he can receive all the other effects as soon as he renounces his bad dispositions (LXIX. 9, 10).

Other than the effects proper to Baptism, are there certain effects attaching to the ceremonies of Baptism?

Yes, but they are of an entirely different order, and they are over and above the grace properly so-called of Baptism; they have reference rather to the removal of obstacles which might prevent one from receiving Baptism with all its fruits; and this is the reason why these ceremonies have not the nature of a sacrament but only the nature of a sacramental (LXXI. 3).

XXVIII.—OF THE DIGNITY AND OF THE DUTIES OF THOSE WHO HAVE RECEIVED THE SACRAMENT OF BAPTISM

Is there not a peculiar dignity, and certain duties conse quent thereon, attaching to those who have received the sacrament of Baptism with its indelible character?

Yes, for those who have received the grace of Baptism and carry in their soul for evermore the character thereof, according to the measure of their faithfulness to this grace, surpass in dignity and excellence the whole of creatures. They are children of God, and brothers of Jesus Christ; more, they are as it were a continuance of Jesus Christ Himself, who lives again in them. But so high a dignity demands that man lead a life of corresponding goodness, since he is united to Jesus Christ, who is the perfection of goodness.

XXIX.—OF THE SACRAMENT OF CONFIRMA TION; OF ITS NATURE AND NECESSITY; OF THE DUTIES IT IMPLIES; AND OF THE RELIGIOUS KNOWLEDGE NECESSARY FOR THE RECEPTION THEREOF

(A)

Is the grace of Baptism sufficient in order to lead the Christian life in its perfection? ·

No; for the grace of Baptism is as it were only the grace of commencing the Christian life; it gives the spiritual life of grace but it does not make us grow therein (LXV. 1; LXXII. 7, *Obj.* 1).

What are the other graces which have this effect?

They are the grace of Confirmation and the grace of the Holy Eucharist (LXV. 1).

What is Confirmation?

Confirmation is that sacrament of the New Law whereby we receive the grace which makes us grow in the life of Jesus Christ received by the grace of Baptism (LXXII. 1).

In what does this sacrament consist?

It consists in an anointing done in the form of a cross, upon the forehead of the person being confirmed, with the holy chrism, and at the same time the following words are pronounced by the minister of the sacrament: "I sign thee with the sign of the cross and I confirm thee with the chrism of salvation in the name of the Father and of the Son and of the Holy Ghost.   Amen " (LXXII. 2, 4, 9).

What does the holy chrism signify that is used as the matter of this sacrament?

It signifies the fulness of the grace of the Holy Spirit which leads the Christian through life and makes him spread around as it were the perfume of the Christian virtues.   Indeed, the holy chrism is made of olive oil, which symbolizes grace, and the odoriferous plant of balsam (LXXII. 2).

What do the words pronounced by the minister, which are the form of this sacrament, mean?

They mean three things: The source or the cause whence is derived the spiritual strength which is the effect of this sacrament; this cause or source is the august Trinity. They mean also the strength itself conferred by the sacrament when these words are said: " I confirm thee with the chrism of salvation." Lastly, they signify the distinctive mark of a soldier of Christ, armed for the combats encountered in the Christian life; and this mark is the sign of the cross which is the instrument of triumph of our Lord and King Jesus Christ (LXXII. 4).

Confirmation then is, properly speaking, the sacrament of Christian manhood making the child into a man capable of withstanding all the enemies of his life as a Christian?

The sacrament of Confirmation is precisely this; and for this reason its ordinary minister is a bishop to whom it belongs officially to promote perfection in the Church of God (LXXII. 11).

Why is a godfather or a godmother given to those who are confirmed?

Because it is the custom to give instructors to those newly enrolled in an army (LXXII. 10).

(B)

Does the sacrament of Confirmation impress a character?

Yes; and for this reason it can be received only once (LXXII. 5).

If at the reception of Confirmation one is not in the proper conditions in order to receive its fruits, is it possible afterwards, by putting oneself in the proper conditions, to receive these fruits?

Yes; for the character remains and the fruits will come as soon as the obstacles are removed. For this reason it is a good thing to make the grace of this sacrament re-live in us.

Is it necessary for the reception of this sacrament that one be well instructed in the things of faith and in the Christian life?

Yes; and this not only to live a good life oneself, but to be able to defend the true Christian life against all who attack it (LXXII. 4, *Obj.* 3).

XXX.—WHICH OF THE TWO SACRAMENTS REQUIRES THE BETTER INSTRUC TION: CONFIRMATION OR THE HOLY EUCHARIST?

Does not the sacrament of the Holy Eucharist demand a great deal of instruction before one may receive it?

Yes, a great deal of religious instruction is required for the reception of the Holy Eucharist. As regards the degree of instruction required it often happens that the sacrament of the Holy Eucharist is received before that of Confirmation, and in this case not so much instruction is required for the reception of the Holy Eucharist; but for Confirmation the subject should be instructed in things religious, not only to suffice for his own individual life but also to be able to defend them against those who attack them. But during the whole of one's life one should continually seek instruction in these mysteries.

XXXI.—OF THE SACRAMENT OF THE HOLY EUCHARIST

(A)

What is the sacrament of the Holy Eucharist?

It is that mysterious repast in which, after the conse cration (which makes Jesus Christ to be really present in the same state, under the sacramental form, as the victim immolated on Calvary), the body of our Lord Jesus Christ is given to be eaten, and His blood to be drunk, under the species or accidents of bread and wine (LXXIII.-LXXXIII.).

Is this sacrament necessary for salvation?

Yes; for it signifies the unity of the Church, which is the mystical body of Christ, to which everybody who would be saved must belong. But the fruit of the sacrament of the Eucharist can be enjoyed by anyone who has the intention of receiving the sacrament, whether he himself personally have this intention or whether the Church communicate it to him by the reception of baptism as is the case with infants (LXXIII. 3).

By what names is this sacrament called?

In so far as it is a commemoration of our Lord's sacrifice on the Cross it is called a " sacrifice "; in so far as it signifies the unity of the Church, the mystical body of Christ, it is called " communion "; in so far as it fore shadows the glory of future happiness, it is called " viaticum "; and it is called the " Eucharist," which means the " good grace," because it contains Jesus Christ Himself, who is the author of all grace (LXXIII. 4).

(B)

When was this sacrament instituted?

It was instituted on the evening of Holy Thursday on the eve of our Lord's Passion: in order to console men after the departure of our Lord from this world; in order to show the relation of this sacrament with the Passion of our Lord, who is the only source of our salvation; and in order that by reason of circumstances so memorable the cult of this sacrament might be more practised among men (LXXIII. 5).

Was there any special type or figure of this sacrament in the Old Law?

Yes; in so far as it is an outward sign it was prefigured by the bread and wine offered up by Melchisedech. In so far as it is a sacrament containing the true body of our Lord immolated on the Cross, it was prefigured by all the sacrifices of the Old Testament, and especially by the sacrifice of expiation, which was the most solemn. In so far as it is a spiritual nourishment feeding our souls, it was figured by the manna which contained every flavour and

every sweetness.   But it was prefigured in an exceptional
way by the paschal lamb which was eaten with unleavened
bread after it had been sacrificed, and whose blood turned
away the avenging angel (LXXIII. 6).

XXXII.—OF THE MATTER AND FORM OF THE SACRAMENT OF THE HOLY EUCHARIST; OF TRANSUBSTANTIATION, AND OF THE REAL PRESENCE; OF THE ACCIDENTS OF THE HOLY EUCHARIST

(A)

What is the matter of the sacrament of the Holy Eucharist?
The matter of this sacrament is wheaten bread and
wine of the vine (LXXIV. 1, 2).
What happens to the matter of this sacrament?
The substance of the bread ceases to be that of bread, and
the substance of wine ceases to be that of wine (LXXV. 2).
*What becomes of the substance of the bread and of the
substance of the wine?*
The substance of the bread is changed into the body of
Jesus Christ; and the substance of the wine into His
blood (LXXV. 3, 4).
What is this change called?
It is called " transubstantiation " (LXXV. 4).
*By what means does this change or transubstantiation
take place?*
By the almighty power of God alone (LXXV. 4).
*Is only the substance changed or is all changed in the
bread and wine?*
Only the substance is changed, for the accidents of
bread and those of wine remain (LXXV. 2, *Obj.* 3).

(B)

What is meant by the accidents that remain?
By the accidents are meant those external realities
which are perceived by our senses—such as quantity,

colour, taste, etc.; these alone remain, and they are the
same as those which existed in the bread and wine before
transubstantiation took place.

Why do these accidents remain?

In order that we might be assured of the sacramental
presence of the body and blood of Jesus Christ.

*Are the body and blood of our Lord, such as they are in
themselves, here truly present by virtue of transubstantiation?*

Yes, absolutely (LXXV. 1).

(c)

Is the whole of our Blessed Lord in the sacrament?

Yes; except that under the species of bread His body
only is present by virtue of the words of consecration, and
under the species of wine His blood only; but by con
comitance, and because now the body and the blood of
Jesus Christ are no longer and cannot again be separated
(as they were when our Lord died on the Cross), wherever
is His body there also is His blood and His soul; and
wherever is His blood, there also is His body and His soul.
As regards the Person and the Divinity of the Son of God,
these had never been separated since the Incarnation
from any single part of the human nature of Jesus Christ,
not even when the body and soul of our Lord were
separated by His death on the Cross (LXXVI. 1, 2).

*Is our Lord wholly present under each part of bread and
under each drop of wine?*

Yes; He is wholly present, entirely, such as He is in
Himself under each part of bread and under each drop of
wine; but as long as the bread or wine remain undivided
He is present there only once, but according as the bread
or wine is divided into parts, He is present wholly under
each part (LXXVI. 3).

(D)

*Can one touch the body of Jesus Christ in itself by touching
the accidents of bread and wine?*

No; because the accidents are not accidents of our
Lord's body but of bread and wine only (LXXV. 4-8).

Do these eucharistic accidents always remain in the state of eucharistic accidents after the consecration of the bread and wine?

No; for immediately after the communion when they are consumed they begin to alter and pass into another state. They can also alter and become corrupt through atmospheric conditions when they are left for too long a time (LXXVII. 4).

What happens when the eucharistic accidents of bread and wine cease to be accidents of the bread and wine which were consecrated?

Immediately the body and the blood of our Lord ceases to be present (LXXVI. 6, *Obj.* 3).

It is then only by reason of the consecration of the bread and wine and of the permanency of the accidents that Jesus Christ is present eucharistically?

Yes (LXXVI. 6, *Obj.* 3).

How does the consecration of the bread and wine come about?

By the pronunciation, given the proper conditions, of the following words:—For the bread: "This is My Body." For the wine: "This is the chalice of My Blood, of the New and Eternal Testament, mystery of faith, which for you and for many was shed unto the remission of sins."

XXXIII.—OF THE EFFECTS OF THE SACRAMENT OF THE HOLY EUCHARIST

(A)

Are there any special effects of the sacrament of the Holy Eucharist?

Yes, the Holy Eucharist produces in the soul the treasures of grace that are ordained to man's salvation.

Whence is derived this efficacy of the Holy Eucharist?

This efficacy is derived principally from the fact that it contains really and truly the presence of Jesus Christ Himself, who is the author of all grace that leads to salvation. It is derived also from this, that it is the sacrament of the Passion of our Lord which is the cause of our salvation. It is derived also from the particular way in which we participate in the sacrament by receiving the body and blood of our Lord as nourishment. Lastly, it is derived from the fact that it represents the unity of the mystical body of Christ (LXXIX. 1).

Is it owing to these causes that the attainment of heaven is a special effect of this sacrament?

Yes, because Jesus Christ died that we might reach heaven; and the Holy Eucharist is a figure of heaven's banquet (LXXIX. 2).

(B)

Is the remission of mortal sin an effect of the sacrament of the Holy Eucharist?

There is no doubt that this sacrament has the virtue to remit all mortal sins, since it contains Jesus Christ Himself; but since our Lord is in this sacrament under the form of spiritual food and since food is given only to the living, if anyone receive this sacrament in the state of mortal sin he cannot receive the effect of the sacrament. But if anyone approaches this sacrament believing in good faith that he is in the state of grace, whereas he is not, then the Holy Eucharist will blot out the sin (LXXIX. 3).

(C)

Does this sacrament remit venial sin?

Yes, for it is a food which restores and refreshes the soul; and it compensates for little defects of the love of God which every venial sin implies (LXXIX. 4).

(D)

Does this sacrament remit all punishment due to sin?

As a sacrament its direct effect is not to remit the punishment due to sin but to restore spiritually by a renewal of fervour which unites the soul to our Lord. But by concomitance and by reason of the fervour of love it produces, indirectly it remits the punishment due to sin, not in its entirety, but according to the degree of fervour and devotion which is caused in the soul. As a sacrifice in so far as the victim of Calvary is offered to God this sacrament has the power of expiation; but this depends upon the amount of devotion with which one offers the Victim to God. This is the reason why even as a sacrifice, although it is of infinite value, its effect is not to remit all punishment due to sin but only to do so according to the measure of one's fervour and devotion (LXXIX. 5).

(E)

Does this sacrament preserve man from future sin?

Yes; and this is one of its direct and most wonderful effects, for it fortifies man interiorly against all that might endanger his life as a Christian. As the sacrament of the Passion of Jesus Christ, it is a sign that puts to flight the devils who were conquered by the Passion (LXXIX. 6).

(F)

Has this sacrament any effect upon others apart from those who receive it?

Considered as a sacrament that refreshes the soul spiritually it has an effect upon him only who receives it. But as a sacrament of the Passion of Jesus Christ as a sacrifice it can have an effect upon those for whom it is offered up according as they are in the state to receive the fruit thereof (LXXIX. 7).

(G)

Do venial sins impede the effect of this sacrament?

If venial sin is committed at the moment of receiving the sacrament, for instance if one is wilfully distracted, or the heart is occupied with other things, there is an effect of the sacrament which is necessarily impeded; and it is that spiritual sweetness, all divine, attaching to the reception of the sacrament. But there is always a certain increase of habitual grace produced in the soul. If, however, it be question of past venial sins, there is no impediment whatsoever to any effect of the sacrament provided one approaches it with the proper fervour and devotion (LXXIX. 1).

XXXIV.—OF THE RECEPTION OF THE SACRAMENT OF THE HOLY EUCHARIST

(A)

Are there divers ways of receiving this sacrament?

Yes, one can receive it spiritually or sacramentally (LXXX. 1).

What difference is there between these two ways?

This difference: those who receive the Holy Eucharist sacramentally only do not receive its effects; whereas those who receive it spiritually receive the effects thereof, whether this be by reason of the desire which moves them, or by reason of the actual reception of the sacrament which carries with it always the fulness of the sacrament's effect (LXXX. 1).

Can only man receive this sacrament spiritually?

Yes, because only man can believe in Jesus Christ, having the desire to receive Him as He is in this sacrament (LXXX. 2).

Can this sacrament be received sacramentally by sinners?

Yes, sinners who have the faith and who know what is the sacrament of the Holy Eucharist can receive it sacramentally whatever sins they may have on their conscience (LXXX. 3).

Does the sinner who receives this sacrament with the consciousness of his sins commit a sin in receiving this sacrament?

Yes; he commits a sacrilege, because by receiving this sacrament which contains Jesus Christ Himself, and which signifies the unity of Christ's mystic body which cannot exist except by faith and charity, he violates this sacrament, because without charity he endeavours to unite Jesus Christ to himself; and it is only charity which unites Jesus Christ to His members (LXXX. 4).

Is this sin especially grave?

Yes, because it insults the sacred humanity of Jesus Christ in the sacrament of His love (LXXX. 5).

Is this sin as grave as the external profanation of this sacrament?

No; for this latter sin implies the direct intention of insulting Jesus Christ in His sacrament, which is a sin of greater gravity (LXXX. 5, *Obj.* 3).

What is necessary in order to receive, as it behoves, this sacrament sacramentally?

First of all the use of reason, and the state of grace, and also the desire to gather the fruits of the spiritual life attaching to the reception of the sacrament (LXXX. 9, 10).

(B)

May one dispense altogether with the reception of the Holy Eucharist sacramentally?

No, unless there is no possibility of receiving it; and the reason is because no one can be saved without the grace of this sacrament; but it is impossible to have the grace of this sacrament unless one has at least the desire to receive it sacramentally as soon as occasion offers (LXXX. 11).

Are there certain times fixed by the Church when one is bound to receive this sacrament sacramentally?

Yes; and these times are for every man as soon as he has attained the age of reason and is sufficiently instructed in the nature of this sacrament; and during life at least once a year, during paschal time; and lastly, when one is in danger of death, when the sacrament is received under the form of the viaticum (*Code*, Canons 854, 859, 864).

(C)

May one receive the Holy Eucharist sacramentally every day?

Yes, provided the conditions aforementioned are kept, so as to receive it in a fitting manner '(LXXX. 10).

Is one bound to receive the Holy Eucharist sacramentally under both species of bread and wine?

Only priests at the altar in the celebration of the Mass are bound to receive the sacrament sacramentally under both species of bread and wine. As to the faithful they must conform themselves to what the Church has deter mined; and in fact in the Latin Church it is received by them under the species of bread only (LXXX. 12).

(D)

Must one receive this sacrament fasting?

Yes, one must fast from the previous midnight (LXXX. 12).

May one ever receive sacramentally the Holy Eucharist without fasting?

Yes, there are certain occasions when the fast is not obligatory; for instance, in order to prevent the sacred species from being profaned. But apart from this case, one may receive the Holy Eucharist under the form of the viaticum when in danger of death. As regards those who are sick and who have been obliged to keep their beds for a month, and for whom there is no hope of immediate recovery, these may receive the Holy Eucharist once or twice a week even though they may on the same morning have already taken medicine or even food provided it is taken in a liquid form (*Code*, Canon 858).

XXXV.—OF THE MINISTER OF THE SACRAMENT OF THE HOLY EUCHARIST

(A)

Whose duty is it exclusively to consecrate the Holy Eucharist?

It is the duty of the priest exclusively, who has been validly ordained according to the rite of the Catholic Church (LXXXII. 1).

Is it also the priest's duty to dispense this sacrament?

Yes. But a deacon has the power to dispense the

precious blood in a chalice on those occasions when the Church permits communion under both species; he is also able in case of need and in extraordinary circum stances to dispense communion under the species of bread (LXXXII. 3).

Can a priest who is in the state of mortal sin consecrate and dispense this sacrament?

He can do so validly, but he sins gravely in doing so (LXXXII. 5).

Has the Mass of a bad priest the same value as that of a good priest?

The value of the Mass is absolutely the same in either case in so far as it is of the sacrament of Christ's Passion. But as regards the prayers said during the Mass, those of the good priest have an efficacy such as those of the bad priest have not. But all these prayers have the same efficacy on the part of the Church in whose name they are said (LXXXII. 6).

(B)

Can an heretical, or schismatical, or excommunicated priest consecrate the sacrament of the Holy Eucharist?

He cannot do so licitly, but he can do so validly, for he is truly a priest; and provided he does so with the inten tion of doing what the Church intends in the celebration of this sacrament (LXXXII. 7).

Can a priest who has been defrocked validly consecrate?

Yes, because this degradation does not take away the character of the sacrament of Holy Orders, which is indelible (LXXXII. 8).

Can one without sinning hear the Mass of an heretical, schismatical, excommunicated, or of a notoriously unworthy priest, and receive communion from him?

It is absolutely forbidden under penalty of grave sin to hear the Mass of such a priest; or even of a notoriously bad and unworthy priest if by a public sentence the Church has deprived him of the right to celebrate; but otherwise one can hear his Mass and receive communion from him without sinning (LXXXII. 9).

XXXVI.—OF THE HOLY SACRIFICE OF THE MASS

What is meant by the celebration of the sacrament of the Holy Eucharist or of the Holy Sacrifice of the Mass?

It means that the act whereby this sacrament is confected constitutes a veritable sacrifice in the sense that it is an immolation according to the rite existing in the Catholic Church (LXXXIII. 1).

In what does this act consist?

In an immolation of the only Victim that is pleasing to God, namely of Jesus Christ Himself.

How is this act an immolation of Jesus Christ?

Because it is the sacrament of the Passion by which Jesus Christ was immolated on Calvary (LXXXII. 1).

What is meant by saying this?

By this is meant that just as on Calvary at the moment when Jesus Christ gave His life for the expiation of our sins His Body and His Blood were separated, so the act by which this sacrament is confected separates sacramentally the Body of Jesus Christ from His Blood; and this by the fact that there is a separate consecration for the species of bread and a separate consecration for the species of wine.

What follows from this?

It follows that the sacrifice of the Mass is the same as the sacrifice on the cross.

Is it a reproduction of the sacrifice on the cross?

Properly speaking, no; because the sacrifice of the cross took place only once; on the other hand, the Mass is not a reproduction of this sacrifice, it is the sacrifice itself.

May one say it is a representation of the sacrifice on the cross?

Yes, if by this one means that the Mass makes that sacrifice present for us; but it would be incorrect if one meant to say that it was only an image or a likeness thereof, for it is the sacrifice itself.

But how can it be the sacrifice itself since that sacrifice exists no longer, and, further, in the sacrifice on the cross Christ died, whereas now He can die no more?

In this sacrament there is truly the sacrifice on the cross as there is Jesus Christ Himself. For just as Jesus Christ is here present in Himself but under another form, since He is here under the species of the sacrament, in the same way the Passion and the immolation of Jesus Christ which took place on Calvary is here, not indeed under the same violent form but under the form of a sacrament: in such wise that under this sacrament there is in the same state of separation, which constitutes the immolation of the Victim, the same Body and the same Blood of Jesus Christ which were really separated on Calvary.

When one assists at the celebration of this sacrament, is it as if one assisted at the immolation of Jesus Christ on Calvary?

Yes; and we cannot perform an act of religion more pleasing to God, since it honours and glorifies Him above all else.

Is it for this reason that the Church desires we should assist as often as possible at the Holy Sacrifice of the Mass?

Yes; and the Church has even determined that on Sundays and certain feast days it is obligatory to hear mass (*Code*, Canon 1248).

Does one sin gravely unless one attends Mass on these days fixed by the Church?

Yes; unless one is absolutely impeded from being present.

What must one do in order to fulfil the obligation of assisting at Mass on the days aforementioned?

One must be present in the place where it is celebrated, and one must not do anything which is incompatible with so august a sacrifice; moreover, one must not be absent from its principal parts.

What are these principal parts of the Mass?

They come between the offertory and the communion inclusively.

What is the best way to hear Mass?

It is to be united with the priest, following him from part to part so as to pay attention to all that is said and done during the Mass.

XXXVII.—OF THE SACRAMENT OF PENANCE: OF ITS NATURE AND VIRTUE

(A)

What is meant by the sacrament of Penance?

It is that holy rite which gives back to men the life of grace which Jesus Christ gave them at baptism; and this by communicating to them again the fruit of His Passion if they have had the misfortune to lose it by sin (LXXXIV. 1).

In what does the sacrament of Penance consist?

It consists in certain acts and words, which show on the one hand that the sinner has quitted his sin, and on the other hand that God has remitted the sin by the ministry of the priest (LXXXIV. 2, 3).

Is this sacrament of particular importance to man, and one for which man ought to be especially grateful to our Lord, who instituted it?

Yes, of a truth; for owing to the fragility of our fallen human nature, even after having received the grace of Baptism, which brings the supernatural life to man, it is possible for him to lose this grace; and if Jesus Christ had not instituted this sacrament of Penance, man would have had no external sacramental means of getting back his life of grace (LXXXIV. 6).

If after having received this sacrament, man falls again into sin, can he receive it again?

Yes; for Jesus Christ in His infinite mercy towards the sinner has fixed no limit to the number of times one may receive this sacrament, which carries with it always remission and pardon of sin, the only condition being that man should be truly repentant (LXXXIV. 10).

(B)

Is there any special virtue which corresponds to this sacrament?

Yes, it is the virtue of penitence (LXXXV.).

In what does the virtue of penitence consist?

It is a quality of the supernatural order which inclines man's will when he has had the misfortune to offend Almighty God, to make good this offence by making satisfaction spontaneously to the Justice of God in order to obtain from Him pardon of the sin (LXXXV. 1, 5).

Does this virtue of penitence presuppose the concurrence of the other virtues?

It implies the concurrence of the other virtues. For it implies faith in the Passion of Jesus Christ, which is the cause of the remission of sins; it implies also the hope of pardon and the hatred of sins in so far as they are opposed to the love of God, and this presupposes charity. Further, since it is a moral virtue it presupposes the virtue of prudence. On the other hand, since it is a species of the virtue of justice, whose object is to obtain pardon of God by making voluntary satisfaction for an offence, it has to make use of the virtue of temperance by abstaining from what brings pleasure, and of the virtue of fortitude when it takes upon itself things that are hard and difficult, or when it supports them (LXXXV. 3, Obj. 4).

What is the object in view of the virtue of penitence in its act of compensation?

It is the appeasing of our sovereign Lord and Master, who has been justly offended by our sin; it is to come once more into the good graces of the best of Fathers whose love has been wounded (LXXXV. 3).

The act of the virtue of penitence is then something of great import, and one cannot renew it too often if one has offended God?

In some sort this act ought to be uninterrupted in so far as it implies an interior sorrow for having offended

God; and as regards exterior acts of satisfaction, it is true there is a limit beyond which one is not bound to go; but if one has reason to think that his satisfaction is imperfect, it is to his interest to do his best in order to be entirely quit of debt towards God. It should also be remembered that in practising the virtue of penitence, one practises all the other Christian virtues (LXXXIV. 8, 9).

XXXVIII.—OF THE EFFECTS OF THE SACRAMENT OF PENANCE

(A)

Is the proper effect of this sacrament to remit sins?

Yes, provided one receives it with true sorrow in the heart (LXXXVI. 1).

What sins does the sacrament of Penance remit?

It remits all sins that a man can have on his conscience and that come under the power of the keys as having been committed after baptism (LXXXVI. 1).

Can these sins be remitted without the sacrament of Penance?

If it is a question of mortal sins, these can never be remitted unless the sinner have the will, at least implicit, of submitting them to the power of the keys by the recep tion of the sacrament as soon as he is able to do so; but as regards venial sins, if the person is in a state of grace a fervent act of the love of God suffices without having recourse to the sacrament (LXXXVI. 2).

Does it follow then that only those who have mortal sins on their conscience have need of this sacrament?

No; for although the sacrament is necessary for them, it is of great help to those in a state of grace; first of all in order to purify them the more from past sins if per chance any of their past sins were mortal; and also to purify them from venial sins, and to strengthen them against future venial sin by an increase of grace (LXXXVII. 2, *Obj.* 2, 3).

If by the sacrament of Penance man has received pardon for his sins, and he should fall again into the same grave sins, is his state worse by reason of this second and perhaps repeated fall?

Yes, his sin and his state of soul is worse; not that his past sins which were remitted are imputed to him again by God, but by reason of his ingratitude and despisal of the great goodness of God (LXXXVIII. 1, 2).

Is this contempt and this ingratitude another sin added to his fall?

Not unless he has, in falling again, the direct intention of contemning the goodness of God; but his repeated fall is a circumstance which aggravates the gravity of the new sin (LXXXVIII. 4).

Is it then certain that by confession God pardons sins, and that once pardoned they are never imputed again to him who committed them?

Yes, this is absolutely certain (LXXXVIII. 1).

(B)

As regards the good in the soul which sin destroys, does the sacrament of Penance by its power make that good to re-live?

Yes, most certainly; the virtue of this sacrament makes that good which was destroyed by sin to re-live; and in such wise that if it be question of an essential good, which is grace, and the right to the vision of God which one loses by grave sin, both grace and this right to heaven is given back when one receives this sacrament in good dispositions. If these dispositions fall short in fervour of one's former dispositions, the essential good is in a measure lessened somewhat; but the whole of former merits re-live and one will receive proportionate recompense for them in heaven (LXXXIX. 1-4, 5, *Obj.* 3).

It is then important to receive the sacrament of Penance in the best possible dispositions?

Yes, for the effect of the sacrament is proportioned to the dispositions of him who receives it.

XXXIX.—OF THE PART OF THE PENITENT IN THE SACRAMENT OF PENANCE; OF CONTRITION, CONFESSION, AND SATIS FACTION

(A)

Has the penitent a part in the effect of this sacrament?

Yes, because the acts he performs are part of the sacrament itself (XC. 1).

In what way do the acts of the penitent form a part of this sacrament?

The acts of the penitent make part of the sacrament of Penance, because in this sacrament the acts of the minister give the form whilst those of the penitent constitute the matter (XC. 1).

What are these acts of the penitent which constitute the matter of this sacrament?

They are contrition, confession, and satisfaction (XC. 2).

Why are these three acts required as the matter of the sacrament of Penance?

Because it is the sacrament of reconciliation between a sinner and God. But in a reconciliation of this nature, the sinner must give to God some compensation which is pleasing to Him in such wise that the sin is pardoned and its effect blotted out. For this three things are necessary: (1) That the sinner have the will to offer that compensation such as it pleases God to determine; (2) that he come to the priest who stands in the place of God to receive the conditions of this compensation; (3) that he offer the compensation and acquit himself thereof faithfully. These three things are fulfilled by contrition, confession, and satisfaction (XC. 2).

Can the sacrament of Penance exist without one or other of these parts?

It cannot exist without a certain exterior manifestation of these different parts; but it can exist without the interior reality of contrition or without the fulfilling of the satisfaction; but in either case the virtue of the sacrament is hindered or paralyzed (XC. 3).

(B)

What is meant by contrition?

It is that sorrow, of the supernatural order, which the sinner has in thinking of the sins he has committed; thereon he resolves to go to the priest, the minister of God, in order to confess them and to receive some penalty in satisfaction which he resolves to perform faithfully (*Supplement,* I. 1).

What is necessary for this sorrow to be supernatural?

In order to be supernatural it is necessary for this sorrow to be caused by some motive which refers to the order of grace; this motive may commence with the fear of punishment with which, as one knows by faith, God threatens the sinner; so with the hope of obtaining pardon one does penance, whereby one comes to detest the sin in itself which threatens death to the soul, or at least in so far as it is contrary to one's supernatural good and perfect life, and above all, by reason that it offends God, the supreme object of our love (I. 1, 2).

If one detest sin for the sole reason of the punishment which God will inflict for sin either in this life or the next, would one have contrition?

No, for to have contrition it is necessary to detest sin because of the evil it does the soul; this evil is the loss of God, who can be possessed by us in this life through grace, and in the next life by glory (I. 2).

What then is that sorrow called which consists in detesting sin only because of the fear of punishment?

It is called attrition (I. 2, *Obj.* 2).

What then is the precise difference between attrition and contrition?

The first is sorrow for sin caused by a motive of servile fear; whereas contrition is caused by a motive of filial fear or of the pure love of God (I. 2).

Does attrition suffice in order to obtain pardon of one's sins in the sacrament of Penance?

With attrition one may approach the sacrament of Penance; at the moment, however, of receiving the grace of the sacrament by the absolution of the priest, this attrition is succeeded in the soul by contrition (I. 3; X. 1; XVIII. 1).

Must contrition be directed to all sins committed?

Yes, and in particular at the beginning of the move ment of sorrow for sins, especially if the sins be mortal; but at the end of this movement of sorrow it is sufficient that sorrow be directed in a general way towards the sins committed by detesting sin as an offence against God (II. 3, 6).

(c)

How may one make an act of contrition?

In this wise: " O my God, I am sorry from the bottom of my heart for having committed many sins which deserve to be severely punished by Thee; my sins have taken away Thy grace from me because they have wronged Thine infinite goodness. Have mercy on me and deign to pardon me; give me once more Thy holy grace that I may live and grow therein until the day of my death. Willingly I accept from Thy hands all the pains and the sufferings Thou hast destined for me; and I unite them with the sufferings and death of my beloved Saviour Jesus Christ in expiation of my sins, so that I may never be separated from Thee again."

(d)

What must the sinner do after having conceived sorrow for his sins, whether this sorrow be attrition or contrition?

He must go to the priest and confess his sins (VI. 1-5).

When does the Church oblige one to confess?

For all the faithful once a year, at Easter time by preference, by reason of the Easter communion which no one may receive if he have mortal sin on his soul (VI. 5; *Code,* Canon 906).

Why is confession necessary in order to receive the sacrament of Penance?

Because it is only by confession that the penitent can make known his sins to the priest, whose duty it is to judge whether the penitent is worthy to receive absolu tion, and to impose some Penance as satisfaction for the sins committed, in order that a just compensation might be offered to God for the renewal of His grace (VI. 1).

What does confession entail for the sacrament to be valid?

As far as possible the sinner must make known to the priest in detail the number and the species of mortal sins committed; and he must confess them with a view to obtaining the sacramental absolution from the priest (IX. 2).

If at the moment of self-accusation the sinner lack both contrition and attrition for his sins, does the absolution given by the priest remit the sins?

No, they are not remitted; but they would be con fessed, and there would be no need of repeating them to the priest again in order for them to be remitted by the virtue of the sacrament; it is sufficient for the sinner to conceive contrition for them and to accuse himself in his next confession of the want of contrition in his pre ceding confession (IX. 1).

If one has forgotten to confess some mortal sin in con fession, and afterwards one remembers, is one bound to confess this sin in the next confession?

Yes, because every mortal sin must be submitted directly to the power of the keys (IX. 2).

In what capacity does the priest receive the confession of the sinner?

He receives it in the name and in the place of God Himself; and this in such wise that in his life as man, and outside his ministry as confessor, he knows nothing whatever of the sins confessed to him (XI. 1-5).

(E)

After the confession what must the penitent do?

He must with the greatest care perform the Penance im
posed upon him by the priest in the name of God (XII. 1, 3).

*What are the different kinds of Penances one may perform
in satisfaction for sin?*

They all come under these three good works: almsgiving, fasting, and prayer. Indeed, for satisfaction's
sake, we should deprive ourselves of something in order
to offer it to God in His honour. Now there are three
sorts of goods which we can thus offer to God: the goods
of our fortune; the goods of the body; and the goods
of the soul. The offerings of the first come under the
name of almsgiving; of the second under the general
name of fasting; and of the third under the general name
of prayer (XV. 3).

*If one does not perform the Penance imposed by the
priest, does one lose the grace of the sacrament?*

No, unless one voluntarily omits it through contempt;
but if it come about by forgetfulness or by negligence,
the grace of remission in the sacrament endures; but
always, in justice to God, the penalty due to the sin must
be paid either in this or in the next world; moreover, the
grace of the sacrament does not receive that increase
attaching to the performance of the sacramental Penance
(*Third Part*, XC. 2, *Obj.* 2).

XI.—OF THE MINISTER OF THE SACRAMENT OF PENANCE, AND OF THE POWER OF THE KEYS: OF ABSOLUTION; OF INDUL GENCES; OF THE COMMUNION OF SAINTS; AND OF EXCOMMUNICATION

(A)

What is meant by the power of the keys?

It is nothing more than that power which opens the
gate of heaven by removing an obstacle which prevents

entrance thereto, namely sin and the punishment due to sin (XVII. 1).

Where is this power?

First of all it is in the Holy Trinity as in its primary source; then in the sacred humanity of Jesus Christ, by the merit of whose Passion the twofold obstacle above mentioned was removed, and which also by its own power removes this obstacle; also because the efficacy of the Passion of Jesus Christ lives in the sacraments, which are channels, as it were, of His grace by which men participate in all its merits. It follows then that the ministers of the Church, who are the dispensers of the sacraments, have also the power of the keys which they have received from Christ Himself (XVII. 1).

(B)

In what way is the power of the keys exercised in the sacrament of Penance?

It is exercised by the act of the priest judging the state or the dispositions of the sinner, and in giving him absolution and a penance; or in refusing him this absolution (XVII. 2).

Is it at the moment that the priest gives absolution, and is it by virtue of this absolution that the effect of this sacrament is produced, namely the remission of sins?

Yes; and without this absolution there would be no sacrament, nor would there be deliverance from sin (X. 1, 2; XVIII. 1).

Have priests only the power of the keys?

Only priests validly ordained according to the rite of the Catholic Church have this power (XIX. 3).

Is it sufficient for a priest to be validly ordained in order to have this power of the keys over any baptized person who wishes to receive the sacrament of Penance?

No; it is also necessary for him to be approved by the Church in order to hear confessions, and also that the person who desires the sacrament of Penance be under his jurisdiction (XX. 1-3).

Has every priest who has the power, and whose duty it is to hear confession in a certain place, the right to absolve all who present themselves before him?

Yes, unless these persons accuse themselves of sins that are reserved to a higher power; and of this he him self judges in hearing the confession of those that present themselves.

(c)

Is there in the Church, attaching to the power of the keys, a power which frees man from the penalties due to sin, other than by sacramental absolution and the imposition of a Penance?

Yes; and it is the power of the indulgence (XXV. 1).

In what does this power consist?

It consists in this, that the Church from the infinite and inexhaustible treasures of the merits of Jesus Christ, of our Blessed Lady, and of the saints, can take, in satis faction for sin, what corresponds in all or in part to the satisfaction which the sinner owes to the justice of God in this or in the next world. The power also extends to this, that an indulgence can be applied to certain par ticular individuals, and by the effect of this application they are freed from their debt towards the justice of God (XXV. 1).

What is required in order to make this application?

Three things are necessary: he who makes this applica tion must have the authority to do so; there must be a state of grace in him to whom the application is made; and a motive of piety which is the reason for making the application, that is, something that refers to God's honour or to the welfare of the Church, as pious practices, works of zeal or of the apostolate, almsgiving, and the rest (XXV. 2).

These works which are the motive or the reason of the indulgence, are they the price thereof?

In no wise, for an indulgence is not the remission of a penalty which can be bought (XXV. 2).

Is it only those who fulfil the conditions above mentioned who benefit by the indulgence?

They may themselves give this benefit to another, by gaining the indulgence for this other; for instance an indulgence may be gained for the benefit of the souls in purgatory when he who concedes the indulgence gives such faculty (XVII. 3, *Obj.* 2; *Code*, Canon 930).

(D)

Who can thus concede indulgences?

He alone has the power to concede indulgences to whom the treasures of the merits of Christ and the saints are confided, by reason of the power he has received of binding or loosing those who belong to the mystical Body of Jesus Christ on earth, that is to say the Sovereign Pontiff. But also bishops may grant certain indulgences, according as is determined by the Sovereign Pontiff, to those who come under their jurisdiction (XXVII. 1-3).

What follows from so marvellous a power existing in the Catholic Church, and in it alone, by reason of the supreme authority of the Sovereign Pontiff?

From this marvellous power, joined as it is to the power of the keys in the sacrament of Penance, and in a general way in all that touches the communication in the merits of Jesus Christ, it follows that there can be no greater blessedness for man on earth than to be incorporated, by Baptism, in the Catholic Church, and to have the power of participating in all the rights and privileges which Baptism confers. He is thereby in perfect communion with all its members and with its head, the Roman Pontiff to whose care are confided all the treasures of those spiritual goods that can be distributed among men.

(E)

Can it happen that one who is incorporated into the Catholic Church by Baptism does not participate in the privileges that Baptism confers?

Yes, it is the case of those who have fallen under the

censures of the Church; and the worst of all is excommunication (XXI. 1, 2).

Are heretics and schismatics excommunicated?

Yes; they have no part in the communion of saints.

It is then only Catholics subject to the Roman Pontiff and not branded with censure who can fully enjoy the privileges of the Church?

Yes; and in order to participate in the privilege of indulgences they must be by grace and charity in the communion of saints.

(F)

What precisely is the communion of saints?

It is that union among the members of the mystical Body of Jesus Christ, who are yet on earth, or who are in purgatory, or who are in heaven, whereby without ceasing they communicate with each other by reason of eternal happiness which one day will be common to all in heaven.

XLI.—OF THE SACRAMENT OF EXTREME UNCTION

(A)

What is the sacrament which, when he is about to die, prepares man for his entrance into heaven?

It is the sacrament of Extreme Unction (XXIX. 1).

What is this sacrament?

It is that holy rite instituted by Jesus Christ, that consists in anointing with the holy oils one who is about to die; God is asked to remit whatsoever remains of spiritual weakness which is due to past sin, so that the soul might recover fully and perfectly its spiritual health; with this renewed vigour of soul man is prepared to enter the glory of heaven (XXIX.–XXXII.).

Does this sacrament remit sins?

No, for it is not ordained either against original sin as is Baptism, nor against mortal sin as is Penance, nor in a sense against venial sins, as is the Holy Eucharist; but its object is to restore strength to the soul after the evil of sin has been taken away. However, by reason of the special grace it confers which is incompatible with sin, it can remit indirectly the sins which are in the soul, provided there be no obstacle on the part of the person; that is to say if the person is in good faith and has done all he can to get rid of them (XXX. 1).

Does Extreme Unction also bring back health to the body?

Yes; indeed it is one of the proper effects of this sacrament to do this, and in such wise that always, provided the person puts no obstacle in the way, the virtue of this sacrament brings back physical strength and bodily health; and this it does in such measure that the spiritual health may be benefited thereby, for this latter is the primary and principal effect of the sacrament (XXX. 2).

(B)

When may one and when ought one to receive this sacrament?

One may receive it in sickness or bodily failing which puts one in danger of death; one should strive to receive the sacrament in the full state of consciousness so as to receive it with the greatest possible fervour (XXXII. 1, 2).

May one receive this sacrament several times?

One may not receive it more than once in one and the same danger of death. But if after having received it health is recovered, or at least danger of death ceases, one may receive it as often as there are subsequent dangers of death, by reason of the different sicknesses; and if one and the same sickness is prolonged to a great length of time, the sacrament may again be received (XXXIII. 1, 2).

Is Extreme Unction the last sacrament instituted by our Lord to give to men the benefit of the life of His grace?

Yes, it is the last sacrament to give grace to man in so far as he is an individual. But there are two other sacraments of great importance which bring to men this life of grace in so far as they form part of a society, and these are the sacraments of Holy Orders and Matrimony.

XLII.—OF THE SACRAMENT OF HOLY ORDERS; OF PRIESTS, BISHOPS, AND THE SOVE REIGN PONTIFF; AND OF THE CHURCH, MOTHER OF SOULS

(A)

What is the sacrament of Holy Orders?

It is that sacred rite instituted by Jesus Christ in order to confer on certain men a special power whereby they are enabled to consecrate His Body for the benefit of His mystical Body (XXXVII. 2).

Is this power that is conferred one or manifold?

It is manifold; but this does not prejudice the unity of the sacrament of Holy Orders, for the inferior orders are a participation of the higher order (XXXVII. 2).

What is this higher order?

It is the order of priests who receive at their conse cration the power to consecrate the Holy Eucharist (XXXVII. 2).

And what are the inferior orders?

They are all the orders below the priesthood whose duty it is to minister to the priest in the act of consecration. First of all come those who serve the priest at the altar, namely the deacons, sub-deacons and the acolytes: the first of these have the power of distributing the Holy Eucharist at least under the species of wine on those occasions when the Holy Eucharist is distributed under both species; the second prepare the matter of the sacrament in the holy vessels; and the third present this matter. Then come those whose office it is to prepare the recipients of the sacrament, not by sacramental absolu tion which the priest alone has the power to give, but by turning away those that are unworthy, or by instructing the catechumens, or by exorcising the possessed: all of which offices had their *raison d'etre* in the primitive Church, and they have always been kept in the Church in order to safeguard the integrity of its hierarchy (XXXVII. 2).

Which of these orders are called major orders, and which minor orders?

The major orders are the priesthood, diaconate, and sub-diaconate. The minor orders are four in number, viz., the acolytes, the exorcists, the readers, and the door keepers (XXXVII. 2, 3).

Where are these orders to be found, as a general rule, with the exception of the priesthood?

They are to be found in ecclesiastical establishments, where the members of the clergy are educated and are prepared for the priesthood.

(B)

Has the priest a special character which distinguishes him from other men in the Church of God?

Not only the priest but all the members of the ecclesi astical hierarchy have a certain special character impressed upon their soul when they receive the sacrament of Orders. This character is more marked in the major orders, and more still upon those who have received the priesthood, to whom is given the power to consecrate the Body and Blood of Jesus Christ, and to remit sins.

In truth then the faithful owe all to the priest as regards the boons of grace and salvation that are attached to the sacraments?

Yes, with the one exception of the sacrament of Con firmation, which is ordinarily reserved to the bishop. It is the priest who gives to the faithful the sacraments which are ordained to the welfare of their individual life, viz., Baptism, the Holy Eucharist, Penance, and Extreme Unction. It is also the priest who has that supreme power of making really present among men and of offering up in sacrifice the Body and Blood of our Lord Jesus Christ.

Is it not also the priest who gives to the faithful that inestimable benefit which is the knowledge of the mysteries of the Christian religion, and of the truths of salvation?

Yes, it is the priest's office and duty to teach them all these truths.

(c)

From whom does the priest receive these powers?

He receives them from the bishop (XXXVIII. 1; XL. 4).

In what way is a bishop superior to a priest, and how can he give these powers to the priest?

The bishop is superior to the priest not as regards the consecration of the Body and Blood of Jesus Christ in the Holy Eucharist, but as regards what refers to the mystical Body of Jesus Christ, which are the faithful in the Church. It is for the welfare of this mystical Body that the episcopal power was instituted by Jesus Christ. This power comprises all that is necessary for the coming into being and the organization of the mystical Body in order to communicate in its fulness the life of grace through the sacraments. Consequently a bishop pos-sesses the fulness of the priesthood, being able not only to consecrate the Body and Blood of our Lord as every priest is able to do, but also without reserve to administer all the other sacraments, including Confirma tion; further, he gives to priests and to the lesser ministers their power of order by consecrating or ordaining them, and he gives them their power of jurisdiction over the faithful (XL. 4, 5).

In some sort then the whole life of the Church is con-centrated in the person of the bishop?

Yes, this is so.

What is required for a bishop to be this principle of life in his diocese?

He must be in full and perfect communion with the Bishop of Rome, who is the head of all the Churches in the world over which he has supreme authority, and which form the Church of Jesus Christ (XL. 6).

(D)

Has the Bishop of Rome or the Sovereign Pontiff powers which other bishops have not?

As regards the administration of the sacraments his powers are the same as those of other bishops. But as regards the power of jurisdiction, which refers to the government of the Church, and to the administration of the sacraments to such and such particular individuals, his power is absolute and extends to the Church in the entire universe; whereas the power of jurisdiction of other bishops extends only to a part of the universal Church, viz., to their own diocese; but even as regards their own diocese, their power derives its nature and its exercise from the power of the Sovereign Pontiff (XL. 6).

Why does this supreme power in the order of jurisdiction belong to the Sovereign Pontiff?

Because the perfect unity of the Church demands that this supreme power should belong to him alone. For this reason Jesus Christ charged Simon Peter to feed His flock; and the Roman Pontiff is the one and only legitimate successor of St. Peter unto the end of time (XL. 6).

It is then from the Sovereign Pontiff that depends every man's union with Jesus Christ through the sacraments, and consequently his supernatural life and eternal salvation?

Yes; for although it is true that the grace of Jesus Christ is not in an absolute way dependent upon the reception of the sacraments themselves when it is impossible to receive them, at least in the case of adults—and that the action of the Holy Ghost can supplement this defect provided the person is not in bad faith; it is, on the other hand, absolutely certain that no one who separates himself knowingly from communion with the Sovereign Pontiff can participate in the grace of Jesus Christ, and that in consequence if he dies in that state he is irremediably lost.

Is it then in this sense that it is said no one can be saved outside the Church?

Yes, for no one can hold God as his Father who does hold the Church for his Mother.

XLIII.—OF THE SACRAMENT OF MATRIMONY; OF ITS NATURE, IMPEDIMENTS, DUTIES; OF DIVORCE; OF SUBSEQUENT MAR RIAGE; AND OF ESPOUSALS

(A)

What is that sacrament instituted by Jesus Christ which by grace perfects the life of those whose duty regards the continuance of human life in the society?

It is the sacrament of Matrimony (XLII.).

In what way is this sacrament ordained to the good of society in the supernatural order?

By the fact that it is ordained to the propagation of the human species whose members are called to be part of a supernatural society (XLI., XLII.).

What is the sacrament of Matrimony?

It is a union between man and woman, indissoluble until the death of one of the parties, and which of itself excludes all participation of a third. This union is con tracted between baptized persons by mutual consent; by this contract each is given to the other, so that each in regard to the other has the right to certain acts, that children may be born to them for the continuance of society (XLI., XLII.).

Why has this union at the moment it is contracted the nature of a sacrament?

Because Jesus Christ wished it so; and He wished to elevate Matrimony to the dignity of signifying His own union with the Church (XLII. 2).

(B)

What is necessary on the part of the two who wish to make this contract?

It is necessary for both parties to be free to dispose of themselves, and that there be no obstacle opposing their union.

What obstacles can oppose this union?

They are those that are called the impediments of Matrimony.

Are all these impediments of the same nature?

No, for some of them make Matrimony illicit, whereas others make it null and void: the former are called prohibitory impediments, and the latter diriment impediments (*Code*, Canon 1036).

(C)

What are the prohibitory impediments?

They are the simple vow of virginity, the vow of perfect chastity or of not getting married, the vow of receiving Holy Orders, the vow of embracing the religious state; legal parentage, which results from adoption, in those countries where the civil law makes this a prohibitory impediment; lastly, the mixed marriage when one of the two baptized parties is a member of an heretical or schismatical sect (*Code*, Canons 1058, 1059, 1060).

When one of these impediments exists what is to be done so that marriage may take place?

It is necessary to ask the Church's dispensation from the impediment; and this the Church does not grant except for grave reasons, especially in the case of a mixed marriage; in this latter case the Church exacts that the non-Catholic party shall do nothing to hinder the other from practising the Catholic religion, and that the children born of the marriage shall receive both Catholic baptism and bringing up (*Code*, Canon 1061).

If one of the parties, without belonging to an heretical or schismatical sect, be notoriously impious and have rejected the Catholic faith and have joined some society condemned by the Church, would there in this case be an impediment of marriage?

No, not in the sense that the Church's dispensation is necessary, but the Church desires that all the faithful should avoid such unions because of the perils of all sorts attaching thereto (*Code*, Canon 1065).

(D)

What are the diriment impediments of Matrimony?

The following, and they are such as are to be found in the new Code of Canon Law: (1) Immature age, that is before sixteen complete years for the man, and before fourteen complete years for the woman; (2) impotency anterior to marriage and perpetual, whether on the part of the man or on the part of the woman, whether known or not known, whether absolute or relative; (3) the fact of being already married even though the marriage has not been consummated; (4) disparity of religion when one of the parties is not baptized, and the other has been baptized in the Catholic Church, or has returned to the Church by being converted from schism or heresy; (5) the fact of being in Holy Orders; (6) the fact of having taken solemn vows in religion, or also simple vows provided the Holy See has determined that these simple vows render marriage null and void; (7) rape or detention by force with a view to marriage, until the person so detained have the full use of liberty; (8) adultery with the promise, or the civil attempt, of marriage, or adultery followed by murder of the married partner committed by one of the two delinquents—or the co-operation, without adultery, whether physical or moral, in the murder of the married partner; (9) con sanguinity in direct line of descent always, and collater ally to the third degree inclusively, and this impediment is multiplied according as the root or stock common to the two parties is multiplied; (10) affinity in the direct line always, and collaterally to the second degree inclusively, and this impediment is multiplied according as the impediment of consanguinity which is the cause is multiplied, or by a subsequent marriage with a blood relation of the dead partner; (11) public honesty arising from an invalid marriage whether consummated or not, and from public concubinage—this makes marriage null and void in the first and second degree in the direct line between a man and the blood relations of the woman, and *vice versa;* (12) spiritual parentage contracted between a person baptized and the one who baptizes and the godfather or the godmother; (13) legal parentage by adoption—if the civil law holds this as an obstacle to the validity of marriage it becomes by the virtue of Canon Law a diriment impediment (*Code,* Canons 1067-1080; L.-LXII.).

(E)

Does the Church ever dispense from these diriment impedi-ments?

She never dispenses and indeed she cannot dispense from those diriment impediments that arise from strict natural law or the divine law, as are, for instance, impotency, or the consummated marriage, or consanguinity in the direct line, or in the collateral line between two very nearly related as brother and sister. But as regards the other impediments which in the main are due to her own ruling she can dispense from them, but only does so for very grave reasons.

Is there not a diriment impediment that does not refer to the condition of the contracting parties, but is extrinsic to them?

Yes; and it is the impediment of clandestinity.

What is clandestinity?

It is a law of the Church which declares null and void the marriage contracted between baptized Catholics, or those who sometime or other were Catholics—and between baptized and non-Catholics whether the latter be baptized or not—and between Latins and Orientals—if the marriage is not contracted before the parish priest or before the bishop of the place, or before a priest delegated for this purpose, with at least the presence of two wit nesses. If the parish priest or the bishop absolutely cannot be present or only under the greatest difficulties, and there is danger of death to one of the parties, or the difficulties be of such nature that it is impossible for either the parish priest or the bishop to be present for the space of a month, the marriage can be contracted validly with the testimony of two witnesses only (*Code,* Canons 1094-1099).

(F)

When all necessary conditions are present what must the two to be married do in order to receive the sacrament, and who is the minister of the sacrament?

The two parties must give themselves each to the other, actually, by free consent, without constraint or being forced thereto by grave fear; the consent must be formal and mutual, manifested by words or signs about which there can be no mistake; and the two contracting parties are themselves the ministers of the sacrament of Matri mony (*Code,* Canons 1081-1087; XLVII. 1-6).

(G)

If there is any error on the part of those contracting marriage, is the consent, which makes the marriage, invalid?

If this error touches the person of either party the marriage is null; but if it touches the qualities of the person it is illicit (*Code,* Canon 1083).

Is it a good thing on the occasion of the celebration of marriage for the contracting parties to assist at a special Mass in which their union is blessed by the priest?

Yes; and the Church wishes that all her children before receiving this great sacrament in which a special grace is conferred on them that they might fulfil the duties of their married life, should dispose themselves to receive this grace in all its fulness by a good confession and a fervent communion (*Code,* Canon 1101).

(h)

What is the special grace attaching to the sacrament of Matrimony?

It is the grace of perfect conjugal harmony which inspires a true, lasting, and supernatural affection; it is of such nature that it is able to resist all that might com promise this affection, until death; at the same time this grace brings with it a generosity whereby short comings and trials are overcome as regards the children which by the blessing of God may be the fruit of this union; and to this effect that they do nothing whatsoever that may hinder the coming into the world of their children. Moreover, this grace helps the parents to watch over their children with jealous care so that they may be healthy and strong both in body and soul (XLIX. 1-6).

(i)

Can a validly contracted marriage be dissolved by civil divorce?

No. For no human law can separate what God has joined together. Even after a civil divorce the two parties are united by the bonds of matrimony, and if one or the other re-marries, in the eyes of God and the Church this new union is simply concubinage.

(j)

If one of the parties die may the surviving one re-marry?

Yes; this is permitted although, in itself, the state of remaining unmarried is more honourable. But in the case of re-marriage, the woman who has already received once the solemn nuptial blessing may not receive it again (LXIII.; *Code*, Canons 1142, 1143).

(k)

What are solemn espousals which are celebrated before marriage?

They consist essentially in the promise made by two

aspiring to marriage to contract marriage with each other at some future time.   For them to be valid in conscience and before the world it is necessary for this promise to be made in writing and that it be signed by both parties, and by the parish priest or the bishop of the place, or at least by two witnesses.   If one does not know how to write or is unable to do so, the fact must be mentioned in the document and another witness brought forward as testimony thereof (XLIII. 1; *Code*, Canon 1017).

Do espousals or an engagement to marry give the right to the use of marriage before the marriage is celebrated?

No.   Those fiances who act thus, apart from the fact that they commit a mortal sin, arouse the anger of God, who, later on, may make them pay dearly for the abuse of the holiness of their espousals.

XLIV.—OF THE INTERMEDIARY STATE OF THOSE SOULS WHO AFTER DEATH ARE AWAITING THE DAY OF THE LAST RESURRECTION; AND OF PURGATORY

(A)

To what end does Jesus Christ, who conquered sin and death by His Blood, lead the human race?

He leads it to that end which is life eternal in the glory of heaven through all eternity.

Are men given this immortal life in heaven immediately by the action of the redeeming power of Jesus Christ?

No; for although Christ's sacred humanity and the power of the sacraments could bring human nature imme diately to this life of glory, it is fitting according to the divine wisdom that human nature should run the course of its evolution.   Hence all those who have received baptism and participate in the sacraments of Jesus Christ, even after their personal sanctification is accom plished, have to remain in this life subject to its penalties, and to the worst of all, which is death (LXIX. 1).

It is then only at the end of human generations that death will be definitely conquered, and that men who were bought by the Blood of Jesus Christ will be fully compensated by the glory of both their body and soul in heaven?

Yes, only then will they receive their full compensation; and in the meantime they are in an intermediary state.

What is meant by this intermediary state?

By this is meant that they do not receive immediately the recompense of their meritorious life. All will receive either recompense or chastisement, as the case may be, in its fulness on the day of the resurrection, and whatever it be it will endure for all eternity (LXIX. 2).

(B)

What is that intermediate state of those souls that cannot receive the reward of their meritorious life owing to some obstacle?

It is called purgatory (LXXI. 6; *Appendix*, II.).

What souls are in purgatory?

The souls of the just who die in a state of grace, but who at the moment of death have not given satisfaction to God for the temporal punishment due to sin (*ibid.*).

Purgatory then is a place of expiation where one must satisfy the justice of God before being admitted to the reward of heaven?

Yes; and there could be nothing more in harmony with the mercy and justice of God (*ibid.*).

How is the mercy of God shown in the expiation of purgatory?

Because even after their death God gives the just the means of satisfying His justice. God's mercy is also shown by the communion of saints in that He permits the living to offer up in the form of suffrages their own prayers, good works, and penances for the benefit of the souls in purgatory.

(C)

What is the best offering that can be made to God on behalf of the souls in purgatory?

The offering of the Holy Sacrifice of the Mass.

Is it important that he who offers up some good work for the souls in purgatory should do so with the greatest possible fervour?

Yes; for although God without doubt takes into account the worth of what is offered to Him in expiation—and in the oblation of the sacrifice of the Mass this worth is infinite—He takes into greater account the fervour of him who offers it; whether he himself offer it up as does the priest, or whether he offer it through the ministry of another, as when the faithful ask the priest to offer up the Holy Sacrifice of the Mass in their name and for their intention (LXXI. 9; *Third Part*, LXXIX. 5).

These offerings to God in expiation, whether offered for the souls in purgatory in general, or for a particular group, or for this or that soul in particular, are they applied by God according to the intention of him who makes the offering?

Yes (LXXI. 6).

Are the indulgences that one gains (such as are applicable to the souls in purgatory) also applied according to the intention of him who offers them?

Yes, all depends upon the intention of him who gains them in conformity to the intention of the Church, who fixes the limits of such offering (LXXI. 6; *Code*, Canon 930).

As soon as sufficient satisfaction has been offered to God for their past sins, are the souls which were detained in purgatory for this end immediately received into heaven?

Yes, they are received into heaven as soon as the satisfaction for past sin is completed (LXIX. 2; *Appen dix*, II. 6).

XLV.—OF HEAVEN

(A)

What is heaven?

It is that place where the holy angels have lived since the beginning of the world and to which are admitted all the just who have been redeemed by the Blood of Jesus Christ since the day of His glorious Ascension.

What is necessary for the just to be admitted into heaven?

They must have reached the term of their mortal life, and must have no debt to pay to the justice of God (LXIX. 2).

Are any souls of the just admitted into heaven imme-diately after their death?

Yes; they are those souls who have received in their full effect the application of the merits of Jesus Christ; or who, whilst on earth, in union with the satisfaction of Jesus Christ have offered to God full satisfaction due to their sins (*ibid.*).

Children that die after having received baptism and before they have come to the age when they would be capable of sinning, are they admitted immediately to heaven?

Yes, because original sin, which for them was the only obstacle, has been washed away by baptism.

Is the case the same as regards those adults who, although they have committed mortal sins, receive baptism in good dispositions and die immediately afterwards or before they commit sin again?

Yes, because the sacrament of Baptism applies in all their fulness the merits of the Passion of Jesus Christ (*Third Part*, LXIX. 1, 2, 7, 8).

And those who having committed sins, even mortal, since their baptism, and who have not made complete satis faction for them, but who nevertheless at the moment of dying offer their life to God by a perfect act of charity, are they received into heaven immediately after their death?

Yes; especially when this perfect act of charity is martyrdom (*Second Part: Second Section*, CXXIV. 3).

(B)

What happens to the souls of the just as soon as they enter heaven?

They immediately behold the vision of God which renders them supremely happy (*First Part*, XII. 11).

Is it by their own power that they can thus see God, or must they receive some new perfection which strengthens their power of vision?

It is necessary for them to receive a further super natural perfection other than grace, virtues, and gifts which they already possess (*ibid.* XII. 5).

What is this ulterior perfection called?

It is called the Light of Glory (*ibid.*).

What is meant by this?

It is a quality infused by God into the mind of the blessed which strengthens and elevates it, making it capable of receiving within it as the principle of its act of vision the Divine Essence itself in all its splendour (*ibid.*).

What results from this union of the Divine Essence with the mind of the blessed?

The result is that the blessed see God as He sees Himself (*ibid.*).

Is this the vision that is called Face to Face?

Yes, such as is promised us in the Holy Scriptures; and such as makes us like to God as far as it is possible for a creature to be.

Is it in order to communicate this vision to the blessed that God created all things, and rules and guides them all, from the beginning to the end of the world?

Yes. Moreover, when all the places He has marked in heaven shall be filled the actual course of the world will come to an end; and He will re-establish this world in a new state which will be that of the resurrection.

Can we know when the end of the world will come?

No; this depends entirely upon the counsels and providence of God.

(c)

Do the happy elect who enjoy the beatific vision take any interest at all in the things that take place on earth and among human beings?

Most certainly they interest themselves with things that happen on earth.

Do the elect in heaven see all that passes on earth?

They see in the vision of God all that in this world refers to the mystery of God's predestination and its fulfilment.

Do they hear the prayers addressed to them, and do they know the spiritual and temporal needs of those who were dear to them on earth?

Most assuredly; and they are always answering these prayers, and provide for the wants of those on earth by interceding to God (LXXII. 1).

Why then do we not always feel the benefit of their intercession?

Because they see our bequests and needs in the light of God, in which that which oftentimes seems a good to us is not in reality so according to the ordering of the divine providence (LXXII. 3).

XLVI.—OF HELL

(A)

Is there a place of eternal damnation?

Yes, and it is called hell (LXIX. 2).

What is hell?

Hell is a place of torments to which are condemned all those who by their sins have revolted against God, and have remained in their sins.

Who are these?

Among the angels all those that sinned; and among men those that die in the state of final impenitence (LXIX. 2).

Since the damned are rooted in evil in such wise that they never repent what is the consequence?

The consequence is that the torments which they have merited by their sins will last for ever.

But could God not put an end to these torments?

Yes, He could do so by His absolute power; but according to the order of His wisdom He will not do so, for according to this order those who arrive at the term of their life are fixed for always either in good or in evil, and since the evil always remains so must the punishment always remain (XCIX. 1, 2).

(B)

What are the torments that the damned will suffer always?

They are twofold: the pain of loss and the pain of sense (XCVII. 1, 2).

What is the pain of loss?

It is the privation of the infinite good which is the beatific vision in heaven.

Whence is it that this punishment will be cruelly felt by the damned?

It arises from this, that having arrived at the term of their life they see the nothingness of all the things they sought in life to the prejudice of the infinite good; they will then appreciate the greatness of the good they have lost, and they will realize that they lost it through their own fault entirely.

Is not this perpetual consciousness of having lost so great a good as the vision of God called by the Gospel "the worm that never dies"?

Yes; and this will be the most terrible punishment of their guilty conscience (XCVII. 2).

(c)

Must one understand in a metaphorical and purely spiritual sense the other punishment of which the Gospel speaks and which it calls " the fire that never dies "?

No; one must understand these words of material fire; for they signify the pain of sense (XCVII. 5).

But how can material fire act upon spirits or upon souls separated from the body?

By a special ordering of His justice, God communicates to this material fire the preternatural power of serving as an instrument of His justice (LXX. 3).

*Will all the damned be tormented by the fire of hell in
the same way?*

No, for since it is used as an instrument of the divine
justice, its action will be proportioned to the nature,
number, and gravity of the sins committed by each one
(XCVII. 5, *Obj.* 3).

XLVII.—OF THE JUDGMENT WHEREBY A SOUL IS SENT TO PURGATORY, HEAVEN, OR HELL

(A)

By what act is a soul sent to purgatory, heaven, or hell?
By the act of judgment.
What is this judgment?
It is that act of the justice of God which pronounces
definitely on the state of a soul with regard to its reward
or punishment.
When does this judgment take place?
It takes place immediately after death as soon as the
soul is separated from the body.
Who makes this judgment?
It is made by God Himself; and after the Ascension
of Jesus Christ to heaven it is made through the sacred
humanity of the Word made flesh.

(B)

*Does the soul that is judged see God or the sacred humanity
of Jesus Christ?*
God is not seen in His essence, nor is the sacred
humanity of Jesus Christ seen who is in heaven, except
by those souls who according to a judgment in their favour
immediately enter heaven.
*In what way does the judgment take place of the other
souls?*
There is as it were a light whereby they see instantan
eously [the whole course of their life, and which shows

them immediately the place to which they are allotted whether in hell or in purgatory.

It is then as it were in the same instant that the soul, as soon as it leaves the body, is judged and its place allotted to it in purgatory, hell, or heaven?

Yes, since all this takes place by the almighty power of God, whose action is instantaneous.

Can sometimes the very last act of man, before the soul leaves the body, decide the fate of the soul for all eternity, and guarantee for the soul eternal happiness?

Yes, but this comes about sometimes only by the great mercy of God; and it may be that there were other acts during man's life which in some way prepared him for this great grace, or by reason of the prayers of saintly souls who inclined God to perform this act of supreme mercy.

XLVIII.—OF THE PLACE OF THOSE WHO ARE NOT JUDGED, VIZ., OF THE LIMBO OF INFANTS

(A)

Are there any human beings who at the moment of death are not judged?

Yes. All children who die before attaining the age of reason, or those who though adults never had the use of reason (LXIX. 6).

Is there any allotment at all as regards infants and those who have not had the use of reason?

Yes, but this is not by reason of their merits or demerits; and it is not made by way of judgment. It comes about by the fact that some have received baptism and others have not. Those that have received baptism immediately go to heaven; whereas those who have not received this sacrament go to a place reserved for them which is called Limbo.

(B)

Is Limbo distinct from purgatory and hell?

Yes, because these two latter are places where punishment is inflicted for personal sins (LXIX. 6).

Do infants who have died without baptism suffer the pain of loss in Limbo?

Yes, to a certain degree, for they know they are deprived of the vision of God; but this has not the character of torture such as those in hell suffer (*Appendix*, I. 2).

Whence arises this difference as regards the pain of loss?

It comes from this, that although they know they are deprived of the vision of God, they also know that this is not by reason of any personal sin but by reason of their being born of Adam, who sinned (*ibid.*).

For them, then, there is no horrible worm that gnaws their souls such as torments the damned in hell?

No. But they live in a state without any kind of suffering or sadness, except that they are conscious of that supreme happiness which would have been theirs had the merits of the redemption been applied to them and which they will never have, not by any fault on their part but because the inscrutable counsels of God have arranged it so (*ibid.*).

(C)

Do the souls of these infants know the mysteries of the redemption?

Most certainly.

Have they the light of faith?

No, they have not faith in the sense of that interior supernatural light perfecting the mind whereby in a certain intimate manner it penetrates revealed mysteries and generates in the soul a strong desire towards them; they know these mysteries very much in the same way as those who cannot help but assent to the truth of the divine mysteries revealed by God, but who are not drawn by an impulse of grace to cling supernaturally to these mysteries, and as a consequence they do not penetrate the intimate meaning of them.

(D)

Besides this Limbo of the souls of children who die before baptism, is not mention made of another Limbo in the language of the Church?

Yes, it is that Limbo where formerly the just were detained, that is, those in whom there was no personal hindrance as regards entrance into heaven, but who had to await the coming of the Redeemer (LXIX. 7).

Is there anyone now in this Limbo of the just?

Since the day when Jesus Christ at the moment of His death descended there and left it on the day of His Resurrection, bringing with Him all the souls of the just, this place ceased to be occupied by those for whom it was primarily destined; but it may be that since then it is the place where children go who die without baptism, so in this case it would be the same as the Limbo of infants.

XLIX.—OF THE END OF THE WORLD AND THE SEQUEL THEREOF

In what will the end of the world consist, and what will follow upon it?

The end of the world will be immediately followed by two great events, viz., the resurrection and the judgment. Moreover, the Apostle St. Peter teaches us that the end of the world will be by fire at the moment when Jesus Christ shall come in His glory to judge the living and the dead (LXXIV. 1, 2).

Will this universal conflagration which will destroy the present world be as it were a preparation for the judgment?

Yes, by purifying all things and making them worthy of the new state so as to be in harmony with the glory of the elect (LXXIV. 1).

Will this final conflagration act by its own virtue, or also as instrument of the divine power?

It will act also as an instrument of God in particular

for the purification of those souls which would have perhaps remained in the flames of purgatory for a long time (LXXIV. 3-8).

These souls then will be purified and made worthy to be admitted among the elect as it were instantaneously?

Yes; and the purifying virtue of this fire will be pro portioned by God to the degree of expiation necessary in each case.

Do we know when this conflagration will take place?

No; but it will be preceded by certain signs which will herald the near advent of the Sovereign Judge.

What will these signs be?

There will be unheard-of upheavals in the whole of nature which, as the Gospel says, will make men quake with fear.

L.—OF THE RESURRECTION

(A)

What will happen immediately after the great conflagra-tion?

There will be heard an order, a voice, the sound of a trumpet, so speaks St. Paul in his First Epistle to the Thessalonians, which will awaken the dead from their tombs, and command all men to stand before the Judge of the living and the dead; and this Judge will descend from heaven in all the glory of His majesty (LXXV. 1).

Which are those who will come to life at this moment?

All those who were already dead; and also all those who are still living when Jesus Christ appears.

But how can these last also rise from the dead?

In this wise: if all comes to be as it were instantan eously as St. Paul seems to say (1 Cor., chap. xv., ver. 51), by the power of God all those human beings who are living will die an instantaneous death, and will rise again immediately in the state which they have merited and which will be theirs for all eternity (LXXVIII. 1, 2).

Will the bodies of all the just who rise from the dead be instantaneously transformed and become glorious?

Yes.

But will these bodies now resplendent with glory be the same bodies that the just had when they lived this life?

Yes, they will be the same bodies with this difference, that there will be no imperfections or troubles or sicknesses such as they were subject to on earth; on the contrary, these bodies will have perfections that will in some sense spiritualise them (LXXIX.-LXXXI.).

How can all this come about?

By the almighty power of God, who having created all things can change and transform them as He wills.

(B)

What are these new perfections or properties of the glorified risen body?

They are impassibility, subtlety, agility, and clarity.

What is impassibility?

It is that property of the glorified body whereby the soul has perfect dominion over the body in such wise that no defect and no suffering or sickness whatsoever can be in the body (LXXXII. 1).

Will this impassibility be the same in all?

Yes, in the sense that there can be no defect in the body which is perfectly under the dominion of the soul; but the power of this dominion will be proportioned to the glory of the soul, which will be different according to the degree in which the soul participates in the beatific vision (LXXXII. 2).

Will it follow from this impassibility that the glorified body will be devoid of sensibility?

In no wise; it will have, on the contrary, a sensibility that is exquisite in the highest possible degree, with no admixture whatsoever of imperfection. Hence the eye of the glorified body will see in an incomparable degree more readily and more piercingly than in this life; the ear will have a sensitiveness without compare. So with all the other senses; each will attain its object with an intensity of perfection impossible for us now to imagine, and this without an object ever injuring the sense as so often happens in this life (LXXXII. 3, 4).

(c)

What is the property of subtlety in a glorified body?

Subtlety will consist in a superlative perfection of the body due to the influence of the glorified soul; this influence will impart to the body something so pure and ethereal that it will cease to have that heaviness or density that it has now on earth; but this property in no way detracts from the true nature of the body as though it thereby becomes unreal, aeriform, or a phantom.

Will a glorified body on account of its subtlety be able to occupy the same place as another body? and is it itself independent of all place, or does it occupy space?

The glorified body cannot occupy the same place as another body, for it retains always its own dimensions or quantity, and consequently it will always be in a place and in space (LXXXIII. 2).

It was not then by reason of the property of subtlety that the risen Body of our Lord passed through closed doors?

No, this was a miracle and was performed by the divine power of Jesus Christ; in the same way it was by the divine power that our Lord was born without prejudicing the virginity of Mary His Mother (LXXXIII. 2, *Obj.* 1).

(D)

What is the property of agility in the glorified body?

It is a certain perfection in the body derived from the glorified soul whereby the body will obey in the most marvellously ready manner all the movements of the soul which is its motive principle (LXXXIV. 1).

Will the saints make use of this property?

They will most certainly use it when they have to come

to the judgment of Jesus Christ on the last day, and when they ascend to heaven with Him. It is also probable they will use this gift according as they will in order to manifest the divine wisdom in conferring this gift upon them; and also in order to appreciate better the beauty of all things in the universe in which the wisdom of God will shine forth (LXXXIV. 2).

Will the bodies of the saints be moved instantaneously by virtue of agility?

No; their movements will always require duration in time, except that so rapid will be their movement that this duration will be imperceptible (LXXXIV. 3).

(E)

What is the fourth property which is called clarity?

By this is meant that the splendour of the soul will shine as it were through the body, so that the body will be as it were luminous and transparent; but this will not detract from the natural colour of the body, but will rather harmonize with it, imparting to it the most exquisite beauty (LXXXV. 1).

Will this clarity be the same in all?

No, it will be proportioned to the degree of glory proper to each soul; and for this reason St. Paul speaks of a variety among the glorified bodies: "One is the glory of the sun, another of the moon, and another the glory of the stars. For star differeth from star in glory" (First Epistle to Cor., chap. xv., ver. 41).

Will it be possible for the eye of a non-glorified body to see this clarity of the glorified body?

Yes; and the lost will perceive it in all its splendour (LXXXV. 2).

Will it be in the power of the soul to permit or not to permit this clarity of its glorified body to be seen?

Yes, for this clarity comes entirely from the soul and is entirely subject to it (LXXXV. 3).

(F)

In what state or at what age will the bodies of the blessed rise?

They will all rise at that age in which human nature is in its most perfect state of development (LXXXI. 1).

Will it be the same as regards the bodies of the damned?

Yes, except that they will have none of the four qualities of the glorified body (*ibid.*).

Does it follow that the bodies of the damned will be corruptible?

In no wise, for corruptibility and death will be no more (LXXXVI. 2).

They will then be at the same time passible and immortal?

Yes, God has so arranged in His justice and power that the bodies of the damned will never corrupt or be destroyed, and yet all things, especially the fire of hell, will be for them a cause of suffering and torture (LXXXVI. 2, 3).

(G)

As regards children that die without baptism what will the state of their bodies be?

They will rise in the most perfect state of a human being in nature, but without the properties of the glorified body; but they will never suffer any sorrow or pain (cf. *Appendix*, I. 2).

LI.—OF THE LAST JUDGMENT

As soon as men rise from the dead will they immediately be in presence of the Sovereign Judge?

Yes (LXXXIX. 5).

Under what form will the Sovereign Judge appear at the moment of judgment?

He will appear under the form of His sacred humanity in all the glory which is due to His union with the Person of the Word (XC. 1, 2).

Will all men see this glory of the Sovereign Judge?
Yes (*ibid.*).

Will all see Him in the glory of His divine nature?
No, only the elect whose souls enjoy the beatific vision will see this glory (XC. 3).

Will all men who appear be judged?
No, only those who have had the use of reason during this life; but they will be present that they may behold the sovereign justice of the judgments of God and the glory of Jesus Christ (LXXXIX. 5, *Obj.* 3).

Will all men who have had the use of reason be judged?
They will all be judged as regards the separation which will take place between the good and the bad. The good will be placed on the right hand of the Judge to hear His sentence of benediction; and the bad on His left hand to receive His sentence of malediction. But the good will not be judged in the sense that their bad acts, if any, will be judged before all heaven and earth; in this sense only the lost will be judged (LXXXIX. 6, 7).

Will this convincing of sin in the face of all bring con-fusion to the lost?
Yes, it will be inexpressible torture for them, because behind every sin, especially mortal sin, there is hidden pride; and on the day of judgment they will be forced to confess all before the Sovereign Judge, who will leave nothing hidden.

Will all the evil done by the lost during life be brought to light before all present?
Yes, whatever evil it be it will be brought to light: all that was committed in their individual and private life, or in the family or in the society (LXXXVII. 1, 2, 3).

In what way will this manifestation of an entire life take place?
In the same way as in the particular judgment when by a light the whole of one's life is instantaneously present, so in the general judgment all consciences will be laid bare to the gaze of all instantaneously (*ibid.*).

Will the consciences of the just and all their life also be made manifest to all?

Yes, but this will be a triumph for their humility in life (LXXXIX. 6).

Will all the sins one has committed during life, but for which penance has been done, be also made manifest?

Yes, but this will be to the glory of the just by reason of their penance (LXXXVII. 2, *Obj.* 3).

Will there be certain of the just who will also assist at the last judgment in the capacity of judges?

Yes; all those who after the example of the Apostles left all to give themselves up entirely to God, and whose life has been in some sort a proclamation of the Gospel in its perfection (LXXXIX. 1, 2).

Will the angels also be judges on the last day?

No, because those who help Jesus Christ to judge must resemble Him; but it is as man that the Son of God will exercise the function of Sovereign Judge (LXXXIX. 7).

Will the angels be judged on the last day?

No, except that the good angels who have helped in the actions of the just, and the bad angels in the actions of the wicked, will receive an increase of happiness or of punishment respectively (LXXXIX. 3).

What will be the ending of the last judgment?

To those on His right Jesus Christ will say: " Come, ye blessed of My Father, and possess the Kingdom pre pared for you from the constitution of the world." To those on His left He will say: " Depart from Me, ye accursed, into hell fire, which was prepared for the devil and his angels."

LII.—OF ETERNAL PUNISHMENT

Will the sentence of the Sovereign Judge with regard to the lost be carried out by the demons?

Yes; the lost will immediately be seized by the demons and dragged to hell, where in addition to their own sufferings they will be tormented for ever by the demons (LXXXIX. 4).

Will the fact that the lost have now their bodies be a new cause of suffering?

Yes, for henceforth they will suffer not only in their soul but also in their body; but the suffering of the body will not be the same for all, for the punishment will be pro portionate to the number and gravity of sins committed by each one (XCVII. 1, 5).

Will the sufferings of the lost ever cease or become less intense?

No, because their will is fixed in evil, and hence they will always be in the same state of wickedness (XCVIII. 1, 2; XCIX. 1).

LIII.—OF ETERNAL HAPPINESS

(A)

Will the elect immediately enter heaven after their sentence has been pronounced?

Yes.

Will the happiness of the elect be increased by the fact that their bodies are now united to their souls?

Yes, they will have an increase of accidental happiness, their essential happiness consisting in the vision of God (XCIII. 1).

Will there be distinct places for the elect in heaven?

Yes, for the degree of charity or of grace will determine the degree of glory (XCIII. 2, 3).

In this assembly of the elect will men have something that the angels will not have?

Yes, for men will form the Church triumphant, but the angels will not have the same relation to Jesus Christ, who is the King of the Church triumphant (XCV. 1, 2, 4).

In what will this difference consist?

In this, that the elect belonging to the human race resemble Jesus Christ, who has the same human nature; but this will never be so with the angels. The elect therefore will have certain intimate relations with Jesus Christ which the angels have not.

(B)

What will be the result of this intimate relation between the Church triumphant and Jesus Christ?

The result will be that on its entrance into heaven Almighty God will bestow upon it the most inestimable gifts which are called the dowry of the blessed (XCV. 1).

What is this dowry?

It is threefold in the glorified soul from which it is reflected, as it were, in the body under the form of the four properties whereby the body is glorified (of these latter we have already spoken); this dowry will consist in the *vision, possession,* and *fruition* of the divine essence (XCV. 5).

(C)

May one say that the elect in heaven will be invested, as it were, with a royal dignity?

Yes, because the beatific vision unites them to God, and thus they participate in the divinity of God; and since God is the immortal King of ages, the elect participate in this sovereign royalty and its glory (XCVI. 1).

Is it then by reason of this that the blessed are said to receive a crown in heaven?

Yes, it is for this precisely (XCVI. 1).

(D)

Do the blessed also have what is called an aureola?

Yes; but although the crown is common to all, only certain ones will have an aureola (XCVI. 1).

What is the reason of this difference?

It comes to this: the crown is the result or the resplendency of essential happiness which consists in the vision of God; whereas an aureola is a resplendency of an accidental order caused by the joy of certain of the elect on account of certain works they performed while on earth which were specially meritorious (XCVI. 1).

Will the angels have aureolas?

No, for they had no such meritorious works to accom-plish (XCVI. 9).

What kind of meritorious works did certain of the elect perform which gives them the right to an aureola?

Some were martyrs, others virgins, and others preached the Gospel (XCVI. 5, 6, 7).

Why will these three kinds of good works merit an aureola?

Because they make men resemble Jesus Christ in a special way in so far as He was victorious over the flesh, the world, and the devil (*ibid.*).

Are there not in the Sacred Scriptures words which concern the eternal happiness of the elect in heaven?

Yes, in the Apocalypse of St. John, chap. xxii., ver. 5, we read these words: " Night shall be no more: and they shall not need the light of the lamp, nor the light of the sun, because the Lord God shall enlighten them, and they shall reign for ever and ever."

EPILOGUE

Prayer to Our Lord Jesus Christ

O Jesus, most sweet Son of the glorious Virgin Mary, and the only-begotten of the living God; together with Thy Father, who begot Thee from all eternity in the womb of His infinite nature, and who communicates to Thee this same infinite nature; and with the Holy Ghost, who proceeds from the Father and from Thee, who is Thy Father's Spirit and Thine, who is Thy Father's subsisting Love and Thine, and who received from you both the same infinite nature;

I adore Thee and I acknowledge Thee as my God, the only true God, one and infinitely perfect;

Who created all things out of nothing, and who main tains and governs them with infinite wisdom, with sovereign goodness and with almighty power;

I beg Thee, in virtue of the mysteries of Thy sacred humanity, to cleanse me in Thy Blood and wash away all my sins; I beg Thee to impart to me Thy Holy Spirit with an abundance of His grace, His virtues, and His gifts;

I beg Thee to make me believe in Thee, to hope in Thee, and to love Thee, that by each one of my acts I may strive to merit Thee, who hast promised one day to give Thyself to me in all the splendour of Thy glory in the presence of Thy holy angels and saints.   Amen.

(On January 22nd, 1914, Pope Pius X. granted *in perpetuum* 100 days' indulgence, applicable to the souls in purgatory. This indulgence may be gained once each day by all the faithful who with devotion and a contrite heart recite the above prayer.)

Printed in England